Engaging Imagination

Engaging Imagination

Helping Students Become Creative and Reflective Thinkers

Alison James and Stephen D. Brookfield

JB JOSSEY-BASS™
A Wiley Brand

Cover design by Michael Cook

Cover image : © Sergey Nivens/Thinkstock (RF)

Published by Jossey-Bass
A Wiley Brand
One Montgomery Street, Suite 1200, San Francisco, CA 94104-4594—www.josseybass.com

Jossey-Bass books and products are available through most bookstores. To contact Jossey-
Bass directly call our Customer Care Department within the U.S. at 800-956-7739,
outside the U.S. at 317-572-3986, or fax 317-572-4002.

Wiley publishes in a variety of print and electronic formats and by print-on-demand.
Some material included with standard print versions of this book may not be included
in e-books or in print-on-demand. If this book refers to media such as a CD or DVD that
is not included in the version you purchased, you may download this material at http://
booksupport.wiley.com. For more information about Wiley products, visit www.wiley.com.

Library of Congress Cataloging-in-Publication Data has been applied for and is on file
with the Library of Congress.
ISBN 978-1-118-40947-3 (cloth)
ISBN 978-1-118-83619-4 (ebk.)
ISBN 978-1-118-836118- (ebk.)

Printed in the United States of America
FIRST EDITION
HB Printing   10 9 8 7 6 5 4 3 2 1

The Jossey-Bass Higher and
Adult Education Series

Contents

List of Figures

All photographs are the authors' own unless otherwise indicated.

Preface

This book is a tale of two coffees. It had its origins in a London café in summer 2011, when we met for the first time to share mutual interests in student reflection. Alison had contacted Stephen by e-mail to let him know she had been using his Critical Incident Questionnaire (Brookfield, 2006) in her teaching at the London College of Fashion. Because Stephen would be visiting London a few months later, we decided to get together and chat about the different ways we each worked with students to develop reflective and critical thinking. Although Stephen had done some workshops at the Fashion Institute of Technology in New York, the world of creative arts education was unfamiliar to him. But he was intrigued to find out more about how Alison worked within that setting.

As we talked, we both agreed that visual and kinesthetic approaches to teaching reflective thought and practice, although central to certain creative arts disciplines, are largely unknown to teachers in other areas. We agreed that these kinds of approaches hold the possibility of migrating effectively from creative arts teaching to multiple settings. We wondered about drawing together our different experiences of teaching reflection under the umbrella of engaging imagination. We both want our classrooms to be ones in which students are engaged as learners, and we talked about the link between the use of imaginative activities and the creation of enlivening and engaging classrooms.

Eventually our conversation morphed into a book proposal and then into the book you now have in your hands (or on your screen). We decided to collaborate partly because this would open us up to each other's different worldviews and practices. Our assumption is that a strong part of becoming a better teacher is committing to learning new ways of thinking about, and doing, our pedagogic work. Our collaboration across a physical ocean and two continents, and across different intellectual paradigms, has been mutually engaging, and we hope this spirit of playful creativity comes through in our writing. An English College of Fashion and an American Catholic university are certainly very different environments. Yet we believe that colleagues in both institutions are equally interested in helping students become critically reflective and in creating lively classrooms that engage students.

In *Engaging Imagination* our purpose is to show how students develop and sharpen their personal, professional, and political understandings through an engagement in multiple classroom activities. We draw on multisensory approaches to learning—visual and verbal, kinesthetic and cognitive, online and off-line, solo study and group work, large and small numbers of students—and travel across domains of time and space. Our focus, as befits our different backgrounds, is interdisciplinary, but what unites us is the focus on using creativity, imagination, and play to help students learn how to be critically reflective. We recognize that our approaches are not for every unit of study or every classroom; learners, teachers, outcomes, contexts, purposes, and subjects are all deciding factors in selecting what techniques to use and determining what will work. Some of you may have come across some of the activities described in this book in some guise already. What you decide to use, as with any teaching ideas, materials, or theories, will be a matter of personal preference, teaching style, and selection according to curricular purpose.

This is a book about practice, yet we would classify it not so much as a "how to," but as more of a "what if?" book. What if we take more imaginative approaches and integrate them into what we do already, in whatever form that exists? What if we change the reflective questions, prompts, and structures that we, and our students, are used to using? What if we, and our students, step outside our comfort zone and do something differently? What if we are playful in our approaches to learning? What do we risk, lose, or gain?

Risk and uncertainty are things that we try to prepare our students to deal with in our volatile and unpredictable social, professional, financial, political, and educational climates. Trying new things in our teaching can be exhilarating but also risky; what if my students don't like new approaches and disengage from learning? Is the devil I know better than the one that's untested? Will playfulness be seen as anti-academic, as somehow not properly intellectual? The idea of playfulness is sometimes hard to fit with the kind of serious, high-minded endeavors that we expect of college and university students. Is this going to be a book about being silly?

Well, no, it is not about being silly. In fact, the ethic of play is a serious matter. When we use activities and approaches that seem like an entertaining distraction from "proper" study on the surface, we always have a deeper intent. We want to jolt ourselves, and students, out of our normal and routine ways of understanding and practicing. In this we build on Herbert Marcuse's (Reitz, 2000; Miles, 2012) argument that aesthetic experiences induce breaks and ruptures from the familiar. When students who are used to text- and teacher-dependent modes of learning switch into a playful mode, they are learning very differently. They are temporarily estranged from the typical experience of listening to a lecture, adding notes to PowerPoints projected during that lecture, and then being split into small-group discussions. Marcuse would argue that they are lifted into a different way of being.

Stephen once heard English philosopher Marghanita Laski on the BBC radio show *Start the Week* speaking about the notion of everyday ecstasy—the way listening to music for a few minutes, smelling or tasting a new food, or letting your eyes linger on something you thought to be beautiful took you into a different and heightened sensuous way of being for a brief time each day (Laski, 1980). We think what Laski was talking about was essentially the same as Marcuse's: the idea that an aesthetic experience challenges the normal ways of thinking and feeling in everyday life. By extension, we believe that creativity, imagination, and play also accomplish this rupture with ordinary experience, and that students remember imaginative classroom moments as some of the most powerful events in their learning trajectories.

Engaging Imagination offers a mixture of things: exercises, activities, theories, positions, approaches, and people. It is a text of different voices: stories, case studies, anecdotes, and project descriptions. It is a book about questions and assumptions, about dialogue and spaces. We seek to add to the library of resources on alternative modes of learning and assessment and to link the literature of creativity, imagination, and play explicitly to reflective practice. We are not about shutting out traditional approaches to reflection but about extending and adding to them. As we know already, and as you will see further illustrated, writing, the most dominant of these approaches, can be creative, imaginative, and playful as well.

How Should You Use This Book?

The shortest answer to this question is "In any way you like!" Although we have tried to group our chapters into themes, there are recurrent issues, approaches, and theories, such as identity and metaphor, that permeate them all. As befits a text on creativity, imagination, and play, we are fine with a serendipitous skimming, dipping in and out of chapters as particular paragraphs engage you. We also urge you to read the book in conjunction with the Web presence we have created to accompany the text. At http://www.engagingimagination.com you can watch demonstrations of many of the activities we describe in the following pages and also hear from their originators or enactors.

In terms of how the contents can be used in teaching, we have sought to provide all sorts of ideas and activities for encouraging reflective learning that can easily be integrated into a range of settings, whether for five minutes, two hours, or much longer. They can be used at student orientations, to support career progression, to enable someone to write a dissertation, to help with essays, to enhance classroom learning, to complete projects, to assist in formulating design ideas, to prepare for tutorials, to aid private introspection or decision making, to weigh choices, to work out whether a proposal is valid or has originality, or for any other tasks for which the teacher deems them relevant.

Although the theories and models adopted originate in a wide variety of disciplines, several of the case studies are taken from creative arts contexts. If you are an educator working outside these creative fields, do not let this put you off—or not at least until you have read the book and know what you are discarding. After all, one of us—Stephen—teaches in a typically text-dependent, content-heavy discipline. The field of the creative arts is huge and multifaceted. A small part of it might be about designing clothes or artifacts, but its other spheres of activity include creative and visual conception, commercial practice, business and management strategy, local and industrial-scale production systems, and community mobilization. To give just one example, the various encampments of the Occupy Wall Street movement involve cartoons, collage, free-form drawing, found poetry, music and drama, as well as more traditional modes of political education. So we see the possibility of adapting imaginative approaches that have their genesis in the creative arts to multiple disciplines and subject matter contexts.

What This Book Is Not

As we have already stressed, this book does not pretend to be a box of magic wands. Although the ideas and techniques we offer have been successful in a range of contexts, we cannot guarantee that they will be popular with everyone. One of Alison's best friends is managing director with a global corporation. One day as the two of them were mucking out horses and chatting over buckets and pitchforks she asked Alison, "So, what's your book actually about then? You've told me the title but I did not quite get it." Alison said something along the lines of "It's all about how we can use creativity, imagination, and playfulness, with things like Lego and labyrinths, to reflect on our learning in different ways." "Ah," said her friend conversationally, "I'd hate that."

Being a generous, as well as honest, person, Alison's friend was quick to recognize, however, that this was a personal view, at the same time noting how many playful or unconventional approaches are increasingly popular for fostering organizational learning. Go to any team-building or communications workshop offered by an organization, and chances are that you will be asked to engage in something kinetic (such as falling backward, trusting that colleagues will catch you before you hit the ground), visual (such as drawing what a productive day looks like), or physically risky (such as undertaking a ropes course that requires you to overcome a fear of heights). Of the two of us, Stephen is notoriously wary of "touchy-feely" exercises, so your authorial team has a built-in skeptic. Yet some of the most memorable moments of Stephen's own learning autobiography involve music, not words.

We have already stated, and will reiterate throughout the book, that part of the success in using imaginative approaches is to allow for freedom and flexibility of choice wherever possible. Just because a particular strategy or exercise has been received enthusiastically by physicists or welders does not mean it will necessarily appeal to the same extent to tutu makers or critical theorists.

Equally, we may have assumed that approaches that suit product designers won't work with elite sports faculty, and then find to our astonishment that we were wrong.

One thing we do know is that some of the approaches we propose can appear to some colleagues as self-indulgent navel gazing, or pseudo-therapy in disguise. Or they may hear the term *reflective practice* and see institutional monitoring lurking in the not-so-dim background. We know from experience that suggesting imaginative or playful approaches is often met with the response "My students would never go for that," or "That sounds fine for artists but it just doesn't fit with engineering, geography, or medicine." We know that attending to gut feelings is important, but we also subscribe to the cliché that you never know until you try.

Overview of Chapters

We begin the book with a chapter arguing that engaging imagination fosters reflective thinking and in which we propose three axioms of student engagement. We define what we mean by *reflection* and explore fourteen elements of reflective thinking in students. Chapter 2 then considers how best to introduce students to reflective thinking by clarifying what it entails, beginning with modeling, and using students' testimonies. The connection between creativity and reflective thinking is the focus of chapter 3. We also explore the notion of multiple intelligences, connect imagination to creativity, and clarify the meaning of play. In chapter 4 we set out the case for creative reflection in visual form, illustrated by diverse aspects of visual theory: perception, literacy, and visual intelligence. We present activities that include ways of seeing and not seeing, such as visual research, visual dialogue, and visualization. We look (pun intended!) at a number of activities, including Jastrow's duck/rabbit, the use of urban and rural walks, sketchbooks and look books, paper tearing, the plait, and collaging classroom discussions.

Our attention shifts to narrative, story, and especially metaphor in chapter 5, where metaphors such as dyslexia as the bully in the playground are examined. Our analysis investigates the "Tell Us about It" initiative, diagrams as story triggers, the use of timelines, and how metaphors can act as parables. Playing seriously through the use of Lego building blocks and through labyrinth walking are considered in chapter 6, where we outline a workshop in which students use Lego materials to construct physical metaphors of their learning journeys. Then we examine how labyrinth walks can be used to engender creative reflection and insights. The focus of chapter 7 is on the impact of space on students' readiness to engage in reflective learning. We look at permanent, temporary, natural, and human-made spaces and discuss adjustments to the physical environment and the creation of outdoor spaces. The chapter introduces the Reflective Pod, the spliff bunker, postcards and patchworks, and the connections between inner and outer space.

We mine the fields of psychology and clinical therapy to analyze how to ask good questions in chapter 8, drawing on Kelly's personal construct psychology to help students challenge their assumptions and clarify their thinking through self-characterization, laddering, and pyramiding. The chapter also examines the use of clean questions as a means of allowing someone to reflect without imposing the values, views, and opinions of the questioner on the person's thought processes. Etienne Wenger's notion of communities of practice is our basis for exploring creative and imaginative approaches to working collaboratively in groups, networks, and communities in chapter 9. We provide case studies such as Maps, Memberships, and Mazes; the Picture Group; Six Degrees of Separation; wikis; and the Digital Transformations project.

Chapter 10 scrutinizes how the peaks and troughs of student energy and engagement should be managed. We review a wide range of approaches to understanding students' energy levels by employing animal analogies such as frogs and bats, as well as paper plates, timelines, and reflectionaires. Csikszentmihalyi's concept of flow is central to our analysis, and we use that, our version of the Life Wheel, and Covey's Circles of Concerns to understand best how to channel students' energies as learners. The Emotional Pathfinder and the Nesta Creative Enterprise Toolkit provide additional techniques for keeping morale for learning high.

Chapter 11—our final chapter—concludes with some personal reflections on our experience of co-authorship. The two of us write about the ways our own imaginative capacities have been engaged and expanded during the writing of this book.

Audience

Our audience for this book is potentially enormous—any teacher who wishes to use imagination, creativity, and play in order to engage students in reflective and critical thinking. Most of the activities are probably best suited to university and college students and to different forms of adult education and training. But we also know that a lot of them can be adapted to K–12 primary and secondary classrooms. As we were writing this book, we received requests about the techniques it demonstrates from teachers as diverse as further education teachers, university lecturers, community and technical college instructors, staff and professional developers, art college instructors, organizational and corporate trainers, fashion institute teachers, adult basic education tutors, social movement activists, military trainers, community group facilitators, seminarians, online program designers, parent educators, health education professionals, proprietary school teachers, and environmental educators. We believe that's an accurate representation of the kinds of teachers, trainers, and instructors who will find this book helpful.

Acknowledgments

Alison acknowledges the expertise and contributions of the many people who feature in this book, as well as those who have supported its development less directly. All have variously and freely offered time, content, stories, activities, photographs, and recommended readings; made good suggestions; and opened their address books. In particular she thanks the following individuals:

At the London College of Fashion/University of the Arts, London:

David Garner, Clare Lomas, Rob Lakin, Terry Finnigan, Benedicta Kilburn, Janice Miller, Sina Shamsavari, Nicky Ryan, Shibboleth Shechter, and Professor Hilary Grainger

And externally:

Nick Reed, Pat Francis, Julian Burton, Caitlin Walker, Professor David Gauntlett, Stuart Nolan, Jan Sellers, Sonia Overall, Gary Pritchard, Ian Bride, Lynne Dorling, Bernard Moss, Hilary Wilson, Noam Austerlitz, Kay Sandor, and Alex Irving

She is also immensely grateful to David Brightman at Jossey-Bass for having had faith in the book from its earliest stages.

A debt of gratitude and respect is also due to the many authors and educators cited in this book whose work has been enjoyed and respected and has shaped the ideas expressed.

Finally, her warmest thanks go to Stephen, an ideal writing partner who has always been generous and wise; thanks to his expertise and insights she has had the opportunity to view academic practice through wider, different eyes.

Stephen acknowledges and thanks Alison for inviting him on the ride of co-authorship of a book that truly widened his own imagination. As anally compulsive as he is, Alison's continual introduction of new exercises and activities kept Stephen in a constant state of productive uncertainty, never knowing what was coming next! He is immensely grateful to her for everything he has learned. Stephen also makes special acknowledgment to the University of St. Thomas, and particularly to Sue Huber, executive vice-president and provost, for supporting his visits to London to work intensively with Alison on the writing of the manuscript.

Finally, we extend our thanks to all our students, named, "aliased," or anonymous, those of you who have taken part in the exercises and practices included, as well as those of you who haven't. You are why we teach.

About the Authors

Alison James is associate dean, Learning & Teaching, at the London College of Fashion, and in her higher education career has focused on working with creative arts staff and students. Her first degree (1978) was in modern foreign languages (French and Italian), and she did her best to avoid going into education for eight years after graduation, working, among other things, as an interpreter and reflexologist, as well as for institutions as diverse as the Royal Institute of British Architects and a natural medicine clinic. The moment she took up a teaching post, she wondered why it had taken her so long.

As a mature student she achieved a distinction in her MA in education and followed this swiftly with a PhD in the life and work of the Royal Academician Dod Procter, and a monograph on this same artist, *A Singular Vision* (2007). While studying she worked in full-time learning and teaching roles and developed her long-standing interests in alternative and creative pedagogies, identity and self-construction in learning contexts, reflective practice, and personal and professional development. She has presented widely on all of these subjects and published in creative arts journals and edited collections. In 2013 she received an excellent teaching award from the University of the Arts, London, for her work with Lego Serious Play and student learning. She is married to Glyn, and they have six children: Kimberley, Michelle, Tom, Ashley,

Rachel, and Poppy. The family is currently being expanded by one grandchild, two horses, four cats, and mysterious numbers of fish in the garden pond.

The father of Molly and Colin, and the husband of Kim, Stephen D. Brookfield is the John Ireland Endowed Chair at the University of St. Thomas in Minneapolis–St. Paul. He received his BA degree (1970) from Lanchester College of Technology (Coventry, UK) in modern studies, his MA degree (1974) from the University of Reading (UK) in sociology, and his PhD degree (1980) from the University of Leicester (UK) in adult education. He also holds a postgraduate diploma (1971) from the University of London, Chelsea College (UK), in modern social and cultural studies and a postgraduate diploma (1977) from the University of Nottingham (UK) in adult education. In 1991 he was awarded an honorary doctor of letters degree from the University System of New Hampshire for his contributions to understanding adult learning. In 2003 he was awarded an honorary doctorate of letters from Concordia University for his contributions to adult education. In 2010 Muhlenberg College awarded him an honorary doctorate of letters for educational leadership in the scholarship of teaching.

Stephen began his teaching career in 1970 and has held appointments at colleges of further, technical, adult, and higher education in the United Kingdom and at universities in Canada (University of British Columbia) and the United States (Columbia University, Teachers College, and the University of St. Thomas). In 1989 he was visiting fellow at the Institute for Technical and Adult Teacher Education in what is now the University of Technology, Sydney, Australia. In 2002 he was visiting professor at Harvard University Graduate School of Education. In 2003–04 he was the Helen Le Baron Hilton Chair at Iowa State University. He has run numerous workshops on teaching, adult learning, and critical thinking around the world and delivered many keynote addresses at regional, national, and international education conferences.

In 2001 he received the Leadership Award from the Association for Continuing Higher Education (ACHE) for "extraordinary contributions to the general field of continuing education on a national and international level." In 2008 he received the University of St. Thomas John Ireland Presidential Award for Outstanding Achievement as a Teacher/Scholar, and also the University of St. Thomas Diversity Leadership Teaching and Research Award. Also in 2008 he was awarded the Morris T. Keeton Medal by the Council on Adult and Experiential Learning for "outstanding contributions to adult and experiential learning." In 2009 he was inducted into the International Adult Education Hall of Fame.

He is a six-time winner of the Cyril O. Houle World Award for Literature in Adult Education: in 1986 for his book *Understanding and Facilitating Adult Learning: A Comprehensive Analysis of Principles and Effective Practices* (1986); in 1989 for *Developing Critical Thinkers: Challenging Adults to Explore Alternative Ways of Thinking and Acting* (1987); in 1996 for *Becoming a Critically Reflective Teacher* (1995); in 2005 for *The Power of Critical Theory: Liberating Adult Learning and Teaching* (2004); in 2011 for his book with John D. Holst, *Radicalizing Learning: Adult Education for a Just World* (2010); and in 2012 for *Teaching for Critical Thinking: Tools and Techniques to Help Students Question Their Assumptions* (2011). *Understanding and Facilitating Adult Learning* also won the 1986 Imogene E. Okes Award for Outstanding Research in Adult Education. These awards were all presented by the American Association for Adult and Continuing Education. The first edition of *Discussion as a Way of Teaching: Tools and Techniques for Democratic Classrooms* (2nd ed., 2005), which he co-authored with Stephen Preskill, was a 1999 Critics Choice of the Educational Studies Association. His other books are *Adult Learners, Adult Education and the Community* (1984), *Self-Directed Learning: From Theory to Practice* (1985), *Learning Democracy: Eduard Lindeman on Adult Education and Social Change* (1987), *Training Educators of Adults: The Theory and Practice of Graduate*

Adult Education (1988), *The Skillful Teacher: On Technique, Trust and Responsiveness in the Classroom* (2nd ed., 2006), *Teaching Reflectively in Theological Contexts: Promises and Contradictions* (co-edited with Mary Hess, 2008), *Learning as a Way of Leading: Lessons from the Struggle for Social Justice* (co-authored with Stephen Preskill, 2008), *Handbook of Race and Adult Education* (co-edited with Vanessa Sheared, Scipio Colin III, Elizabeth Peterson, and Juanita Johnson, 2010), and *Powerful Techniques for Teaching Adults* (2012).

Engaging Imagination

Part 1

Understanding the Role of Imagination in Learning

1

How Engaging the Imagination
Fosters Reflective Thinking

Imagination is the key to human progress. Without the capacity to imagine a different world that is more beautiful than the one in which we live, change is impossible. Why would we strive for something better or different if we didn't have the imagination to conceive of a more beautiful way of living? The capacity to imagine is part of what makes us human. It is essentially a creative impulse that people build on as they conceive of, and realize, new social forms and artistic processes. Imagination is also often playful and elusive. It revels in serendipity, in unexpected connections, chance meetings, and seeing the everyday and familiar in new ways.

The unpredictability of engaging the imagination makes it hard to adapt to classroom environments ruled by rigid assessment protocols. If we have decreed in advance the evidence we will use to measure whether or not learning has occurred, there is little room for divergence or the unexpected. This virtual outlawing of so many facets of creativity is one of the travesties of higher education. If education is supposed to draw students out, to help them understand new ideas, practice new skills, and make meaningful personal connections to learning, then it makes no sense to declare in advance that certain modes of expression are off the table.

To pose a provocative challenge: Why shouldn't doctoral science students dance their PhDs (Bohannon, 2011)? Why are we not open to varied expressive modes—video, art, drama, poetry, music—to gauge students' learning? If there are multiple intelligences (Gardner, 2011), if students' diverse histories, cultural backgrounds, racial identities, and personalities mean teaching and learning is inevitably complex (Allen, Sheve, and Nieter, 2010), then shouldn't our approaches to helping and assessing learning exhibit a similar variety? Even in something as highly structured as online education it's clear that creativity, variety, and imagination are crucial to retaining student interest and participation (Conrad and Donaldson, 2011, 2012).

This book is about finding ways to increase the number of imaginative moments that students encounter in contemporary classrooms. We both work from the assumption that when students learn something using different senses and when they study the same content through different modalities, there is a depth and complexity to their learning that is absent when only one format—filling in the lines next to PowerPoint slides projected during a lecture, for example—is adopted. For learning to "stick," whether it is understanding a complex new concept, applying existing knowledge in unfamiliar contexts, or honing a newly developed psychomotor skill, the fullest range of our imaginative faculties needs to be engaged. Both of us love listening to well-constructed and delivered lectures and reading well-written texts. Equally, however, we both know that the broader the range of imaginative activities we're involved in, the more engaged we are with the learning.

Allied to imagination is the notion of engagement. Exercising imagination is inherently engaging, so a classroom in which students use their imaginations to study content, play with ideas, and imagine new possibilities should be an engaging one. Engaging students is something we hear about all the time, but we know that some colleagues assume that student engagement means "teaching-lite." "Teaching-lite" is a view of teaching whereby teachers are deemed to use superficial activities, social media, and games to convince students that learning is "fun," thereby securing favorable student evaluations. Effort, hard work, and struggle seem excluded in this stereotype. Colleagues subscribing to this caricature usually assume that *engagement* means going easy on students and never asking them to take on anything challenging. A false dichotomy is then created between engagement and "real learning"; that is, between learning that is superficial and that which is substantial, important, not much fun, and requires enormous effort.

We agree that learning sometimes is fun. But equally we know that learning is sometimes difficult, frustrating, and a long hard slog. We acknowledge that although classroom learning is certainly enjoyable at times, it also involves struggle, arduous work, and, yes, boredom. Before we can engage creatively and critically with ideas and practices, we often have to struggle to learn the fundamentals of a discipline, the grammar of a subject. We need to understand axiomatic principles, practice basic skills to a point of expertise, and assimilate foundational building blocks of knowledge. One of us (Stephen) teaches critical social theory, a dense, jargon-ridden body of work for which both a dictionary and considerable powers of perseverance are necessary to make progress. Stephen is the first to admit that his continuing struggle to understand this material is one that involves a lot of hard, and often frustrating, labor.

But living with frustration, motivating oneself for the long haul of learning, and negotiating continual challenges is helped considerably by moments of imaginative engagement. When we come at difficult material in new and unexpected ways, when we try to convey complex meanings visually or kinetically rather than through language (dancing our PhD!), and when we ask the question "What would this look like if…?," we often find our energy for the hard slog is renewed. The important point about using imagination is that we are using it to engage students with the most challenging, difficult, and substantial learning that we judge they need to undertake. Engagement is precisely what it says: helping students engage with knowledge, concepts, ideas, and skills to an

ever-higher degree of expertise. There is nothing inherently superficial or unchallenging about engagement; in fact it's the opposite
of superficiality. Indeed, we would argue that it is the only hope of
ever getting students to understand complex content or develop
exemplary skillfulness.

The Three Axioms of Student Engagement

In engaging students—in helping them to develop deeper
levels of understanding and to demonstrate higher levels of
accomplishment—we need to be imaginative in thinking about
different ways to teach that provoke learning. Our position regarding the importance of imagination in teaching is built on three
essential pedagogic axioms:

1. Student learning is deepest when the content or skills being
   learned are personally meaningful, and this happens when
   students see connections and applications of learning. Connections and applications occur when creative synthesis takes
   place, when people suddenly see unexpected patterns emerging, and when new questions are posed. Doing these things involves creativity and imagination.
2. Student learning "sticks" more (in other words, retention of
   knowledge and skill is increased) when the same content or skills
   are learned through multiple methods. A monochromatic approach that adopts one pedagogic strategy overwhelmingly (always using discussions, always lecturing, always studying inde-
   pendently, always using language to communicate learning) is
   at odds with the empirical reality of students' multiple intelligences, different models of information processing, and variety
   of culturally preferred learning styles.
3. The most memorable critical incidents students experience
   in their learning are those when they are required to "come
   at" their learning in a new way, when they are "jerked out" of

the humdrum by some unexpected challenge or unanticipated task. We naturally remember the surprising rather than the routine, the unpredictable rather than the expected. One of the best ways to create memorable learning moments is to ask students to use their imaginations to ask "What if?" Upending the normal and familiar can be threatening and confusing, but it is usually also unforgettable. So a large part of student engagement entails creating moments of productive discomfort when expectations are reversed and different faculties are called into play—as, for example, when students are asked only to draw or dance their ideas, or to use Legos to build a model of their developing understanding of a topic.

Our belief in the importance of engaging imagination rests on these three axioms, so let's say a little more about them.

Engagement Is Personally Meaningful

The first axiom focuses on meaningfulness, on students appreciating that the knowledge and skills being learned are important and necessary in some way. Now, importance and necessity are not the same as utilitarian. We can study something that has no immediate vocational application yet find it enthralling. An artist can be fascinated by the scientific principle of falsifiability (the idea that unless something is open to empirical disconfirmation it cannot be considered scientific), and a scientist can be enthralled by the creativity of a Cyril Power or the Clash. But we believe that the scientist and the artist in these two examples are captivated because something about scientific falsifiability or artistic creativity "speaks" to them.

In other words, some truth, which might not be able to be concretely articulated, rests in the respective objects of contemplation. Perhaps the artist finds falsifiability an interesting notion because it is so contrary to her experience, and therefore poses an interesting challenge. Or perhaps falsifiability is intriguing because its emphasis on the importance of direct experience is also compelling for her in artistic expression. The scientist, at the same time, may find that Power's linocuts, or Joe Strummer's vocals, prompt an immediate visceral response that is very different from the pleasure derived from science. Maybe there is a suggestion of the erotic or animal, or a fascination with line or form that seems totally unrelated to scientific convention. But in both instances the connections with new forms of understanding are personally meaningful; they are not apprehended at a distance, but rather felt as somehow personally significant.

Of course, it is much easier to see learning as personally meaningful in situations in which students understand that a direct application to their life, work, or self-awareness is entailed. Thus, studying philosophy is often justified as preparing students to work through ethical dilemmas or to live with the ambiguity they will find in adulthood. Social work or engineering courses are deemed to provide vocationally necessary skills that will secure employment and advance a career. Psychology is taught to help students develop insight into their own actions and the justifications for these so that they become more self-aware. Our position is that where such clear connections are absent, it is still pedagogically important to find imaginative ways of helping students discover personal meaning in learning.

Learning "Sticks" When Multiple Methods Engage the Imagination

This axiom regarding engaging imagination is much less philosophically dense than the first. As researchers into student engagement have shown (Barkley, 2009; Bean, 2011), asking students to "come at" the same knowledge or skills in different ways has multiple benefits. First, it is more successful in promoting "deeper" learning (Ohlson, 2011); that is, learning where students understand the complexity of content and the contextual application of skills, and where they can reinterpret experience to change their understanding of the world. It also keeps student interest at higher levels. The more you change up different teaching methods and ask students to try out different classroom, online, or homework activities, the more they stay awake and involved. Alternating verbal and visual modalities, silent and oral ways of communicating, individual and group activities, kinesthetic and cognitive activities, and abstract and concrete ways of processing information keeps the class moving as it calls on different elements of students' personalities and skill sets.

Stephen has spent twenty years collecting data from students across multiple disciplines and institutions regarding their reactions to classroom learning. Through the use of a Critical Incident Questionnaire (CIQ; http://stephenbrookfield.com/ Dr._Stephen_D._Brookfield/Critical_Incident_Questionnaire. html)—an anonymous student response form—he has found that the most enduring reality of college teaching is that the greater the modality of teaching methods used, the higher the level of student engagement; that is, the more students were successful in actively striving to comprehend material, make connections, and apply concepts. The CIQ specifically asks students to identify moments when they were most and least engaged as learners, and actions that helped or hindered this engagement. Repeatedly, students say that the classes where they were most engaged were those where three or four different teaching modalities or learning activities were used.

Students Are Engaged When Something "Jerks" Them Out of the Routines

The most charismatically engaging lecturers and the most responsively alert discussion leaders can still occasionally fall victim to routine. For students, nothing wakes up attention to learning more than being asked to do something unfamiliar and expected. When a student is asked to represent his or her understanding of a concept by building a Lego model, or when a group is asked to draw the discussion they have just had for the whole class to interpret, a level of productive dissonance, of helpful creative panic, is introduced. The disorienting nature of a surprisingly new learning task or unanticipated classroom activity is always vividly remembered, precisely because of the risk involved. Risk is inherently unsettling, and adrenalin runs as we go into retreat or avoidance. But it is that same adrenalin-infused panic that makes the activity, and then the resultant learning sticks.

Whenever the two of us use activities and approaches that seem like an entertaining distraction from routine, we always have a deeper intent. We want to jolt ourselves, and students, out of our normal and routine ways of understanding and practicing. In this we build on Herbert Marcuse's (Reitz, 2000; Miles, 2012) argument that aesthetic experiences induce breaks and ruptures from the familiar. When students who are used to reading texts and following PowerPoints while listening to lectures switch into a different mode they are learning very differently and temporarily estranged from the familiar routines of learning. This is startling and memorable, a classroom equivalent of the kind of "disorienting dilemma" Jack Mezirow (1991) regarded as the precursor of transformative learning.

One way to help students manage their feelings of danger and risk is by modeling our own willingness as teachers to do exactly what we are asking of them. Instead of standing at the side and observing while students take all the risks, we need to take them first in front of the class. For example, as this chapter was being written, Stephen Brookfield was running a professional development workshop with his sometime co-author Stephen Preskill in which they asked students to summarize their small-group discussions visually or musically. The two Stephens then tried to model stretching themselves in this activity in front of the class by drawing their discussion in terms of a surfer riding the infamous "mavericks" wave off Santa Cruz, as they sang a reworked version of the Beach Boys' song "Catch a Wave."

How Does Engaging Imagination Connect to Reflection?

How does engaging imagination connect to reflective thinking? We think there are two categories of connection—one for teachers, one for students. For teachers our notion of imaginative teaching necessarily entails them trying to see their pedagogic actions and reasoning in new and creative ways. This requires them to pay attention to the myriad of ways that different students understand, experience, and respond to the same curricular content or classroom activity. We need also to solicit different colleagues' readings of our practice. One of the joys of team teaching is that you have a built-in observer (your colleague in the team) who will notice things you miss, provide different interpretations of what went on that day in class, and open you up to new aspects of the material you are teaching. Both of us learn so much from the colleagues we teach with. In fact, we rely on them to keep the content fresh for us.

Teachers also can have their familiar perspectives and assumptions challenged and upended by literature. For example, Stephen's study of Michel Foucault (1980) was an imaginative stretch for him that provided a wholly new and very different perspective on his practice. Things that to Stephen had seemed wholly positive examples of empowering students—for example, using discussion circles or refusing to develop curricula in an attempt to encourage student empowerment—were challenged by Foucault's analysis. Stephen began to understand that to some students the circle was an unwarranted attempt to coerce students into participating in the class and an experience in surveillance. Similarly, refusing to develop curricula or specify evaluative criteria was likely to be seen by many students as evasive, as holding back or playing a game in which students were disempowered because they were not privy to the rules Stephen was keeping to himself. This analysis sparked Stephen's imagination and caused him to rethink completely the dynamics of small-group discussion, and to work very differently when clarifying his power and authority. Now, instead of being coy about his power, and pretending almost to be a friend of the students, Stephen is eager to make an early disclosure of how he seeks to exercise the positional authority he has, and to encourage students (through the CIQ) to critique his use of power.

For students, engaging imagination requires an attempt to see things from multiple, and very different, perspectives, and to be open to multiple ways of learning something. Before we explain in detail how imagination enhances reflective thinking in students, we need to explain what we mean by that term.

What Does It Mean to Be Reflective?

According to the *Oxford English Dictionary*, reflection is simply serious thought or consideration. Among the many who amplify this rudimentary understanding Dewey suggests reflection is the "active, persistent and careful consideration of any belief or supposed form of knowledge in the light of the grounds that support it . . . and the further conclusions to which it tends" (Dewey, 1933, p. 18). This is something that both parents and natural scientists understand. These two groups build knowledge by continuously subjecting their theories to empirical scrutiny, and they change those theories as they find evidence to refute or modify them. But although experience provides the vital raw material for reflection—its evidence, if you will—on its own, it does not suffice as a basis for learning. It is what we do with that experience—how we convert its complex constituent elements into knowledge or understanding—that constitutes learning.

Perhaps the most influential work on reflection in the past few decades has been that of Donald Schön (1987), who differentiated between *reflection-in-action* (conscious, critical thinking that simultaneously reshapes what we are doing as we are doing it) and *reflection-on-action* (a post facto evaluation of behaviors and decisions that have taken place). Related to this distinction is the difference he drew with Chris Argyris between *espoused theory* and *theory in use* (Argyris and Schön, 1974). At its most simple, this can be described as the tension between what we say we believe or do and how we live out, or deviate from these beliefs, in particular contexts. Argyris and Schön also argued that two forms of reflective practice were apparent, based on single- and double-loop learning. Single-loop learning built on Kolb's (1984) notion of the learning cycle as a means of reviewing how things are done and how they can be bettered. Double-loop learning moved reflection to a process through which things might be transformed rather than just improved (Brockbank, McGill, and Beech, 2002). Subsequent critiques of these models suggest that their neatness does not allow for nonlinear, multidirectional, and multilayered manifestations of reflection, nor do they take account of the opacity and mess that often surround the chiseling out of new insights or paradigm shifts.

Educators typically envisage reflection as a cognitive process, yet humans perceive through all our senses (see Robinson, 2011) in an embodied, mobile existence; consequently we reflect through all of these senses too. There are variations in the rhythms of reflection, the ebb and flow between purposive and judgmental kinds of thinking and those that are fluid and undirected. Reflection involves multiple pursuits and responses: mulling over, letting go, chasing after, homing in, asking why, leaving be, pulling apart, reassembling, stirring, sifting, critiquing, analyzing, evaluating, observing, intuiting, looking, feeling, waiting. It may involve conscious or unconscious decisions to deliberate in the hope of forcing insights, or walking away from an internal wrangle, thereby loosening the pressure valves of concentration in the hope that a solution will naturally present itself. Having probed our experiences we may reassemble them in a different configuration and find that our initial readings of a situation have shifted shape, perspective, and intensity as a result.

Claxton has an interesting categorization of these variances in our patterns of thought, idea, and response, between when we are deliberating and when we decide to let go. He calls this the difference between "hard" and "soft" thinking. Hard thinking—purposeful and deliberate—is sometimes experienced as an antidote to innovation. When we try too hard, or put pressure on ourselves, this "leads to self-consciousness, tension and a loss of expertise" (Claxton, 1999, p. 149). Our attention narrows when we reflect to order, against the clock, or within the confines of a learning situation that is not conducive to us. Claxton cites stress as an inhibitor of learning and evokes the pitfalls that can arise when we are too conscious of what we are doing, or when reflection is a form of compliance to meet external performance appraisal or accreditation.

Soft thinking, however, involves being in a relaxed state, able to allow one's thoughts to bubble up and disperse freely, without nailing them down or only allowing in the ones that fit with a preset framework. It is a process that takes time to emerge and cannot be rushed. In describing a study involving fine art students in Chicago, Claxton (1999) noted that the most successful students were identified as those who "played with more objects, and in more imaginative ways, before choosing which they wanted to paint, and their choices were more unusual" (p. 156). Taking the time to mull over their choices and change their minds was part of the slow thinking required to achieve better results in the long run.

Pink (2011) and Kane (2004) are also spiritually aligned with the value of soft thinking, noting that the first solutions generated or the most swift, articulate answers provided are not necessarily the best or right ones. Both authors recognize that intuition is both undervalued and underdeveloped in formal education. We agree and argue that we need to make space for and honor our inner voices, personal antennae, and gut feelings. While the sense of this is something all teachers can recognize, we are equally aware that our educational climate today does not favor the slow approach or value intuition. Rather it encourages technical rationality, analysis, and logic over other kinds of knowing.

Fourteen Elements of Reflective Thinking in Students

Based on the foregoing analyses, what should teachers look out for as examples of reflective thinking in students? We believe that reflective thinking happens when students do one or more of these fourteen things:

1. Check the assumptions that inform their actions and judgments
2. Seek to open themselves to new and unfamiliar perspectives
3. Attempt intersubjective understanding and perspective taking—trying to understand how another person reasons, understands content, or views knowledge
4. Make their intuitions and "gut" feelings the focus of study
5. Study the effects of their actions with a view to changing them
6. Look for blind spots and omissions in their thinking
7. Identify what is justified and well grounded in their thinking
8. Accept and experiment with multiple learning modalities
9. Value emotional dimensions of their learning as much as the purely cognitive
10. Try to upend their habitual ways of understanding something
11. Connect their thinking conducted in one domain to thinking in another
12. Become more aware of their habitual epistemic cognition—the typical ways they judge something to be true
13. Apply reflective protocols in contextually appropriate ways
14. Alternate cognitive analysis with an acceptance of an unregulated, unmediated flow of emotions, impulses, intuitions, and images

Encouraging these fourteen elements of reflective thinking is what the rest of this book is about. In the subsequent chapters we look at specific approaches and particular activities that encourage these different aspects of reflective thing. Our survey covers a range of different approaches such as Lego model building, story, metaphor, labyrinth walking, visualization, inflatable pods, and clean language. But before we start to delve into particular activities and exercises, we want to say a few things concerning the dynamics of teaching imaginatively.

Creativity and Playfulness Are Important

Whenever the term *thinking* is employed, the discourse typically lurches immediately to mental maps, cognitive pathways, ladders of inference, and so on. In this discourse, thinking is typically equated with purposeful analysis tied to some predetermined goal. However, as David Lodge's novel *Thinks* (2001) nicely demonstrates, even supposedly rigid formulaic thought is continually interrupted by images that pop into our heads and take us by surprise, by random questions that suddenly surface, by an awareness of smells, by the way the touch of a keyboard produces a misspelling that leads to a new line of analysis, or by a pre-conscious process of biofeedback when our bodies move into lulls or come alive with adrenaline. At one point in *Thinks* the protagonist (a university-based cognitive scientist) decides to study, deliberately and purposefully, his own thoughts. He is shocked at how random these are and how little control he has over them.

In this book we emphasize these creative, playful, and imaginative elements. The discourse of cognition with its formal mental protocols gets enough coverage, and we value it and learn from it. But we want to explore alternative approaches to engaging student reflection. By working with visual, auditory, kinesthetic, discursive, and written modalities of teaching and learning, we hope to show how learners can broaden and deepen their understanding of knowledge and open their minds to other ways of construing the world and their futures.

A Degree of Student Freedom Is Essential

No matter how charismatic, knowledgeable, and gifted teachers might be, they cannot make every student learn in the ways they expect. The approaches and activities we explore presume an element of freedom for students in trying out and adopting reflective techniques and environments. Take reflective writing as an example. Journaling, writing up learning logs, keeping portfolios, compiling critical practice audits are all things Stephen has explored, because this is both familiar territory to him and constitutes the most organizationally accepted mode of recording reflection. This is also precisely how accreditation agencies define evidence of students' developing reflective capacities.

But although writing has many advantages and attractions, a significant number of students find the process of textual reflection a turn-off. Requiring a certain number of pages to be turned in documenting the student's engagement in appropriate reflection can be constraining and deadening. If we are to challenge the hegemony of written representations of learning, we need to insist on a degree of freedom for students to document their learning in alternative formats. Poetry, music, artworks, video, collage, graphics, drama, dance—some students will find some of these a far more interesting way of communicating what meanings they have drawn from content, or what skills they are developing, than a written assignment.

This does, of course, raise political problems for teachers. What if our head of department has told us that the impending accreditation visit requires that we apply written protocols to collect evidence of student progress? If we refuse to comply we are imperiling our future contract renewal, jeopardizing our tenure, as well as earning a reputation for ourselves as institutional loose cannons. Then again, we may have little or no experience in working in alternative formats. Stephen, for example, has had no training in using anything other than written evaluations of student learning. For him, evaluating poetry, collage, or video is very intimidating. We explore how to negotiate this dynamic at various points in this book.

Not only is a degree of freedom important to students, but teachers also need to have mind-sets that are open to possibilities. Much of the work around encouraging student reflectivity involves trying to create an openness to methods of learning that sometimes appear to be unconventional or "abnormal" for their field. Of course, this is not to say that only unconventional approaches instigate imaginative or more engaged learning. Slavishly and uncritically applying divergent strategies is as narrow minded and unresponsive as only sticking to lectures. But we both feel it's important to ask the questions whether and where imaginative engagement may be missing from student reflection and why this might matter.

The Hegemony of Written Reflection Must Be Challenged

This problem was touched on in the preceding paragraphs. In some measure writing has become synonymous with "degree-ness"—a sign that academic thresholds have been crossed and intelligence suitably demonstrated. Students' ambivalence over writing is not just confined to one single sector, or simply a matter of specific learning difficulty. It crosses disciplinary boundaries and educational levels. Avoiding writing for whatever reason may also have been a deciding factor in the choice a student has made of a degree program, community college certificate, or further education course. One of Stephen's friends has built an enviable and flourishing academic career analyzing poetry because it involved less writing and reading than conducting literary analysis of novels. Other students choose STEM (scientific, technical, engineering, and mathematics) subjects because these don't require much writing. Sometimes academic writing is demoralizing:

"It feels like when I put my thoughts on paper and try to fit them into the structures and rules of academic writing, my own thoughts become alien to me and I no longer understand them or see the logic of them in the same way" (from Line, a student of Alison's from Scandinavia).

With the advent of Web 2.0 technologies there has been an increase in the use of other modes of reflecting, including podcasts, video and audio diaries, and social media; however, the dominant mode of expression is writing, not least where evidence of reflection is required for assessment. Reflective activities that are commonly used include producing accounts of self-assessments of reflective skills and capabilities, compiling reflective curriculum vitae, writing personal platforms, assembling reflective portfolios, or completing learning audits. Some of the materials used have been designed for specific professional sectors, such as health care and education, and are related to particular aspects of professional practice—dentistry is one example.

Faced with the task of writing reflections, students are not always sure what they should write about and how. They ask whether they can use "I," if they can relax their observation of academic conventions (such as avoiding theoretical references), or if a more colloquial voice is permissible. How they are advised on these matters will depend on local circumstances and protocols, or the criteria specified for the reflective task. For example, Stephen has built on Robert Nash's idea of scholarly personal narratives (Nash, 2004; Nash and Bradley, 2011; Nash and Viray, 2013) to supervise dissertations that follow a personal narrative format. However, along the lines advocated by Nash, he requires that such narratives contain regular citations of relevant theory and research that illuminate the story's arc. He is well aware that without these being included, students would have a much harder time convincing potential committee members of the academic legitimacy of their work.

Students who are highly articulate verbally and who can talk imaginatively and with passion about their work are not automatically or necessarily fluid writers, although we frequently assume that one goes with the other. Compared to writing, less attention appears to have been paid to the other kinds of reflective practice that people engage in, and of alternative ways of evidencing this. This is a recurrent issue in the creative arts and design, where there is a higher proportion of students with dyslexia than in other disciplines. Their preference for visual or kinesthetic activity, as opposed to reading or writing, and their discomfort in producing written reflective accounts show that an opportunity is being missed to play to these students' strengths. We note too that in the world of work some of the behaviors most often identified with good leadership and organizational effectiveness—chairing a meeting well is a prime example—have nothing to do with the capacity to write well academically.

A Degree of Resistance Is Normal

Students schooled in top-down, instrumental ways of working, when the question at the forefront of their minds is "Is this on the test?," may well see reflection as pointless, "touchy-feely," and "soft," compared to traditional academic conceptions that learning is always textually based and reproduces what an expert does or says. They dismiss reflection as narcissistic navel gazing or directionless dithering. However, as Atherton (2012) recognizes, the importance of reflection is to some extent decided by the discipline—in some it is integral to academic study and practice, while for others it may appear irrelevant and inappropriate.

Telling students that we are opening up opportunities for them to practice reflective thinking will not always be welcomed. Students may take a purely instrumental approach to this, slipping quickly into a "Just tell me what you want me to do and how you want me to do it" mode. Being imaginative is probably not the first thing that springs to students' minds when they are asked to reflect on their learning. And things become even more complex when they are told that being reflective involves elements of self-appraisal. Students underwhelmed by the prospect of a foray into their own metacognition may prefer an instrumental approach concerned with "getting reflection done" as opposed to fully exploring all its possibilities. Our book tries to counter this instrumentalism by shifting the spotlight onto imagination and its counterparts of creativity and play.

Reflection Can Be Used for Control

Another cause of resistance to reflective practices is the notion that this is being used to control students. In *Beyond Reflective Practice* (Bradbury, Frost, Kilminster, and Zukas, 2010), the book's contributors draw on Foucault's work to argue that reflection, far from being a liberating experience in expanding perspectives and transformative realizations, is an example of disciplinary power in which people keep themselves in line because they feel themselves under the threat of constant surveillance.

Disciplinary power is the power we exercise on ourselves to make sure that we do not transgress acceptable boundaries of thinking and acting. When we monitor our own conduct out of fear of being observed by an unseen, powerful gaze, then the perfect mechanism of control—self-surveillance—is operating. There is no need for the coercive state apparatus to spend enormous amounts of time and money making sure we behave correctly because we are watching ourselves to make sure we don't step out of line. What makes us watch ourselves so assiduously is the sense that our attempt to stay close to the norm is being watched by another, all-seeing, presence. We carry within us the sense that "out there," in some hidden, undiscoverable location, "they" are constantly observing us. It is hard to deviate from the norm if you feel your thoughts and actions are being recorded (figuratively and sometimes literally) by cameras hidden in every corner of your life.

Formal protocols of reflection carry within them the possibility of controlling self-surveillance. When an institution decides what you will reflect on, and prescribes the mechanisms by which that reflection will be carried out, there is clearly the possibility of a controlled abuse of power. This is not always the case, though. After all, insisting that students reflect on the ways they have uncritically accepted social norms, how far dominant ideologies (patriarchy, White supremacy, and so on) have got their hooks in them, is a form of directed reflection that challenges dominant power.

Much of the mandated reflection the two of us have come across is tied to institutional goals, which are themselves tied to the kinds of learning outcomes that accreditation and licensing bodies desire. Performance appraisal formats typically require that the employee reflect on his effectiveness in the preceding year, and that he set goals for the coming year based on that reflection. The reflective effort is completely framed by the judgment of how well the individual serves institutional ends. Nowhere have we come across performance appraisals that ask for a reflection on the degree to which the sponsoring organization is racist, sexist, homophobic, ableist, and so on. In the American and Canadian universities where Stephen has worked, the tenure process typically involves the candidate submitting a number of reflective self-evaluations on her development as a professional. He has never read an evaluation in which the compiler focused on her success in challenging and subverting organizational norms and practices; neither has Stephen ever submitted such a reflection.

Any time we tie reflection to the evaluation and assessment of students' reflection it becomes an exercise of teacher power. Of course, pretty much anything we do in our formal role as teachers is an exercise of power, and often this power is used for good, is enacted ethically, and is fully justifiable. But we should also always remember that when we require students to reflect, and when we grade their efforts, we are not working solely from a student-centered ethic. Certainly we hope students will learn from their mandatory reflections, but it is naïve and disingenuous for us to pretend that there is not the continual potential for students to experience those same reflections as a constraining and controlling exercise of teacher power.

Summary

Having enumerated several difficulties of getting students to think reflectively, at about this point you may be wondering "Why bother?" Rest assured the chapters following this one answer that question and provide multiple examples of activities and exercises that students have found helpful. We end this opening chapter, however, by stressing the importance of teacher modeling. By *modeling* we don't mean providing an exemplary demonstration of something so students can aspire to emulate our flawless perfection. Indeed, one important aspect of modeling reflective thinking is demonstrating that it has uncontrollable aspects, long pauses, and regular episodes of confusion.

We need always to remember that for many students the different aspects of thinking reflectively are inherently intimidating, particularly if students are encouraged to experiment with imaginative approaches that don't use writing or follow preset and familiar protocols. As teachers we need to demonstrate for students that we also find this difficult, but that we believe strongly enough in the benefits of using imaginative approaches that we voluntarily and publicly commit to doing everything we are asking students to—and doing it first.

Throughout this book the two of us—Alison and Stephen—try to model how we implement and adapt the exercises we describe. In doing this we adhere to the same modeling dynamic that students say they appreciate. We assume that you as a reader will appreciate our doing our best to model for you how we try out the various activities we propose.

2

Introducing Reflective Thinking to Students

In this chapter we explore the ways teachers can introduce reflective thinking—and the broader notions of reflection and reflective practice—to students. Much has been written on the generation of millennial students, although, as Bonner, Marbley, and Howard-Hamilton (2011) have pointed out, any attempt to reduce a group of people who display a dizzying array of identities and experiences to a set of broad characteristics is fraught with peril. Interestingly, however, three of the top eight defining events of the lives of millennials interviewed by Dungy (2011) were Web related: social networking, YouTube, and Wikipedia. All of these represent in different ways an overarching emphasis on immediacy of access to information—personal, popular, and academic.

In stark contrast to this emphasis, *reflection* sounds dull and passive, the province of those whose lives are so insignificant or unimportant that there is no need for them to be accessing information at the touch of a fingertip on a keyboard. So by using terms like *reflective practice* and *reflective thinking*, we already have a strike against us. Yet, even as the two of us fear we are working with an outmoded vocabulary, we are encouraged by the creativity that millennials bring to their study. Like it or not, contemporary college classrooms are rapidly transitioning to multimedia environments, where hand-held devices, Web links, polls, clickers, and video are the norm.

So here we have a situation in which some of the ideas we are trying to link in this book—creativity, engagement, and imagination on the one hand and reflection on the other—are seen by students as being in opposition. Creativity, engagement, and imagination are seen as tied to multiple media, social networking, and student interaction; reflection is seen as tied to an armchair. How do we position reflective thinking to students in a way that convinces them it is necessary for their growth and development?

Clarifying the Elements of Reflective Thinking

An obvious first step in getting students to think more reflectively is to remove some of the opaqueness surrounding the catch-all term *reflection*, which suffers from being woolly and ill defined, and therefore ineffective (see, for example, Atherton, 2012). The widespread espousal of reflection as key to effective learning has meant that its meaning is assumed to be obvious to all. Moon (2005) describes a similar difficulty with the term *critical thinking*, resulting in an inherent vagueness in people's minds as to what the expression really means. To this we can add terms like *transformative learning, empowerment*, and even *social justice*. With regard to this last term, Ayers, Kumashiro, Meiners, Quinn, and Stovall (2010) note that "the phrase itself has overrun its banks and risks being reduced to a slogan without substance, a weak trickle where there should be a raging river....It is easily co-opted and rendered toothless in some places, and in other places it is lifeless, dead on arrival" (p. 61). We both feel reflection is sometimes subject to the same evacuation of meaning.

For example, in a study of conceptions of reflection in the creative arts, all the staff surveyed saw themselves as reflective, with one observing, "I used to be a permanent worrier. Then I did my PG Cert and realized I was a reflective practitioner" (James, 2007, p. 187). However, the study also showed that explaining to students exactly what constituted reflection tended not to happen; rather, reflective habits were assumed to be inculcated implicitly through question and answer, feedback, or learning from example. If a final outcome was good, then it was taken as an indication that a student had reflected effectively on her learning. This is the obscurity approach to defining reflection—"I know it when I see it"—and is confusing for students.

One way to introduce the idea in a colloquial way is to define reflections as the way we "look back to go forward." In other words, reflective thinking takes a situation, or an act of learning, and tries to identify what went well or was clearly understood, what went badly or was misunderstood, how to avoid similar errors in reasoning or understanding in the future, and what steps are going to be taken next in action or learning. Of course, this technical sense of reflection elides questions of focus and purpose; after all, politicians can look back reflectively on how well they've deceived voters by misrepresenting facts and how well they've knowingly told blatant lies that ensured their victory. They can then take steps to ensure that the same deceit and manipulation is successfully repeated in future campaigns. Equally, we can assume that for many years tobacco companies spent a considerable reflective effort working out how to portray smoking as harmless and sexually appealing so that they could increase future profits.

One of the most difficult struggles we have faced as teachers is trying to strike some sort of balance between how much or how little guidance we offer to students. There is a fine line to be drawn between providing a subtle steer as to how someone might approach a reflection and micromanaging the living daylights out of her personal analysis of learning and experience. Uncertain as to what is required and constrained by the mode of reflection and its specified topics, students can feel uncomfortable about producing a truly honest reflection. They are concerned about private issues potentially becoming public, of value judgments being made about their views and activities, and, when reflection is assessed, of grades being arrived at simply according to the intensity of enthusiasm they display for their subject.

In a higher education culture driven by a student quest for perfect grades, there is the danger that if reflection is not assessed, then students do not understand why they have to do it. So much organizational behavior is driven by reward systems, and the ultimate reward system for students is getting an A grade for their work. If told that reflection is either optional or not contributing to their grade, there is the strong possibility that most students will simply not take it seriously. At the same time, when reflection is assessed but no information is given about what that constitutes, all kinds of misunderstandings develop. Myths spring up as to what it is appropriate or desirable to write about and how these will be assessed. Students fear that it will be their actual life experience that is being graded and not the quality of the thinking. Consequently they are tempted to write a public relations account of events to put themselves in the best possible light. Alternatively they try to write what they think a teacher wants them to say or pretend an engagement with reflection that they have never felt.

Although we do not spend time on assessment issues here, an exploration of different kinds of reflective activity renders apparent a number of the key elements to consider when grading reflection—a task that can be notoriously difficult. In essence the assessor needs to concentrate on:

- The quality and evidence of the thinking processes at work in the reflective activity, and not on descriptions of what someone has been up to

- The ability to drill into specifics rather than make generic statements

- The ability to question and to challenge assumptions

- The ability to model conclusion and consequence and link cause and effect

- The ability to be aware of and respect different perspectives

On the general issue of assessment we support practice that allows for student flexibility in how they engage with the process. This includes space for the private choice of media for recording reflection, or multimodal approaches that allow for the many different ways in which students may process information and respond to experience.

In chapter 1 we proposed a template of fourteen typical behaviors, operations, or dispositions that we believe could be described as examples of reflective thinking. We reproduce this list again following. Reflective thinking in our view happens when students do one or more of the following things:

1. Check the assumptions that inform their actions and judgments
2. Seek to open themselves to new and unfamiliar perspectives
3. Attempt intersubjective understanding and perspective taking—trying to understand how another person reasons
4. Make their intuitions and "gut" feelings the focus of study
5. Study the effects of their actions with a view to changing them
6. Look for blind spots and omissions in their thinking and practice
7. Identify what is justified and well grounded in their thinking and practice
8. Experiment with multiple learning modalities to foster deep learning
9. Value emotional dimensions of their learning as much as the purely cognitive
10. Try to upend their habitual ways of understanding something
11. Connect thinking conducted in one domain to thinking in another
12. Become more aware of their habitual epistemic cognition—the typical ways they judge something to be true
13. Apply reflective protocols in contextually appropriate ways
14. Alternate cognitive analysis with an acceptance of an unregulated, unmediated flow of emotions, impulses, intuitions, and images

Any course in which teachers are urging reflection on students needs to break that idea down into some specific behaviors or operations. The previous list is not exhaustive, and we do not anticipate that all or even many of them would be involved in any one particular course or even a specific discipline. And we certainly don't wish to erect yet another set of protocols that become as constraining as any other. But a basic tenet of good teaching is that students need to have some general idea of where you wish them to go, while at the same time feeling they have the freedom to chart a new path of their own making if the one you've laid down doesn't make much sense to them.

Modeling Reflectivity: Examples for Each Reflective Thinking Process

We ended the previous chapter mentioning this theme, and it's worth repeating. Before asking students to think reflectively, and to exercise creativity in doing that, we need to model what that looks like for them. We need, too, to be publicly explicit about that practice. There is little point in striving to model certain intellectual operations for students if these operations are not named as examples of reflective or creative thinking. In more than two decades worth of Critical Incident Questionnaire (CIQ) responses from thousands of students across the disciplines, Stephen has noticed that one recurring theme is students' appreciation of teachers who let students know when and how they are modeling the kinds of tasks and processes they wish students to learn.

In professional development workshops Stephen teaches with Steve Preskill (Stephen's authorial colleague on *Learning as a Way of Leading* (1998) and *Discussion as a Way of Teaching* (2005)), one of the exercises they frequently adopt is a version of the Clearness Committee, a Quaker-based exercise popularized by Parker Palmer (2007). In this exercise a group of critical friends devote their full attention to helping one of their number come to a greater understanding of a seemingly intractable problem she or he is facing. They do this solely by asking open-ended questions that meet two conditions: (1) they do not know the answer to the questions they ask, and (2) questions are asked to help the person who has brought the problem to find his or her own answers to it.

Steve and Stephen model this activity for students, and Stephen Brookfield is usually cast in the role of the questioner. He never knows what problem Steve will bring to him, and he worries that he will fail to ask good questions either because he has no prior relevant experience with the problem, or simply because he's not "on" that day. But he begins the demonstration of the exercise by sharing these doubts with the students so they get used to seeing a credible workshop leader admit to nerves before trying out a technique. Then, when he's in the role of questioner he frequently pauses for a while to show a comfort with silence. He also says out loud those moments when he's finding it hard to think of a good question. On CIQ evaluations of these workshops, one of the most frequent and predictable responses is students saying how much they appreciate seeing Steve and Stephen intentionally model tasks they expecting students to undertake, and how much they warm to the fact that they let students in on their struggle.

Taking each of the fourteen reflective thinking operations listed earlier, here are some examples of modeling we have either seen in practice or adopted ourselves:

1. Check the assumptions that inform our actions and judgments.
When reporting back students' CIQ responses we let students know how they confirm or challenge the assumptions under which we have set up the class. We also often stop in the middle of a presentation or lecture to do an *assumption audit*—this is a quick recap or clarification of the assumptions our arguments are based on, the assumptions that lie behind the ways we respond to specific questions, or the assumptions we have heard during a particular classroom discussion.

2. Seek to open themselves to new and unfamiliar perspectives.
When we have team-taught we have asked our colleagues to bring a new perspective to our attention, or to offer a critique from a position we have not considered. Similarly, we try to take a different perspective from our colleagues and make sure we ask them to consider it seriously. We also try to include readings and videos that take a markedly different view from the one we are known to hold. Finally, the CIQ often provides us with very different perspectives on our classes, and we can report these back to students and talk out loud about what they mean for our teaching.

3. Attempt intersubjective understanding and perspective taking— trying to understand how another person reasons.
Team teaching is again one of the best ways to model this operation. In the way we ask questions of each other, and the way we strive to ensure we have understood an argument in the terms it is put to us by a colleague, we try to demonstrate how comprehension typically precedes critique. When teaching solo we can take a particular reading—preferably one different to our own viewpoint—and painstakingly work through it, sentence by sentence, in front of the class.

4. Make their intuitions and "gut" feelings the focus of study.
When we respond to students' questions we can let them know when our answers are based on specific research or a particular theoretical elaboration, and when they are based on our "sense" that this is the right answer. When the latter happens we can ask ourselves out loud where we think this instinct or gut feeling comes from. Is it rooted in a particular experience? Does it derive from a particular cue we responded to in the way the question was asked? Does our answer confirm one of our strongly held beliefs?

5. Study the effects of our actions with a view to changing them.
Again, the CIQ reporting-back period provides a very useful opportunity for us to show students that we're studying the effects our teaching has on them, and that we're open to changing our practices depending on what we learn from student feedback. We can also include plenty of autobiographical instances when we have changed our actions as scholars or practitioners based on what we learned from research or studying our experience.

6. Look for blind spots and omissions in our thinking and practice.
The Empty Chair is one way we can model this. This is when you place an empty chair at the front of the room—much as Clint Eastwood did during the 2012 Republican Convention (the chair was meant to represent President Obama)—and then talk to the chair as if you were sitting on it. Mentioning yourself by name, you try to critique comments you have just made or demonstrations you have just given. So, if the two of us were doing this, we would turn and face the chair where we are presumed to be sitting and say things such as: "Stephen, I noticed you didn't discuss Smith's research study, presumably because it raises questions that are inconvenient for your argument," or "Alison, why didn't you include a demonstration of Clean Questioning in your attempt to model constructive feedback with Jan just now?"

Again, this is made easier when you are team teaching and you can agree that each of you will continually be striving to bring omissions and blind spots to each other's attention. Sometimes a remark on the CIQ alerts you to one of your blind spots, or queries an omission you made, in which case you can report them back to the class and talk about why you think the gap was there.

7. Identify what is justified and well grounded in their thinking and practice.
Reflective thinking entails an appraisal of why things went well, or what elements of learning were successfully demon-

strated, as well as an attempt to eliminate identifiable errors and mistakes from future practice or reasoning. In reporting on CIQ responses, it is important to stress which of your practices or assumptions were affirmed by students' responses. For example, in an intensive two-day workshop Stephen teaches each year, he asks students to spend forty-five minutes reading the same short reading before discussing it in small groups. Often the CIQs from students comment that the small-group discussion went so well because they had all come from an immediate reading of the same textual excerpt. When Stephen reports this finding back to the class, he stresses that he had designed the exercise that way because his assumption was that a period of private reading immediately prior to a small-group discussion would improve the conversation. He then thanks the students for confirming he was right.

Any time we model a demonstration of a particular technique we can conduct a quick self-evaluation of our performance in front of the students and strive to identify what we think we did well and what we felt could have been improved on. Having done this, we can open up the discussion for reactions to our critique from the class.

8. Experiment with multiple learning modalities to foster deep learning.

All of us grow up with particular learning preferences. Stephen's has been for a self-directed mode of study. He likes to do things on his own, engage in trial and error away from a teacher's gaze, and find his own way through technical difficulties (such as when he learned how to operate a home recording studio a few years ago to record the 99ers first album for Spinout Records). As well as reading and writing, Alison enjoys using tactile, hands-on approaches to learning. She learns by doing and making, as is evident both from her own stories in chapter 5 and also in her building of the Lego models you can find on our website for the book: http://www.engagingimagination.com. Both of us believe that any group of learners we are likely to meet will have multiple learning preferences and habits, and that in the interests of giving everyone a fair shake we need to make sure we use lots of different approaches.

But as we introduce each different activity—building a Lego model of our understanding of a concept, or explaining our understanding of a theory only through images we draw or collages we construct—we also try to engage in exactly the same activity the students are engaged in. So we build our own models, draw our own images, or construct our own collages.

9. *Value emotional dimensions of our learning as much as the purely cognitive.*
bell hooks (1994) has written eloquently of the bourgeois decorum presumed to be appropriate to the conduct of higher education. Teachers are supposed to stay on an emotionally even keel at the same time they are expressing joy in the beauty of a subject, or happiness at the keenness of a student's question. We both like to make a point of telling students how their participation has been so terrific or their work so impressive. One of the turning points in Stephen's career was in the 1980s when he first let himself show how the poignancy or honesty of a student's contribution made him cry.

When expressing other less positive, or more ambiguous, emotions, the picture is far more complicated. Both of us try to let students peek through the windows of our own emotional responses, particularly when we are feeling uncertain, confused, or prone to laceration. Both of us are subject to impostorship, to feeling that we're not "real" academics and that people sooner or later are going to see through our false façade of command and competence. We make sure to talk about this and to let students know how nervous we are as we approach a task we are trying to demonstrate for them. But we also try to clarify that a degree of nervousness, properly funneled, can be a valuable spur to us trying to perform to an ever-higher degree of expertise.

We also like to talk of the emotional ups and downs that accompany our own individual learning projects, of how these are an integral element of learning, and how we need to keep the lows from demoralizing us, or the highs from giving us an unrealistic sense of how far we've come. We talk about the importance of pleasure for us in our learning—pleasure in the beauty of a design, theory, example, or turn of phrase, and pleasure in the feeling of finally "getting" something after trying repeatedly to understand or practice it.

10. Try to upend our habitual ways of understanding something.
Many of the modeling activities we've already discussed have this activity embedded within them: The Empty Chair or team teaching, for example, can both involve looking at things from completely opposite viewpoints. One activity Stephen often tries is called *Practice Inversion*. This asks individuals to respond to the four questions below on their own, and then to compare their responses.

PRACTICE INVERSION

Identify an organizational practice that you have initiated. What do you intend to achieve by instituting this practice? What's the reasoning behind it?

What's omitted from your understanding of the practice? What are the contradictions in your understanding of how the practice works? Which views and interpretations are unrepresented in your framing of the practice?

Who benefits from the practice and who is harmed by it? Why do you not recognize those who are harmed?

How could the practice be reinvented to be fairer, more effective, more inclusive, or more justified by our mission?

Before asking people to do this exercise, Stephen does it himself on one of his own practices. He is trying to model what the process looks like, but also to show that he is willing to look at something he is proud of from a completely opposite standpoint. So, for example, when working with students he will provide the following example:

Assigning Students to Write a Critical Analysis of a Text

1. My intended meaning

I want to develop students' skills of critical analysis so that they can make independent intellectual judgments.

2. Contradictions and omissions

The concept of critical analysis I'm using springs from a Eurocentric Enlightenment tradition that values rationality. This tradition ignores important ways of knowing that are embedded in other cultures. It also downplays the importance of intuitive learning. The feminist emphasis on affirmative and connected modes of knowing is not allowed for. I have also overlain my understanding of the word *critical* with a left-of-center ideology drawn from the Frankfurt School of critical theory. The criteria of what is to be judged a properly critical analysis emanates from me, the teacher. The assignment as constructed seems to preclude the possibility of students already being critical. The assignment could easily be interpreted by the students as a game of "guess the teacher's ideology."

3. Who benefits and who is harmed by the dominant view?

Teachers who see themselves as "critical" intellectuals are best served. Worst served are students who are not familiar with traditions of analytic philosophy or Frankfurt School critical theory, students who have a grounding in alternative intellectual traditions, and students who are uninformed about the teacher's biases.

4. Imagine an alternative structure

What counts as "critical" is publicly discussed according to alternate frameworks of analysis. Students generate what they see as "critical" criteria. Students are encouraged to question the relevance of the assignment and to propose alternatives that seem more connected and significant. Students regularly evaluate the usefulness of assignments, discuss these with the teacher, and place these evaluations on the public record. On the basis of these comments, the group continually reinvents its procedures.

11. Connect thinking conducted in one domain to thinking in another.
Something we've already mentioned several times—team teaching—is very well suited to this. When colleagues from different
fields, or from different orientations within a single discipline, explore how they find connections across seemingly disparate ideas
or knowledge, this models for students the interconnectedness
of ideas. Similarly, when practitioners in allied fields (design and
graphics, social work and education, biology and anatomy) show
how similar assumptions inform their different fields, or how the
same basic analytical frameworks are applied but with different
terms used to describe them, students can see the attempt to build
connections.

Those of us who teach alone and who are not generalists by
nature will find this harder to do. But even within the most rigidly
prescribed subdivisions of disciplines, knowledge is always grouped
into categories and subcategories. As students enter your classroom, you can commit to them to try to find out about the other
courses they have taken in their majors and to seek to build connections across them.

*12. Become more aware of our habitual epistemic cognition—the typi-
cal ways we judge something to be true.*
Once more, making sure we regularly talk out loud our own
reasoning processes is something students across the disciplines
appreciate. When teachers talk out loud the steps they take
in a mathematical proof or the reasons why they believe one
explanation of a sequence of historical events is more accurate than another, they can be explicit in their summary of why
the proof or historical theory rings true for them. In practice-
based courses, teachers can present problems of application and
talk through their own approaches to responding to them, all
the time describing the possible courses of action they considered, why they discarded those they did, and what was the most

compelling evidence or steps of reasoning that led them to take the course of action they did.

13. *Apply reflective protocols in contextually appropriate ways.*

Our book is full of activities, exercises, techniques, and protocols. We work from the assumption that readers will appreciate many specific examples of practice so that they can consider which parts of these might fit their situations. It is easy to critique literature on reflection and reflective practice, but much harder to propose practical possibilities. As soon as you suggest a possible technique or protocol, you open yourself to the charge of having gone corporate or joined the ranks of those using reflection as surveillance.

Despite this, we believe it is our authorial responsibility to suggest as many different practical options as possible. But even as we offer activities for readers to consider, we assume that you—the individual or group reading this—will continually assess the fit between our suggestions and the particular conditions in which you work. So, for example, if there is a reason why one or more of the questions on the CIQ form don't really work for your students, or don't give you the information you're looking for, we assume you'll throw out the troublesome question or questions and insert ones of your own choosing. Alternatively, you might reject the whole instrument and design a new one from scratch that's more contextually appropriate.

Similarly, one of the indicators we use to judge students' development of reflective thinking should be their capacity to judge drop, change, or add elements to the reflective protocols they are asked to apply. So as teachers we need to model this process for them. Again, the reciprocal nature of the CIQ should help with this. As we report back results at the start of each new week of classes, or when we do this online, we can comment on the degree to which we find each of the questions to have produced the most helpful data.

For example, Stephen often finds himself wondering out loud if using the word *most* in four of his CIQ questions results in a wrong estimation of the significance of certain comments. After all, a student could have had a wonderful class, understanding all the material explained, but mention one particular example that didn't quite work for her. In reading her comment we may grant a degree of importance to it that it doesn't really warrant. Again, if a student felt a particular class was of little help to her, she may still respond to the questions about the most engaged comment or most helpful action. We may then read those and get a false read of her overall verdict on the class, deciding wrongly that it was a roughly equal mix of engaging and distancing moments and helpful or puzzling actions.

14. Integrate an unregulated, unmediated flow of emotions, impulses, intuitions, and images into cognitive analysis.
For teachers schooled in the research traditions of academe there is pressure to look and behave professorially. Logic is valued and academic competence is typically associated with precision of speech—defining terms, providing clear and articulate explanations, using suitably impressive disciplinary-specific jargon, and so on. Letting go of this façade, particularly for college teachers who also feel like impostors, is enormously difficult, even risky. Because students have been socialized to expect classrooms to be emotionally even zones, a teacher who is ready to display the emotions that are usually concealed can be seen as unstable or, in American argot, flaky.

But the concepts at the center of this book—engagement, imagination, and creativity—are inherently emotional and unpredictable. If we want students to be open to activities that are risky, and that ask them to break out of their overwhelmingly cognitive ways of being, we need to be ready to model a similar openness. This probably needs to be done incrementally to not confuse students unnecessarily. One useful way is to start by introducing the language of emotions into your teaching activities. Talk about the way you felt demoralized during your struggle to learn something you are now teaching, or the flush of excitement you feel as a discussion catches fire. Then, as students develop confidence in your academic competence, you can signal for them that you are moving into a different teaching mode for a certain period of time.

How this is done will depend on many factors, such as the suitability of the content, the ease of the teacher with the activity, and the teacher's past and present relationship with the class. Maybe you can make an effort to draw your response to student questions every now and then, or to bring in more frequently some autobiographical examples of the emotional highs and lows of your learning or practice. Perhaps you can talk more about the role that instinct or impulse plays in your scholarly work or professional decisions. When students or colleagues do something that takes you by surprise be ready to express your delight. When a seemingly random association or unconnected image pops into your head as you respond to an unexpected question, don't be so quick to disregard or censure it as inappropriately un-academic.

Using Students' Testimony

As well as modeling the fourteen processes of reflective thinking for students, we have also found it helpful to use testimony from other students regarding the value of such thinking. An example of this is an elegant and imaginatively conceived reflective account from a student who had spent seventeen months working for a top designer in New York and was waiting for visa formalities to be concluded so she could stay stateside instead of returning to the UK to finish her university studies. As with many reflective episodes, it began with what Mezirow (1991) calls a "disorienting dilemma"; that is, an unexpected and distressing event that took her by surprise and initiated a process of self-scrutiny. This event was the denial of the expected extension to her visa to stay in the US.

Several months after her plans had gone horribly wrong, she combined story, diary extracts, citations from theory, and purposeful self-assessment to write an account of what she had learned from this experience.

> Journal extract recalling December 2008...
>
> "Dear XXX...Blah Blah Blah," I skimmed over, "and so it is my deepest regret to inform you that we were unable to obtain a visa for your returning to [the company] and the States."
>
> Shock. Dismay. Confusion. My mouth dried up, I felt in one moment completely exhausted and terrified and done. I felt done. Everything I had worked for, risked, tried with everything to make work, was just taken from under me in one small e-mail. I felt wounded. There was a large emotional wound and all I wanted to do was curl up in a ball, and let it heal.
>
> The body is an incredible thing. We are incredible things. Amongst all the dismay and confusion, I woke the next morning and wrote a list.
>
> This moment of innate disappointment, it turns out, has made me the person I am today and has had a direct effect on my every hope, activity and failure of this academic year. This "state of doubt, hesitation and perplexity" (Dewey, 1933 p12) was also the single moment I was forced to reflect and with the "act of searching...to find material that will resolve the doubt, settle and dispose the perplexity" (Dewey, 1933 p12a)....I found my strength. That is the beauty of reflection. It can be your saviour. Instead of leaving the past with a begrudged defeatist attitude, you force yourself to understand your every action, expectation, every consequence, and you move forward. I became obsessed with ensuring the mistakes of my past would not affect my future. I had to go back to finish my final year at University.

This one short extract illustrates the positive power of reflection as perceived by a learner, even though it may be expressed with more emotional intensity (possibly) than a geographer might demonstrate in relation to fieldwork, or a dentist to tooth extraction. The writer combines autobiography, skillful prose, references to the literature, and goal setting in the space of four paragraphs. Her extract later refers to a report on the impact of reflection on learning that serves to bolster our belief in its value within our curricula.

Encouraging this kind of student reflection is not always straightforward, and our systems do not make it any easier. The privileging of the kinds of formal reflection that respond to set criteria, cover prescribed territory, and are constrained in a specified format are born of the ethos of control, and the priority of our current educational system to convert every act of learning into a measurable outcome. The institutional model of reflection sits hand in glove with the logico-rational, read-write, assessment-oriented structure we operate within. It is also supported by what seems to be the dominance of written reflection as the preferred method of gathering evidence of student metacognition and self-appraisal.

Student Resistance to Reflective Control

We have already noted how students can find reflection a bolt-on inconvenience separate from the important issue of learning the stuff of content. Students told they "have to" reflect during a particular module may feel an understandable sense of coercion. There may also be a level of resistance around their expectations of student roles and course content—they came to study X, not engage in self-scrutiny. This position is the antithesis of the open, curious mind we identified earlier as an essential prerequisite for effective reflection.

Treating reflection with disdain is inevitably a self-fulfilling prophecy because assignments generated to fulfill academic obligations are artificially constructed to hit particular markers. As one student of Alison's wrote frankly, reflection on learning

> has always been the part that would be written 30 minutes before hand in, and instead of taking the time to fully reflect back on the work I had done I would write some half-hearted waffle about how much I had enjoyed the subject, how much I had engaged with the work and what I had learnt. Most of which was either a lie, or largely exaggerated.

This is a good example of the kind of confessional practices that Foucault (1980) often spoke and wrote about. The student just quoted felt an implicit pressure to write a reflection that took the form almost of a confession, identifying how the course had changed him, enlarged his perspective, moved him on from earlier misunderstandings, and so on. This is an example of how a reflective learning journal can become an instrument of surveillance. After all, journals could arguably be said to be based on "knowing the inside of people's minds" (Foucault, 1982, p. 214) because their explicit intent is to externalize people's innermost reflections. A norm of "transformativity" often hovers in the background to direct the way such journals are written. Learners who sense that their teacher is a strong advocate of experiential methods may pick up the implicit message that good journals reveal dramatic, private episodes that lead to transformative insights.

Students who don't have anything painful, traumatic, or exciting to confess can easily feel that their journals are not quite what the teacher ordered, that they stray too far from this transformative norm. Not being able to produce revelations of sufficient intensity they may decide to invent some, as the student quoted earlier did. Or, they may start to paint a quite ordinary experience with a sheen of transformative significance. A lack of dramatic experiences or insights to relate may be perceived by students as signs of failure—an indication that their lives are somehow incomplete and lived at a level that is insufficiently self-aware or exciting. The idea of trans-formativity thus constitutes a hidden, but powerful, norm for journal writing that is enforced by "judges of normality" (Foucault, 1977, p. 304); that is, by the teachers who read and grade these journals.

If students feel this way, they are understandably cynical about the purposes of reflection and the intent of those reading it. Some have told us that asking for reflective thinking is more for the ben-efit of teachers who get useful information about how to change teaching, or how to redesign future course assignments.

Summary

In summarizing potential difficulties with student engagement and perception of benefit we have identified a range of tensions or op-positions represented in Figure 2.1

Although this figure may not cover every single example of bi-nary tension that may exist in relation to student reflection, we believe that it demonstrates some of the most common ones we en-counter. As we proceed through the rest of this book, we show how attempts to support students by creating opportunities for reflective thinking typically involves balancing these different polarities.

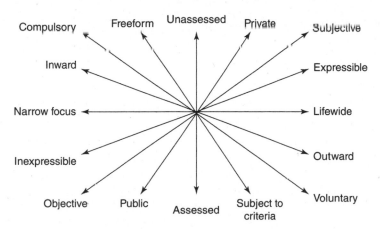

Figure 2.1   Polarities of Reflection

3

Connecting Creativity, Imagination, and Play

In this chapter we turn our focus to creativity and its role in reflective thinking. As the previous chapters have pointed out, most techniques for helping students think reflectively use writing as the central medium for teaching, learning, and assessment. We argue that although this is certainly important, we need to broaden our horizons and consider a number of other creative pathways and modalities. The traditional interpretation of intelligence dominated by deductive reason and ideas of scientific evidence originated as a result of selective ideological and socioeconomic imperatives in the increasingly industrialized eighteenth and nineteenth centuries. Intelligence tests were developed that streamed and labeled pupils in terms of their academic ability and, by implication, their suitability for different work roles within the new industrial economy.

In a postindustrial world, this paradigm is being challenged by research into the complex connections between models of information processing and kinds of learning (Besheti and Large, 2013) and by teaching that builds on knowledge of brain chemistry (Jensen, 2008). One of the most provocative ideas that has emerged from work on multiple intelligences is Goleman's (2011) notion of emotional intelligence. This kind of intelligence seems to be tied to successful organizational functioning, community building, and social movement animation far more than the kind of analytic capacities typically measured by intelligence tests (Mortiboys, 2007). In this chapter we explore this kind of intelligence and propose a model of multimodal forms of reflective thinking. We also try to clarify the interconnections among reflective thinking, play, and creativity. If you're eager to get to the descriptions of techniques and activities, you can find these in chapters 4 through 10.

Emotional Intelligence

Emotional intelligence is embedded both in self-awareness and in an ability to read others' emotions and craft appropriate responses. Goleman argues that mathematically and technically derived notions of IQ have little relevance to success in real life, particularly for members of a growing number of professions that place relationships at their center. Successful practitioners in what are broadly called the "human service professions" (education, social work, management, health care, advertising, training and human resources development, and so on) reach levels of expertise and positions of leadership because of their ability to be aware of their emotions in the moment and over time. This allows them to stand back and change their behavior in ways that build teams, bolster morale, and improve performance. This is because the limbic system of the brain (the part that controls emotions) is far more influential in determining how we respond to situations than is the rational left brain. Hence, anyone working in fluid situations involving colleagues and clients relies far more on the limbic system. By way of contrast, anyone engaged in an isolated analysis of technical data, or facing work conditions that remain stable, taps into the rational part of the brain.

In particular, the fluid ability to read multiple emotional cues and to exercise a meta-awareness of one's own somatic body states and the chains of reasoning that flow from these is strongly correlated with success in working as a change agent. Although Goleman's work is typically framed within corporations, we believe the same is true in social movements (Preskill and Brookfield, 2008; Brookfield and Holst, 2010). Consequently, if we are preparing students to work in these professions we need to develop these skills knowing that they are not best assessed or demonstrated through written tests or reflections calmly drafted long after moments of stress, anxiety, or decision have passed.

The kind of brain research that Goleman has popularized is but the tip of a much deeper and broader iceberg of research and theorizing that has caused a paradigm shift in the comprehension of mind–body relationships and how people process information. In *A Whole New Mind* (2008), Pink draws on this research to articulate differences between left-directed thinkers (analytical, logical, emotionless, objective) and right-directed thinkers (empathic, artistic, conceptual). This has included a complete revision of our understanding of the usefulness of the right side of the brain, the part that controls emotions, creativity, and instinct. From early twentieth-century assumptions of it as a deficient and superfluous part of the organ, there has developed an acceptance of the interdependence of the workings of our two cranial hemispheres. As Robinson (2011) writes, "Academic work focuses on certain sorts of verbal and mathematical reasoning: on writing factual and critical essays, verbal discussions and mathematical analyses. These are all very important forms of ability. But if human intelligence was limited to them, most of human culture would never have happened" (p. 65)

Thomas West, in *In the Mind's Eye* (2009), states the case for moving away from intelligence that is solely measured through read-write traditions to one giving equal legitimacy to different ways of knowing and showing. His book celebrates the visual modes of thought present in many great minds at work, not just in art and design but in science, engineering, medicine, and mathematics. His definition of visual thinking can equally apply to the creative, nonlinear, multilayered emanations of reflection we will explore:

> We may consider "visual thinking" as that form of thought in which images are generated or recalled in the mind and are manipulated, overlaid translated, associated with other similar forms (as with a metaphor), rotated, increased or reduced in size, distorted, or otherwise transformed gradually from one familiar image into another. (p. 21)

West argues that the symmetrical/asymmetrical formation of the two cranial hemispheres accounts for the range in people's thinking abilities. His perspective is driven in some measure by his own experience of being profoundly dyslexic and diagnosed as such well into his adult years. Dyslexia is a classic example of how an alternative mode of processing information in an environment that measures academic success through the written word can put learners at a distinct disadvantage.

We have thankfully traveled a very long distance from the days when dyslexia was wrongly equated with being lazy or stupid; however, associations with the "remedial" still linger in some minds with reference to alternative assessments or modes of learning. The now-extensive literature on dyslexia in general and in the arts in particular argues that students who have difficulties in reading and writing because of dyslexia or a specific learning difficulty may have matching or surpassing strengths in other ways—what Eide and Eide (2012) call the "dyslexic advantage." Most of us have heard of these other strengths—lateral thinking, big picture visualization, alternative ways of problem solving, innovation and entrepreneurship, artistry and creative dexterity—as well as being regaled with lists of famous individuals with dyslexia such as Leonardo da Vinci, Winston Churchill, and Richard Branson.

These limbic strengths are certainly manifested in the domains of the arts and design, but it would be a grave mistake to assume they are limited to these. Essentially, any work that requires formulating responses to unforeseen situations depends on its actors to access these strengths. Teaching—the profession that we assume many readers work in—is a prime example. The one thing you can depend on in a world of what seems like daily exponential leaps in technology, and hence in the ways students access, interpret, and use information, is that whatever you learned in graduate school regarding classroom management procedures, learning design, or student assessment will almost certainly be outdated by the time you enter your first job. Again, in postsecondary classrooms the one constant you can anticipate is the ever-increasing diversity of learners you will have to face. This will be a diversity not only in terms of students' racial and cultural backgrounds, or their identity politics, but also in their levels of readiness for learning and their ways of processing information.

Creative teachers are open to using many pedagogic models, including problem based or inquiry based learning, dependent on the context for learning. They ask themselves what different kinds of students they are dealing with, what they wish the students to be able to know or do, how best to use the time and other resources available to them, and what successful colleagues have done that they can steal. From this mélange of contextual factors, decisions and strategies emerge that are tried out, some of which are then modified further, whilst others are dropped. Unless you choose to sleepwalk your way through your teaching days and ignore how students are responding to learning, no matter what the discipline you teach your work as a teacher is inherently creative.

Figure 3.1 suggests the different kind of domain groupings that can organize our thinking about multimodal and multisensory forms of teaching that foster students' creative reflection. The figure is a visual of the possibilities for practice in an engaging classroom, and we believe it applies to a multitude of disciplines and subject matter boundaries, from fashion design to engineering, art history to real estate management, psychology to business studies. Although these modes are represented cyclically, they also cut across the circle and link in other ways.

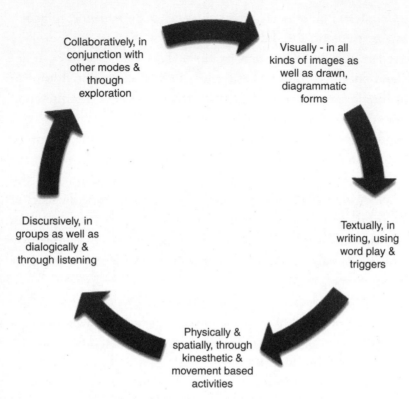

Figure 3.1   Multimodal Forms of Reflection

The Place of Creativity in Student and Teacher Reflection

In his discussion of the location of the creative impulse in brain chemistry or human experience, Robinson (2011) writes that "the creative process is not a single ability that lives in one or other region of the body. It thrives on the dynamism between different ways of thinking and being" (p. 122). We agree. Contrary to the spirit of Cartesian dualism, our physical existence is not divided into the separate domains of mind and body. Creativity is an all-involving process. It is also economically beneficial. Stimulating flexibility, inquiry, and imagination in how students think is fundamental to economic survival. In a world where products, forms of production, markets, services, and consumers continually change, the ability to respond creatively to shifting circumstances becomes the competitive edge that makes the difference between success and failure.

So for all kinds of reasons, educating students about how to awaken their creative possibilities, and helping them learn how these can be applied in different circumstances, is a crucial teaching task. This is why we believe the best teachers create engaging classrooms that display a multitude of different pedagogic forms and a range of assessment modalities. The present curriculum imbalances that favor STEM subjects (science, technology, engineering, and mathematics) over arts, design, and humanities, and that privileges technical, mostly written forms of assessment, misreads the ways education contributes to economic growth. In Robinson's (2011) words:

> Current approaches to education and training are hobbled by assumptions about intelligence and creativity that have squandered the talents and stifled the creative confidence of untold numbers of people. This waste stems partly from an obsession with certain types of academic ability and from a preoccupation with standardized testing. (p. 9)

Robinson is not alone in his articulation of the current crisis in education and the need for different ways of configuring and enlivening learning. His warning as to the risks we run if we undervalue and edit out creativity, imagination, and playfulness from our learning and working is one that colleagues in the creative arts won't need to hear. They know this already. But they are not the only ones drawing on these approaches. Teaching at any level requires creativity on a daily basis as we wonder how to bring subjects alive in ways that resonate with students or make the best of constrained situations in which to learn. And all committed teachers are surely concerned with enabling students to develop their capacity to understand, apply, and internalize knowledge and ideas, applying their imagination and creativity not just to the acquisition of data or production of physical outputs but to their ways of understanding themselves and their world.

Having considered notions of reflection and brain function, we now synthesize three further fields of literature that form the cornerstones of our ethos of how to engage students in creative reflection. The different elements of our understanding of the dimensions of reflection are illustrated in Figure 3.2. Its compartments and rigid boundaries notwithstanding, it is intended to show the interconnecting of different elements that add up to constitute "whole person" reflection.

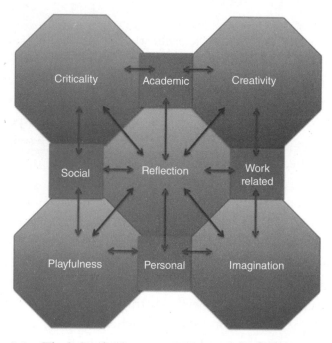

Figure 3.2   The Interplay between Different Constituents of Creative Reflection

Creative reflection as we conceive of it diagrammatically includes three main fields: creativity, imagination, and play. Each of these fields has its own dedicated literature—vast, varied, and sometimes contested—while the knowledge bases behind all three are deep and complex. But at the heart of an engaging classroom, one in which students interact with multiple modes of learning that excite interest and maintain energy, is the presence of creative reflection. Teaching creative reflection is the process by which we help students to look behind the doors, and under the stones, of their usual ways of learning, thinking, and acting. To be able to jerk students out of their usual patterns of interpretation and understanding, we need to come at subjects from a number of different angles. In an engaged classroom, students come to see subject matter as prismatic; that is, as opening itself up to shades of comprehension that shift as students employ new analytical frames, attend to emotional and somatic elements of classroom experience, or engage in new classroom and homework activities. An engaging classroom uses approaches from an eclectic array of sources to stimulate student learning and bring a reenergizing breath of fresh air to our teaching practices.

Our vision of an engaging classroom is one where students have the freedom to bring qualities of creativity, imagination, and play into their formal learning with the same energy and spirit of discovery that they adopt for learning in the other contexts of their lives. After all, you learn about significant friendships and love relationships, or about personal enthusiasms and hobbies, or even about civic engagement, using multiple senses and approaches. Very little of this happens through read-write approaches; so why should classroom learning be any less varied?

For Robinson, creativity "involves breaching the boundaries between different frames of reference" (2011, p. 158), and for us this is a fundamental aspect of reflection. Blending creativity and reflection, and infusing them with qualities of imagination and play, creates a powerful cocktail that enhances learning. If we allow ourselves a brief moment of evangelism, we want the creative reflection cocktail to be imbibed so as to wake up minds, crack open assumptions, shake up thinking, and expand reflective repertoires across the board.

Defining Creativity

We all no doubt have our own local interpretations and definitions of creativity and, depending on context, what creativity looks like varies considerably. After all, creative accounting is one very specific, often illegal, kind of creative practice! In fact, each of the three qualities that are the cornerstones of this book—creativity, imagination, and play—exhibits a paradoxical relationship to reflection. Each is both powerful and simultaneously fragile, and not best elicited by blunt instruments or the step-by-step, predetermined processes that teachers (including both of us) typically use. They are not always measurable or universally explicable, in the same way that it's impossible to explain why you find something funny, when everyone around you is mystified by your mirth.

Creativity is defined most broadly as the bringing into existence of something new, but it has multiple other connotations. A creative person is often seen as someone who has a vision, or a way of doing, that goes beyond the pedestrian, which implies flair, dexterity, difference, or artistry of some kind. Robinson (2011) suggests a more specific definition of creativity as "the process of having original ideas that have value" (p. 151). He stresses, as we noted earlier, that creativity crosses all subject boundaries, from theater to mathematics, from the arts to engineering, and that it is not confined to special roles or select spheres.

With his definition in mind, we need to make clear the boundaries within which we are operating. Our primary interest is not in how to render students more creative in their disciplines through entrepreneurial, innovative, or groundbreaking physical or conceptual outcomes. There are many books out there already that address these goals thoroughly. Rather, we relate creativity to the ways students try to unravel their own potential, question their identity and values, ponder the nature of their work and what counts as its successful performance, clarify their goals, and demonstrate their specific capabilities. As a result, there may well be, and often are, fruitful offshoots in terms of their academic, creative, or professional outcomes, but we cannot promise these.

For our specific purposes it is also helpful to look at Gauntlett's (2011) definition of creativity that offers a counterpoint to those emphasizing the presence of exceptional talent. We lean toward Gauntlett's own view that "we typically think of creativity as something which can happen quite routinely, whenever any of us does something in an unexpected but striking and inventive way" (p. 15). Claxton (2003) echoes this, pointing out that it is not just for artists, or the unconventional or "wacky": "creativity is not particularly artistic, and you do not have to dress weirdly to do it. It is as vital for accountants and receptionists as it is for designers and song-writers" (p. 1).

For Gauntlett, and for us, creativity is both a process and a feeling, a sense of breaking new internal ground that involves mind and body. In the conjunction of the human mind and the material or digital worlds, something is made that is new and that brings joy to the maker. Although many staff and students who are averse to reflection would baulk at the concept of it being a joyous experience (and who may even believe joy is somehow not properly educational), those of us who have found benefit in using the approaches we discuss in this book believe that Gauntlett (and others) have identified an essential ingredient in creative reflection.

Creativity does not simply imply total freedom and lack of control, nor is it something that is either inherently present or absent. We don't believe that there are two groups of people genetically programmed to be creative or pedestrian. Although creativity may be a latent talent in some, others can learn techniques to become more creative. However, we take seriously Robinson's extensive research (1982, 1999, 2010) showing that most people have a lack of confidence in their own levels of creativity. They recognize that they probably were creative as children but think that this capacity has declined as adulthood has advanced.

Creativity is also often visceral, drawing on feelings, instinct, bodily responses, and intuition. We both believe that if the visceral and intellectual are connected and expressed through innovation and/or aesthetics, then we have a richer holistic understanding of learning. Our focus in this book is on encouraging students to go beyond their use of well-known reflective triggers, such as "plan-do-review" models, and bring newness, agility, and personality to the learning solutions they adopt. By opening up students' (and our own) minds to different ways of thinking and by exposing them to multiple perspectives or insights, we hope to see original ideas with value take seed.

Creativity is also not the visitation of the muse, the genesis of genius, or the quick-fix solution that just springs up in your mind unbidden—although this may happen to some people. A quote often attributed to Jack London declares that you can't wait for inspiration, you have to go after it with a club. Claxton's (2003) use of the symphony orchestra as a metaphor for defining creativity as an advanced form of learning is helpful. The commitment, rehearsal, capability, collaboration, and sensitivity to orchestrate critical reflection can be seen as analogous to the performance of complex music or the ability to create something new from a variety of processes over time.

In the noneducational part of Stephen's life he plays in a punk rock-and-roll band, The 99ers (http://www.the99ersband.com). When members rehearse on Monday nights no one knows exactly what will happen, although the "official" purpose for convening is to rehearse new material or go over an established set of songs prior to that week's gig. Invariably, however, one member will start playing a new riff he's been working on over the past few days, and sometimes this takes the rest of the band to a very unexpected end.

The three of us start playing around with that riff, each adding his or her individual embellishments and variations, and each extending the variations introduced by other band members. Sometimes this fizzles out and we leave things for another day. But sometimes this structured and intentional readiness to play around, and with, a musical theme that someone has surprised us with that day, leads to a new song that is played out live and then recorded on our record label (Spinout Records in Nashville, Tennessee: http://www. spinoutmusic.com).

Connecting Imagination to Creativity

Imagination and *creativity* are sometimes used interchangeably; however, while one is often an essential ingredient of, or contributor to, the other, the two are not synonymous. Imagination has varying interpretations. At the closing ceremony of the 2012 London Olympics, John Lennon's song "Imagine" was prominently featured, in which listeners are asked to imagine a world without countries, religions, wars, heaven, or hell. Here imagination is a kind of provocative speculation—what would the world be like if such and such a thing didn't exist? For John Stuart Mill writing in the *London and Westminster Review* in 1838 on the social reformer Jeremy Bentham, imagination involved the ability to enter the mind and circumstance of another being. This is similar to Mezirow's idea of perspective taking (Mezirow, 1991) or Jürgen Habermas's (1987) notion of intersubjective understanding. Another common conception of imagination views it as the act of generating ideas and images not immediately present to the senses, in order to create newness in some form. These departures from the real are what are colloquially referred to as flights of fancy, or fantasizing.

We understand imagination as a means of exploring possibilities, however fantastical (What color is Thursday?), to stretch and warm up the mind to think about what might be. Well-known examples of thinking techniques that can be said to draw on the imagination include Edward de Bono's lateral thinking (http://www.edwdebono.com) and Brian Eno's oblique strategies (http://www.rtqe.net/ObliqueStrategies/). For us, though, it is not a permanent move into fantasy, or speculation without any anchors in reality. Rather, it is the ability to move away from the well trodden, to sniff out the subtle indicators of possibility, and to move sideways and beyond into seeing many different aspects of a situation or individual and their potential. In the words of the classic 1960s hit by the Yardbirds, it is the capacity to see things "Over, Under, Sideways, Down." This kind of imagination is particularly visible in relation to Appreciative Inquiry (Cockell, McArthur-Blair, and Schiller, 2012), in which imagination is equated with the ability to dream and conjure alternatives.

Theories of biographical narrative and inquiry (Nash, 2004; SooHoo, 2006; Smith, 2012) describe imagination in Lennon-esque terms of interpolation, "joining the dots" that accompany the "what ifs" of reflecting forward. Stephen King's *11/22/63* (2011) explores this motif by imagining what the world would be like if the assassination of US President John F. Kennedy had been prevented. In relation to biographical research, imaginative interpolation involves "the ability of mind to speculate upon and to link and assemble ideas" (Erben, 1998, p. 9), which runs directly parallel to the connections we want students to make through reflection. For Mezirow (2012), being able to imagine how things might be different is an essential first step in learning that is transformative.

Imagination may also be interpreted in some situations as creative appropriation, as in the finding of models or exercises in one context that can be reshaped and reused in another, or in mirroring practices of "found objects" and "found photographs." Found poetry is "a qualitative reporting medium that weaves selected words and phrases from participants' research reports into poetry" (Love, 2012, p. 41). This is the literary equivalent of a collage; the words of the poem already exist in research reports but decisions regarding which words and phrases to select and where to place line breaks are left to the poet. Love (2012) describes a Montana experiment for clergy and congregational leaders in which teleconferences were used to build trustful, intense conversations. In reporting the results of this initiative, a series of found poems ("Failure of Logistics," "Out of the Blizzard," "Loving the Questions," "In Need of Circles," and "Over Many Miles That Separate" were some of the poems' titles) were created from responses participants submitted to the evaluators of the project.

The imaginative activities of our brains can be conceived as a combination of both the neural and physiological responses our bodies produce in relation to imagined events as well as the significance of the imagination as a tool for learning. Claxton, Chambers, Powell, and Lucas (2011) note, as do practitioners of NeuroLinguistic Programming (NLP; Vickers and Bavister, 2010), the power of visualizing imaginatively in order to better understand, perform in, or deal with situations. This idea of rehearsal as a learning tool is one that is common in a range of applied fields of practice in community action and in the military. Given the contribution of the imagination in navigating human experience, we are both bluntly critical of the notion that learning imaginatively is something that we should grow out of, to be replaced by intellectual modes of learning that are somehow superior. Our disquiet is something that can equally be applied to considerations of creative learning and play.

The Meaning of Play

Our decision to look at play—or more precisely, playfulness—as part of our triad of reflective thinking qualities (imagination and creativity are the other two) is rooted in the belief that play is a fundamental and lifelong activity that is often misunderstood in the context of higher education. Its importance, particularly in relation to the healthy development of children, is widely held as incontrovertible. An obvious example of this belief is the work of the psychoanalyst D. W. Winnicott, who saw psychoanalysis as a kind of playing together of therapist and client, combining an enjoyable experience with a seeking after meaning. In his book *Playing and Reality* he wrote, "It is in playing and only in playing that the child or adult is able to be creative and use the whole personality, and it is only in being creative that the individual discovers the self" (Winnicott, 2005, p. 54).

However, in other contexts or age groups the appropriateness or benefit of play is often downgraded or sidelined. In Kane's (2004) manifesto for a new way of organizing ourselves, our behaviors, and our values, *The Play Ethic*, the negative perceptions of play are reviewed. He argues that far too often play is seen as trivial, childish, to be kept to the margins of adult society. It is dialectically seen as the opposite of work, as not meaningful, deviant, and something to apologize for. By way of contrast Kane then describes how complexity scientists, artists, educators, and politicians invoke play as a driver of human activity in both its primal and more organized forms.

His definition of the play ethic as a force for deep social and personal change has parallels with what we want creative reflection to do or be. For Kane, play as amusement is the least of its attributes; rather, play is an engine for serious societal restructuring, rebellion, rule breaking, overturning norms, and challenging value systems, all of which are a far cry from fun and games. Kane does not mince his words in arguing the case for play: "Playful scholars are up against the worst kind of industrial-age politics. They are faced by a modern army of clip-boarded Gradgrinds marauding across the developed world, applying tight quantitative measures called 'audits,' 'outcomes' and 'performance indicators'" (Kane, 2004, p. 17).

We all have to find ways of living with, and sometimes outmaneuvering, the measurability agenda that is sweeping educational establishments at a time of financial crisis and future uncertainty. However, Kane's exhortation to find a new way of looking "at the complexity of the educational experience—one that regards the apparent 'messiness' and 'imprecision' of play as a deep resource for understanding…" (2004, p. 18) is apposite. Play has a vital role as an ingredient of what he terms "multi-literacy," an approach that chimes at least spiritually with our own evocation of multimodal creative reflection.

We need to set out our own boundaries here in relation to his theory. Kane is an evangelist for play, and argues for an all-encompassing definition of play that goes far beyond explanation and into the territory of social manifesto. He regularly expresses concern that by extrapolating one aspect of play or focusing on one part as opposed to the whole, we might mistake a few forms of play as the whole story, which would be deeply unsophisticated. We recognize the fullness of play as he describes it, but for the purposes of this book we are opting to concentrate on the quality of playfulness, because we believe this creates a link to the kinds of classroom activities and practices our readers are interested in creating.

At the Smithsonian Institution's Lemelson Center website (http://www.inventionatplay.org), a short video entitled *Does Play Matter?* offers a range of perspectives from inventors, authors, and academics (some of whom may be all three) voicing their opinions on adult play. The many and varied comments evoke play as utility, fun, nondirected, adult skill building, and a means of passing time differently. They are worth reproducing here because they synthesize some of the complexity and contradictions surrounding the place of play in higher learning. Dr. Robert Root-Bernstein of Michigan State University emphasizes the importance of play as being enjoying something for its own intrinsic value. John Fabel, inventor and adjunct professor of design at Hampshire College, describes it as how we get a feel for the shape of the world. Alvin F. Poussaint, MD, professor of psychiatry at Harvard Medical School, notes how we avoid using the word *play* when talking of work for fear of being thought trivial. This charge of triviality has been met head on by the LEGO Group in the name given to their metaphorical modeling techniques for business:—*Lego Serious Play* (hereafter LSP). In LSP, play as safe experimentation and as a means of trying out the "what ifs" runs in perfect parallel to our own ideas of reflecting forward.

Further in the video, David Kelley of Palo Alto consulting firm IDEO argues that playing and being innovative has been "programmed out" of people. Bernard Mergen, MD, author of *Play and Playthings* (1982), points out that competitive games (as in professional sports) appear to be the only kind of play deemed more acceptable in adult life. But simulation, rules, role adoption, or games with an incentive to win in some way are not what we're talking about. Though useful techniques that we both sometimes use, competitive games, or any games that are rule bound, are not what we have in mind as play.

Our interest lies in cooperative, rather than competitive, play. Our book explores focus classroom activities and teacher modeling that encourage the interpretive spirit, humor, lightheartedness, and openness of the curious inquirer. A playful student or teacher is not someone who approaches learning with all the energy and theatrics of a pantomime dame or a mischievous pixie. He is someone who embarks on a process in a spirit of optimistic trust, who is not afraid to suspend his disbelief when faced with the unexpected, and who will travel willingly and curiously to see what it might reveal. Should the process not turn out as intended or expected, that same spirit is drawn on to weigh up the outcomes and take from them the unanticipated thoughts or ideas that may be generated.

The need for playfulness is hard to argue for in a climate in which fear of any criticism of being found guilty of "edutainment" runs rife. We believe the distinction between entertainment and "proper" learning is false. As we have acknowledged earlier, although we don't want to deny that learning is at times a hard struggle, equally we want to celebrate those times when it is inherently joyful. Being creative is something that is often experienced as bringing joy. The "learning versus fun" debate is based on the false premise that it is impossible to enjoy learning while covering content. We reject this premise entirely. There are times when playful enjoyment can aid in the grasp of difficult content, open learners up to multiple, complex interpretations, and help them think more critically.

Summary

In this chapter we have argued that student engagement and creative reflection are two sides of the same coin. Students are engaged when activities and assignments jolt them out of the familiar routines and ruts of listening to the lecture, filling in the PowerPoint slides, and then meeting for small-group discussions of the lecture's themes. When veering toward more traditional, text-based, written formats, the use of metaphor that we explore in chapter 5 encompasses our three qualities of creativity, imagination, and play through its play on words, the images it appropriates to convey meaning, and its creative expression of our most fundamental concerns. What is most likely to open students up to new interpretations and make them more aware of their blind spots, of their taken-for-granted givens, is teaching that embodies what we call "creative reflection." Such teaching is prepared to be playful in the quest for clarification and deeper understanding. Creative reflection is not purely dependent on the activities we are discussing. Once it becomes a set of protocols it loses the unexpectedness and serendipity we believe is vital. A creatively reflective classroom is one in which challenging questions are raised, and in which multiple sensory domains are engaged.

In exploring creative reflection we are conscious that we have to tread delicately, because coercion or overregulation will stifle any flickers of interest that may be sparked. Opinion is divided as to whether or not creativity can be taught. For us the question is not so much how do you teach it, but rather how do you create classrooms in which each of these qualities—creativity, imagination, and playfulness—might be discovered and unleashed by students? So if by teaching creativity, imagination, and play you mean a process by which teachers take students through preordained protocols with a predetermined outcome in mind, then we don't think you can teach these. But if by teaching creativity, imagination, and play you mean purposely varying classroom activities and assessment modalities, arranging opportunities for students to take control of what and how they are learning, paying attention to how emotions, soul, and feelings intersect with learning, and always being ready to try the unexpected with no sense of what will happen as a result—then you are teaching these qualities, particularly if students discover within themselves new ways of experiencing learning. We can, of course, also teach these things through modeling, through showing students how we take the risk of trying something new in our own learning with no idea what might transpire as a result.

With this chapter we end the introductory part of our book in which we have been trying to define our terms, demonstrate the theoretical foundation of our position, and argue for the need to connect student engagement to what we are calling "teaching for creative reflection." From this point on we get practical and concrete, as we start to look at specific teaching approaches and exercises that foster reflective self-awareness in students. In the next chapter our focus is on teaching practices that emphasize visual modes of learning.

Part 2

Engaging Imagination Tools and Techniques

4

Using Visual Methods of
Teaching and Learning

In this chapter we begin the exploration of specific tools and techniques that will take us to the end of the book. We want to begin by looking at visually based teaching and learning partly because the need for visual literacy has never been greater. We are bombarded daily by visual communications that overlay and infiltrate our environments and landscapes. In cities we undergo a kind of visual assault the moment we step outside the door, with media, commerce, and advertising competing for our attention. There is so much to observe that we may fail to see specifics, selectively and clearly, and though we may be attuned to some signals or codes in the visual world, our powers of unguided observation may have gotten rusty through lack of use. In an age in which images can be generated, manipulated, and shared globally and instantaneously, communicating visually is taking pride of place. As a result, the ability to be conversant with the visual language at the workplace and in civil society is essential.

Looking and seeing, like hearing and listening, are not always the same thing. *Looking* involves scanning and taking in the first images that impose themselves on our consciousness, while *seeing* engenders detailed, deeper understanding. This might be understanding better what is being surveyed, or being able to interpret a scene in a particular way by focusing on matters of color, shape, focus, symbolism, inference, relationship, scale, and so on. In this chapter we explore seeing as a mode of learning; that is, the use of pictures, images, and abstract forms to help students understand complex ideas, explore new knowledge, and communicate learning. We begin with a brief description of some basic ideas around visual teaching and learning, and then look at a number of specific examples and activities of how teachers have used visual and drawing exercises to shake up students' settled perceptual frameworks.

Losing Sight of Seeing: A Rural Walk

During the Easter vacation in 2012, Alison went on a walk with one of her daughters in a nearby forest. She was excited to be revisiting a place she had not been to since her children were little and had nostalgic memories of sunny summer days spent picnicking in the heather and tramping through pinewoods. Any recollection of whether or not they whined about the weather, food, or pushing their bicycles up hills had clearly been edited out! Instead, she remembered that, as a mum of young children, a trip to the forest was a simple way of getting back into the wild, despite the encumbrance of a stroller. She remembered tracks that were narrow, windy, and bumpy, paths that were unmade, and a flat paddock masquerading as a car park. There were no signs to direct you in any direction and you could get as lost as you wanted, as long as you didn't mind what time you got home. The only sign of civilization was a tiny Forestry Commission café that provided information on wildlife all year and ice creams in summer. The attraction held in her memory was the natural state of the forest—nurtured but unmanicured.

Inevitably, after more than fifteen years, her visit was a source of multiple shocks. Because it was Good Friday, and a public holiday, the next generation of young families had all been unleashed on the forest in an effort to oxygenate and exhaust the young. Parking the car involved astronomical charges and careful maneuvering in a vast but crowded expanse of tarmac. She was visually bombarded at every turn by signs, directions, and notices reminding her how to pay, where to cycle, what to do with her dog (if she had one), and a litany of prohibitions. If she had wanted to swing through the trees on a climbing system there were even instructions for that! Although the trees and natural landscape were still beautiful, the entire place had been tidied up out of all recognition, paths straightened and "made safe" with bollards. Furthermore, a large café, games area, and information center had been added into the mix. Put simply, much of the remembered magic had gone. She felt flattened by the efforts that had gone into organizing nature as a means of maximizing enjoyment.

As their walk commenced Alison noticed that every hundred meters or so there was something to capture her attention—a spy hole, an artwork, a directive (see Figures 4.1 and 4.2). So much thinking and planning seemed to have been done on the walkers' behalf to make them see and behave in a certain way, yet (access and health and safety issues notwithstanding) Alison wondered why it was all deemed necessary. The efforts to take charge of the forest seemed to suggest that visiting humans had lost the ability to

Figure 4.1   The Hidey Hole; Seeing the Forest from Different Angles

Figure 4.2   Forest Directions

observe, to look, to be captivated by what was naturally there rather than what had been manufactured for their entertainment. The more things that were put in place for people to do, the less there seemed the space for something more unspoiled to be explored.

This story is not just a lament for the days of yore but serves as a visual analogy to the hard and soft thinking we encountered earlier in the book—the tension between when we need to be "helped" to see and learn and when we need to feel our way and gradually uncover the things on our own. The actions of the Forestry Commission (no doubt well intentioned) also suggest a range of decisions and judgments taken on our behalf that consciously or unconsciously tell us what is worth seeing or learning. We have already noted the fine pedagogic balance that needs to be observed between too much and too little guidance. What we see in place thanks to the Forestry Commission is analogous to an excess of instruction for written reflection. While we recognize that there are times when criteria, parameters, and suggestions are useful, freedom from constraint and personal choice in where to direct our attention and learning are also essential. This freedom to learn is important in how we allow reflection to be recorded within our formal curricula.

Visual Intelligence and Visual Literacy

Whether we think about this much or not, we navigate the world, and process our experiences, at least in part using visual intelligence. In so doing, we develop what might be termed *visual literacy*. Students with highly developed visual intelligence are thought to learn best through teaching methods that present content as visual representations (Silver, Strong, and Perini, 2000). Anecdotally we see this in the different ways students take notes during discussions or lectures. Some write lists of facts and observations; others draw mazes and maps. Those who are auditory learners probably take no notes at all, or just doodle. Stephen has written several books while music blares a few inches from his ears.

Visual learners think in pictures, respond to things being presented in image or diagrammatic forms, like to draw their developing understandings of new ideas, and maintain attention through visual stimuli. They are likely to be adept at creating visual representation themselves and have "an eye" for visual composition in whatever form. They are imaginative and creative in the ways they respond to their learning outcomes, and it is all of this that we suggest be harnessed or encouraged in relation to reflective thinking.

In Figure 4.3 we present three images from student essays reflecting on their final year of undergraduate study at the London College of Fashion. The first uses visual metaphors of paths, footprints, dead ends, and destinations, somewhat connected to the labyrinth themes we pursue later in the book. The second is more textually based, presenting a jokey diary-cum-magazine cover. The third is a jigsaw that is partly literal in that it represents the different component parts of someone's education conducted in eight different countries. These three images should reassure readers who fear that teaching visually requires prowess in draftsmanship, or a flair for abstract symbolism. All three images use recognizable

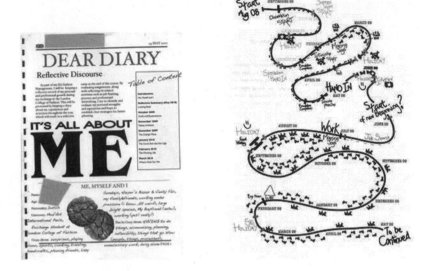

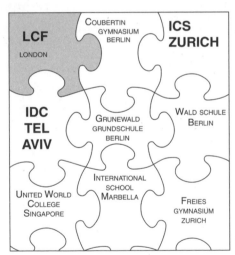

Figure 4.3   Visual Representations of Students' Experiences

tropes, and none need any particular artistic training. We include these images early in this chapter partly to assuage any nervousness you may have around our advocating visually based teaching.

Visual literacy is an allied concept to visual intelligence and is sometimes a synonym for it. In a symposium devoted to the topic the editor opines, "It is amazing that college-level curricula throughout the world continue to be mainly text-based, with intermittent excursions into visual art and culture" (Elkins, 2007, p. 3). He goes on to say, "The possibility of reconceiving first year college education so that it works on a visual model is, I think, the most important and potentially revolutionary problem in current curricular theory" (p. 3). This is not a new observation. In the 1950s and 1960s, Rudolph Arnheim noted that visual ways of learning have traditionally been viewed as inferior intellectual capacities to the logico-rational, text-based models of our traditional academic structures.

Arnheim (2004) argued that visual perception is fundamental to productive thinking, that on the simplest level, for example, we visualize words when we think and write them. When we think of interrelationships between concepts, or how to distinguish between central ideas in an argument and matters of more peripheral importance, we often do so visually. We may write in a logical, linear, fashion, but we think about the "stuff" of writing visually and then order these thoughts on the page or screen sequentially.

Arnheim argued that visual perception is in fact a form of thinking and questions any assumption that thinking begins where the senses end. For him, visual perception is just as much a cognitive operation as any of the other mental processes associated with thought.

John Debes (1969) coined the term *visual literacy* in the 1960s to refer to the visual competencies that humans develop through seeing. Since then multiple disciplines have contributed to the evolution of its definition. For art historians it may represent the kinds of cultural intentions and artistic codes enclosed within a portrait painted at a certain point in history. For war reporters, a photograph may have sociopolitical intent beyond the surface image, while cultural historians can read the value system of a subculture from a visual representation. In *The Visual Literacy White Paper*, Bamford (2003) elaborates different kinds of visual literacy and communication, including the ability to acquire skills in judging the validity and ideological impact of images, and the need for viewers to understand how the images may be deliberately constructed to achieve a certain effect.

For some kinds of creative reflection, visual literacy will be less important because the image or diagram being produced is one that only needs to make sense to its author. Shared visuals such as the Lego models Alison shared with Stephen as the book was developing (http://www.engagingimagination.com) may need explanation for both parties to be in possession of the same codes and understandings, and also for the viewer to grasp where the author is coming from. On the website for this book you can see Alison talking through her intent and meanings for Stephen and for readers of this book.

The Duck/Rabbit: "Seeing As"

We begin exploring the possibility of teaching visually with a very familiar image of the *duck/rabbit* (Figure 4.4).

Jastrow created the duck/rabbit in 1899 as a means of demonstrating that we see with our brains, not just our eyes. Photographer and educator David Garner is a teacher who knows that learning in general, and learning in art and design in particular, is about getting

Figure 4.4   Jastrow's Duck/Rabbit
Source: Wikimedia Commons

students to engage with ambiguity and uncertainty. This is, after all, at the heart of teaching for critical thinking (Brookfield, 2011), something most colleges and universities proclaim in their mission statements. Faced with challenging dilemmas or seemingly insoluble problems students search for rules to follow and focus on adapting existing parameters and categories of knowledge to frame their inquiries. Yet complex intellectual and practical problems are not typified by right and wrong answers, but rather by interpretative and divergent approaches. To help students be open to this realization David Garner uses the ambiguous, bi-stable image of the duck/rabbit.

David describes his ideas for the activity as being motivated by Wittgenstein's inquiries into perception and in particular the notion of aspect perception or "seeing as." It is important to David that students do not only come to an abstract understanding of the ambiguity endemic to perception but that they actually experience visual-interpretative complexity firsthand. As David wrote to Alison in an e-mail, "The duck-rabbit image is *utilized* as a metaphor for ambiguity in visual practice, perception is enacted, interpretations explored, and emotions examined."

In a class that is part of a course designed to prepare students for their experience of college, David begins by telling students they are going to do a drawing exercise and distributes a worksheet with a version of duck/rabbit reproduced. He then gives the deliberately ambiguous instruction "Draw what you see." He also adds the condition that students have to follow the instructions without seeking further clarification. Students immediately ask, "What do you mean?" because they are worried they have seen the wrong thing.

The exercise is intended as a means of engendering discussion about the ambiguity students will experience in a degree course, but this is not mentioned at the outset. Some students mimetically reproduce the full image and others will draw the duck or rabbit they see. As they draw, a ripple of murmuring goes round the room, mostly "I've done it wrong." The next instruction is to "Draw what else you can see." In response students start to interpret the image in their own way and draw anything from driveways to blowfish, monsters to frying pans. At this point there will still be some students who have not seen a duck or a rabbit.

On completion of the drawing the class moves into a discussion of the multiple possibilities that one line drawing can engender. Students often express how hard it is to articulate what they have done. David helps them understand that confidence is required to draw what you see and that this is difficult when operating within the realm of the ambiguous. The point of the exercise is to illustrate that there is no right or wrong way of seeing, but that perception is personal, individual, and valid. To round off the exercise David asks students how carrying out the exercise made them feel. At this point many tell him it has dredged up old school experiences for them, some of which are negative or disempowering. David uses this aspect of their disclosure to introduce students to the notion that there will sometimes be no right or wrong responses to problems they will face in college, because voicing opinions grounded in each person's knowledge, experience, and perception are inherently valid and valuable.

Learning to See Visual Culture: An Urban Walk

The *visual culture walk* has been created by Janice Miller and Sina Shamsavari, lecturers in cultural and historical studies at the London College of Fashion, and is undertaken at the midpoint of an eponymous module with second-year students across a range of disciplines. Having been introduced to theories of ways of seeing, students are given a suggested route to walk around parts of central London as a means of gathering research for an essay on visual culture. This is an opportunity for them to look around and with minimal guidance to see how they can find in their immediate environs evidence of theoretical debates or positions they have been introduced to in class. The idea is to teach students that visual culture is not just present in grand artistic statements but is also found in the ordinary or unassuming, such as the pebble formation shown in Figure 4.5.

Figure 4.5   Pebble Union Jack, Dunwich Beach, Suffolk: Visual Culture in Unexpected Forms and Places

What they pick out and what they miss form the backbone of a discussion when the students gather to share what they have found. Just as with duck/rabbit, there are students who take to the walk productively, and others who return having "seen nothing." For the latter group, what they have *not* seen may teach them as much as what they have. The tutors marshaling the walk at key points on the route feel a continual tension between the desire to point things out and the need for students to develop their own ability to see, select, evaluate, and appreciate. This is, of course, a generic dynamic for any teacher in any discipline concerned to get students to take responsibility for developing their own intellectual judgments. One thing tutors notice is that students are so often on the lookout for the edgy or flamboyant that they miss out on the "subtle stuff."

Sketchbooks and Look Books

In the creative arts, *sketchbooks* and *look books* are mostly used by fashion lecturers—so that students can visualize an emerging collection, or decide on colors, shapes, lengths, and so on. Both are common tools for gathering ideas and inspirations, encouraging immediacy and experimentation when drawing quick representations, or aid memoires, are developed more fully later on. Although look books are primarily used to present a "look" or certain kind of style concept, they can also resemble artists' portfolios, incorporating statements of career intent, curriculum vitae, and reflective statements as tools for future professional self-promotion. They represent another way for students to compile a portfolio that communicates the skills they have developed and the knowledge they have explored. James, a lecturer whose students make extensive use of sketchbooks and look books, notes how students who successfully engage with reflection seem to be able to visualize potential ideas through drawing and collage initially, and of course extensive and exhaustive researching.

There is no reason why sketchbooks and look books should not be used across the disciplines. Students in any practice-oriented subject could benefit from keeping sketch and look books in which they draw emerging understandings of concepts, create maps or diagrams to show connections between different elements of content, and present visuals representing applications of theory in practice. In highly abstract courses visuals will focus on conveying concepts and compiling maps of how the different components of a topic connect and diverge. In practice-based courses the way theory is embedded in practice will be the focus. And in any course in which students are already submitting portfolios of their work, it is not much of a stretch to add an explicitly visual component. Nor is there any reason why a learning journal should not be kept in visual rather than just written form.

Drawing is a powerful means of reflecting, irrespective of artistic capability and aesthetics (Bessette, 2006). Participants using drawing in Alison's classes and workshops have noticed a difference between the things they would say when asked to write a written reflection (often organized around expected or routine topics) and what emerged from their visual representations. Students find it especially revealing to reflect on their experiences through drawing. The symbols or images produced often recur in metaphorical modeling workshops and include representational or recognizable items (people, things) or easily translatable symbols (arrows, sunshine).

Drawing also releases thoughts that are sometimes much more powerful and emotive in their emblematic form than if they are described in words—especially when these involve abstract depictions of mess, tangle, loss, uncertainty, or the unknown (James, 2007, p. 192). The dense black squiggles of confusion like tangled balls of knitting produced by one student are important for what these convey, not for their aesthetic quality. The manner in which this visual was produced was equally revealing; the student responded facially, physically, and through the movement of the pen (fast frustrated strokes, or slow ponderous mark making) while creating this visual. These were all important parts of the reflective experience that would not translate into words in quite the same way, and that form part of our argument for multimode expressions of reflection.

Paper Tearing as Visual Representation

An example of the effectiveness of visual reflection is an icebreaker from Techdis, the leading UK advisory service for technology and inclusion, used to illustrate how we interpret situations differently. It comes from the online JISC TechDis staff pack *Checking the Accessibility of Your E-resources*, produced in 2005, and is used here with permission.

This *paper-tearing* exercise was created as part of accessibility training for staff working with students with disabilities and specific learning difficulties. However, we have found it to be an effective example of playful and creative reflection in a very simple form that is applicable across multiple learning situations. (You might argue, because participants do this exercise with their eyes shut, it is not immediately visual; however, the visual plays an important part in drawing conclusions from the activity.)

The instructions are as follows:

Participants are given a plain piece of paper and everyone is asked to close their eyes (unless they are lip readers, in which case they can follow the teacher's instructions without looking at other participants). The group is told that they will be given a set of simple instructions that they will need to interpret; however, certain conditions will apply to the exercise. No questions can be asked or answered, no conferring between students is allowed, and there is to be no repetition of the instructions. The instructions are to

- Fold the piece of paper in half.

- Fold the paper in half again.

- Fold the paper in half again.

- Tear off the right-hand corner.

- Turn the paper round and tear off the left-hand corner.

Once these steps have been completed, the participants are told to open their eyes and compare their pieces of paper. (See Figure 4.6.) In a large lecture hall it can help to ask students to

Figure 4.6   Paper-Tearing Exercise: One Chilly Winter Morning
Source: By kind permission of Zoe Tynan-Campbell

raise their papers up in the air and to look around the room, so that everyone can see one another's finished articles. Participants will have slightly different interpretations of the instructions, and as such their results may differ. It may be helpful, if working with very large groups, to make sure that people collect all their bits of paper because the exercise can result in the production of considerable amounts of confetti (as Alison found when she did the exercise with 240 new master's students).

What tends to happen as the exercise unfolds is that first students are baffled and disconcerted by why they have to shut their eyes. In the majority of cases when asked what they think the exercise reveals, students say that their papers are all different, and so are they. In some cases a tiny minority will be heard to say, as in the duck/rabbit exercise, "I got it wrong." This, of course, offers useful fodder for reflection as to why the student thinks that way.

Alison has used this exercise countless times as a means of encouraging students to realize that their different interpretations of situations are valid and that a variety of outcomes is not an issue. This exercise might be a problem for a mathematician or in situations when convergent thinking is paramount; but in subjects where divergent thinking and multiple solutions are the most valued it is apposite. As a simple kinesthetic and visual exercise, paper tearing can be flexed to suit a number of purposes. For Alison it embodies neatly for students that their reflections will be as diverse and personal as their paper patterns. The same message can be applied to research proposals and projects, or topics for dissertations, because individual students approach these differently.

The Plait

Visual research and reflection are richly described by Pat Francis in her imaginative book *Inspiring Writing in Art and Design: Taking a Line for a Write* (2009). For our text Pat has given kind permission for two specific activities to be included here as examples of creative reflection. The first is the *Plait*, a metaphor for illustrating how learning, ideas, and ways of working are entwined. Following are her instructions.

> Visualize or make a plait, with three differing strands of material—wool, cotton, ribbon, paper, wire, etc. Each strand can also consist of a number of threads.
> - Begin the plait in the normal way—outside right to middle, outside left to middle...
> - Then change the tension—plait tightly, then plait loosely
> - Then make a deliberate mistake: this is not easy— but try to create a error in the plaiting
> - Then go back to the correct way
> - Carry on till you finish your plait
> - Take a few moments to write down your reflections on this and how it relates to you
> (Francis, 2009, p. 97)

As teachers, you can define what the three elements of the plait represent for you. Pat offers one plait as representing practical work, one representing research, and one representing writing. For our purposes these could just as easily be practice, theory, and reflection, or indeed anything else. The varying tensions and the mistakes are indicative of how the path to a goal is never smooth, and the plait itself represents "the constant interplay and inter-reactions of work and processes" (p. 97) or how parts constitute a whole.

LSD

As Pat explains, the *LSD* exercise is not to encourage drug use but to denote an acronym for its parts: (L) Look back through your work, (S) Select, and (D) Deepen. These three elements are the fundaments of retrospective reflection, which Pat incorporates into a paper fan, with each of the elements marked out on a fold of the paper, to be revealed in turn. Students write on each of the three folds of the fan what they feel they have covered in a course or module (the L stage), what they take as the most important things they have learned (the S stage), and how they will use that learning to frame where they go next (the D stage). Pat recommends the exercise as a strategy to use when you are stuck, with guidance for each of the steps. In the Looking Back stage she reminds students to take their time and really immerse themselves in reexamining every little detail of what they have produced and reappraising the value and relevance of ideas and resources. The Selection stage is about listening to your inner voice as to what to keep, discard, or prioritize. In Deepening students decide what to develop, drill into, or amplify. (See Figure 4.7.)

Figure 4.7   Thinking Laterally: LSD as Pounds, Shillings, and Pence in Old British Currency

Drawing and Collaging Discussion

One of the ways Stephen breaks with speech as the privileged form of classroom communication also involves the visual. In professional development workshops he runs with Steve Preskill, co-author of *Discussion as a Way of Teaching* (Brookfield and Preskill, 2005), the two of them attempt to use *drawing* and *collaging* as alternatives to a talking discussion. The exercise begins with students being assigned a discussion question and supplied with large newsprint to draw on, plenty of colored markers, pens, rulers, scissors, and tape to help them create two-dimensional drawings. They also receive magazine photographs, cloth scraps, and other textured materials for creating a mixed-media collage creation, if they so desire.

Students individually draw (or create an individual collage) on a sheet of newsprint representing their responses to the discussion question. Stephen and Steve stress that abstract drawing with no attempt at representation is fine. This is not an exercise in draftsmanship or aesthetics. After a few minutes students come together in small groups and each person explains his or her drawing or collage to the other group members. The group then prepares a drawing or collage that represents the conversation that ensued as the individual drawings and collages were discussed. Elements of each person's work are included on the newsprint. One member volunteers to take notes of what the group is trying to communicate so she or he can interpret the drawing to the large group and respond to any questions they have.

When all of the groups have completed their task, each group displays their work somewhere in the room for all to observe at their leisure. A blank sheet of paper is posted next to each visual posting. Participants wander the room and on the blank pieces of paper they add their responses—comments, questions, and reactions—to the pictures or collages. They can use drawings or words to give their responses. The group members then gather as a whole class for the chance to talk about each of the postings and the reactions posted to it.

Visual Dialogue

Drawing and collaging discussion shares with *visual dialogue* the intent of breaking with spoken or written language for at least part of the time. For Julian Burton, a practitioner of *visual dialogue*, the ability to look and hear beyond the words that people use to describe their feelings and experiences is a crucial professional skill. Julian is a change consultant and artist (born of an artist father) with a degree in medical illustration—a qualification that straddles the sciences and humanities. His current work differs greatly from his degree study, however. Then he was drawing things that were externally visible; now he draws what is invisible—concepts, ideas, and metaphors. In medical illustration, also, there is the sense of being outside, and detached from the aspect of the body under scrutiny, whereas in drawing the invisible he is working with the inside. (Obviously, when you are drawing sinews and arteries this is inside in a very obvious way.)

Julian came to use visual dialogue while working as a landscape painter and Web designer living in New York. His journey with visual dialogue began when he was given a book on complexity science at a time when this presented a new paradigm of scientific thinking. His interest stimulated, he was invited to a conference at Massachusetts Institute of Technology (MIT) where his contribution was to draw these ideas so that people could better understand them. Back in the UK he was invited to the London School of Economics to draw at further lectures on complexity theory, which led to Julian drawing for organizations at strategy meetings and creating visual records of meetings.

Julian realized that using images is very important to distilling what is most important in a meeting's discussion. Representing information visually can capture what matters *behind* the surface forms of communication—the unspoken issues as well as those that are articulated. Visual images can show complex relationships and lots of information all at once. Visual dialogue is not just effective for organizational learning, however. For Julian, visuals fit in with the new dialogic paradigm of education and present information in a way that is much more easy to talk about. His son describes his work in more straightforward terms: "My dad makes pictures so that other people can talk about them."

In an application of visual dialogue Julian used a set of questions in a twenty-minute period with Alison to elicit what being professional meant to her, what it felt like, how she coped when things went wrong, what it felt like when she was at her best, and what she was able to do to stay at her best. As he questioned and she responded, Julian translated her words into images on a wall that captured succinctly the spirit of Alison's words and presented them to her with strength and emphases she had not anticipated. At the heart of the exchange were two elements that will recur in subsequent chapters: the richly metaphorical aspects of conveying experience, and the use of particular kinds of questions to elicit reflective responses. The image he produced is reproduced as Figure 4.8.

Figure 4.8   Alison's Visual Dialogue with Julian Burton

Source: By kind permission of Julian Burton

At first sight of this image, one may feel a temptation to reach for a phone and ring a therapist; however, the power of the process goes beyond the shock value of seeing one's mental state reproduced in an art form. Through having her images presented back to her Alison was able to see how strongly they expressed her sense of her professional identity. The resulting image was blown up into a poster that she started to show at workshops where students were reflecting on their professional capabilities and identities. Fragments of the poster were also videoed and incorporated into a short movie encapsulating key questions as a back-up to the session. Alison was able to share and reflect on her own experience of asking herself the same questions and then replicate the process (alas, without a professional artist) with pairs of students in classes of many different sizes.

Alison's sharing of her poster with students is an example of the modeling that teachers interested in encouraging reflection need to undertake. She earns the right to ask students to engage in a potentially risky endeavor by first demonstrating her own participation in it. Alison narrates her responses to the questions about the meaning of professionalism, what good work looks like, and so on, for students, making sure to include some easily detectable metaphors in it ("throwing the baby out with the bath water" is one). Students are then invited to consider what being professional means to them, and what it looks and feels like. They can either draw their responses to these questions themselves, or work in pairs drawing for each other. The mood that takes over in this activity is remarkably variable; some pairs step straight into drawing as the most natural medium possible, others intersperse their drawing with repeated and heartfelt apologies for their ineptitude, others are aghast at the prospect of being made so vulnerable as to draw in public. The emphasis is continually reiterated that the quality of the drawing is immaterial, and that thinking in a different way by representing ideas visually is the important part.

Julian's focus is eliciting metaphors on issues, drawing them, and using his images of these as discussion methods for others. His premise is simple: if we understand each other's metaphors, we can understand each other's models of the world better. As a means of eliciting metaphors, Julian incorporated some aspects of *clean language* in order to develop pictures through dialogue. Clean language is a framework of questions developed by the clinical therapist David Grove (http://www.cleanlanguage.co.uk) designed to be devoid, as far as possible, of the preconceptions, intent, interpretations, and manipulation of the person asking them. In chapter 8 we discuss clean language in more detail, so make a detour there now, if this is something that interests you, before reading on.

Visualization Techniques

Techniques of visualization come in many forms and bear different titles. Practitioners of NeuroLinguistic Programming (NLP) use visualization in techniques such as *anchoring* as a means of evoking the strongest multisensory vision in one's head of a memory or experience (http://www.nlpworld.co.uk/nlp-glossary/a/anchoring/). This is then used as a trigger to activate a positive memory or scenario where confidence or situations demand it, which can help a person cope. This technique may be used for all kinds of needs, from public speaking, exam nerves, pre-interview, meeting one's future in-laws, or dealing with the onset of anxiety. In other uses, imaginative visualizing, such as fading out a powerful visual memory from strong colors to sepia, is used as a means of neutralizing prior memories that haunt or obstruct an individual in some way.

Visualization, or the conjuring of images to induce a positive and capable mental state, is also used to help people imagine the outcome they wish to achieve. This technique can be used for sporting activities like mastering horseback riding or any other kind of objective. In his motivational speeches, Paralympian swimmer and multiple gold medal winner Marc Woods (2006) describes advising his team members to "draw the black curtains" every time they entered the water in a race as a means of blocking out any distractions from spectators or media.

In creative reflection, students use visualization as a means of setting their positive learning goals and aiming for them. This may involve creating metaphors for feelings and experiences, as we see in the following essay extract in which one learner attempts to control her tendency to procrastinate:

> To stop myself from falling down this slippery slope [putting things off] I had to get back into a flow if I was to give it my all in my final term. It was at this point my visual interpretation of my future, drawn during a reflective discourse lecture, came into play. The main overriding image was a set of goal posts with an image of myself in a cap and gown underneath. After placing the drawing on a pin board over my desk I found myself staring at it, recognizing that if I fully pushed myself for the next two months I could have those photos along the River Thames with my pink and black cap and gown and my proud parents smiling either side. This picture helped me to regain focus, by imagining the exciting possibilities I was determined to get my dissertation done.

Her use of metaphor shows that we do not necessarily need to instruct students in visualization; they may be doing it for themselves already.

Summary

In this chapter we have looked at visual modes of teaching and learning as alternatives to written reflection and provided some examples of practice based on these. In doing this, however, we don't wish to dismiss all forms of reflective writing. Clearly there is considerable evidence that exists to point up the value of writing reflectively, and Stephen has authored two books dealing with some of these (Brookfield, 1995, 2011). We know too that many students engage more easily in this medium. With this in mind our next chapter is largely devoted to written stories, although the forms that these take, and the origins from which they spring, may vary considerably.

5

How Story and Metaphor
Provoke Reflective Thinking

One of our intentions with this book is to critique higher education's traditional reliance on writing as the best means of assessing student learning across a range of disciplines. But, in the words of a well-used cliché, we don't want to throw the baby out with the bath water. So in this chapter we examine how writing can be used more imaginatively to teach and assess students' reflective thinking. But we are concerned with a particular kind of writing: the narrative form of writing, with specific emphasis on story and metaphor. The use of metaphor weaves throughout our analysis, so we examine conceptual positions on metaphor in some detail.

Stories are everywhere, from Pink's (2008) example of how corporations use stories from personnel to uncover insights about how they function, to stories as doctoral dissertations (Nash, 2004), leadership narratives (Noonan, 2007), and stories of professional practice (Preskill and Smith-Jacobvitz, 2000). There are stories of resistance (Nash and Viray, 2013) and the critical race theory movement uses counter-storytelling (Bell, 2010) to challenge stock stories about race. Digital storytelling (http://digitalstorytelling.coe.uh.edu/) amplifies traditional voiceover narrative with video clips, computer-based images, and music (Frazel, 2010; Alexander, 2011). Story and metaphor are now being adopted in the emerging field of narrative medicine, where, allied with empathy, they provide a means of eliciting patients' narratives as opposed to just their symptoms (Pink, 2008).

Creative Reflection and Metaphor

The quote from the novelist E. M. Forster—"How can I tell what I think till I see what I say?" (1927, p. 99)—evokes the ways in which the acts of writing or speaking transform our vague sense of something into a much clearer appreciation of it. To help us do this we frequently turn to metaphor. Lakoff and Johnson's seminal work, *Metaphors We Live By* (2003), analyzes in depth the pervasive nature of metaphor as a way that humans ascribe meaning to their activities. Lakoff and Johnson elaborate a metaphorical system that infiltrates our entire existence and is expressed and communicated through our language. It is no surprise, therefore, to find student reflections, in verbal, written, or three-dimensional form, are often highly metaphorical.

Metaphor is not just an embellishment of language, the icing on the cake, to speak metaphorically. Lakoff and Johnson argue that it is embedded in daily speech so that what we assume to be ordinary language is in fact metaphorical and our most deeply held values are consistent with our metaphorical system. Common metaphorical systems include physical interiority/exteriority ("taking things in," "out of my mind"), or vertical measures applied to states of mind or personal development ("feeling down," "on a high," "moving up," "aiming high," "sinking low"). Metaphors provide ways of thinking about and acting toward something, as in personifying people as things ("She's a nightmare"), or abstract processes as physical entities (as in inflation being seen as the chief "foe" in a battle for economic prosperity).

According to Sullivan and Rees (2008) people use roughly six metaphors a minute in normal conversation, and the richness of metaphor in everyday speech is immediately apparent if you spend any time listening for it. Alison recently tried this at a university planning meeting, which reinforced her view of the ubiquity of metaphor. In a short space of time, three different speakers evoked aspirations for the future in spatial and directional metaphors (moving/driving/going forward, moving out of silos, being at the forefront, getting our thinking behind something, building up) while evoking the prospect of a "brave new world" and the need to "get under the skin of what students want." Much chiming, resonating, feeding, and capturing also went on, with praise for the existing "strong, vocational threads" and "academic rigorous threads" that would "underpin" student development and help "ease them out of the door."

The moment we start to be aware of metaphors, we find that they are everywhere and give meaning to our most fundamental beliefs and desires as well as our more mundane actions. Perhaps the reason that we speak in metaphor, and why we adopt clichés, is that the expressions work better for us to explain how we feel than other kinds of language. Sullivan and Rees (2008) point out that since the publication of *Metaphors We Live By*, cognitive linguists have done extensive work in the field of metaphor that illustrates the power and presence of metaphor and the way people live by metaphors that remain coherent and consistent over time.

We typically generate our own individual metaphors or lay our own interpretations on existing shared ones. This is important for listening closely to the stories students tell us. The point of seeking out metaphor in student work is both to validate its presence in written work, and to understand the conceptual power of those metaphors that lie behind the accounts of student learning. The metaphors used by students are not just lazy or colloquial language but represent something deeply felt.

Roller Coasters, Rainbows, and Other Learning Metaphors

To illustrate the power of metaphors in communicating learning we turn to a module Alison has taught for several years at a London university that attempts to capture all the insights, experiences, trials, and successes of students as they complete their final assignments in order to graduate. In one particular year, the roller coaster ride dominated as a metaphor for student experiences, with 198 out of 200 students referring to this image at some point in their essays. Moon (2006) cites the view that tired metaphors should be discouraged in student writing, and certainly encouraging the flowering of new ones is a helpful means of developing a student's written and visual vocabulary. However, as Sullivan and Rees (2008) point out, something that seems to be a shared metaphor may in fact conceal specific differences. What each student was evoking by that mention of a roller coaster, how it appeared to her, and why it felt applicable for her experiences, was open to diverse interpretation.

Other common metaphors were about journeys to take, paths to travel, mountains to climb, spirals to endure, dark moments and silver linings to experience, home runs to hit, and projects to give birth to as babies. Metaphorical toolkits were needed, learning curves were traced, slopes were slipped down, hurdles were jumped, and 100 percent was given. In the year of the volcanic eruption in Iceland, the resulting ash cloud, with its attendant metaphors and parallels, was a gift for students (and staff) who had found a powerful new symbol for anything resembling disruption, trauma, or confusion. Learners coined their own imagery, such as pressure storms, mental fogs, energy gremlins, or progress enemies.

Many other essays included single or shorter metaphors. In one, a rainbow was used to represent not just a pastel-colored pretty thing that appears in the sky, but how the student combined insights from multiple mythologies and symbolisms. The rainbow symbolized the coexistence of science, art, Greek and Hindu traditions, with her studies leading her to discover the pot of gold at the end that signified her goals for her future. It is easy to sigh and say that the pot of gold is a well-worn cliché; however, for the student concerned, it represented something important and should not be dismissed.

Student Sarah's essay began with Wilson and Long's *Blob Tree* (Long, 2012) as a visual composed of a tree on which a number of gingerbread people were situated—climbing, hanging, huddling, in isolation, catching, falling, and all with a variety of facial expressions. Originally used as a youth work tool for enabling discussion to unpack emotions and experiences, Sarah used the *Blob Tree* as a means of visually situating herself in the course of her final year. Her essay was populated with metaphors: "on top of the world," "finding myself," "took me under their wing," and having a "network of friends."

Another student took an extract from Philip K. Dick's sci-fi story *Adjustment Team* (subsequently filmed as The *Adjustment Bureau*), in which each element, or individual, follows their Plan—a detailed route through the Sector Board, which looks like the graphic of a computer board but which is a map of their world. The descriptive (and visual) metaphor of the Sector Board was used to show the extent to which that student had deviated from his original plan. A third student took a line from Gandhi—"I will give you a talisman"—to check the degree to which her values and aspirations improved the lot of the starving and homeless. Social responsibility and human rights were at the heart of this student's interests, having spent time studying peace and conflict theory in India. The metaphor of the talisman as a guiding principle for life thus underpinned the entire reflection.

Some students were a little more adventurous in their self-conceptions and envisioning, with more than one student adopting the character of Alice in Wonderland. In so doing they used the vicissitudes and characters of Alice's adventure in a magical and nightmarish otherworld as analogies for their own final-year reflections. Another used the *Pensieve* from Harry Potter as a metaphor for the process of drawing out wisps of memory, feeling, and critical judgment from the cauldron of her mind.

Dyslexia: The Bully in My Playground

Sometimes a metaphor is used throughout an essay to embody a problem or challenge. For Sophie, a final-year student in a management degree course, the challenge was her dyslexia.

> There's a bully in my playground. All this year he watched me in lectures, followed me home and even sat with me in "downtime." I tried to ignore him—in fact I did a pretty good job of ignoring him—and got on with the things that weren't so problematic. I love my specialism; I love my dissertation topic; don't mind researching and I certainly have some ideas of my own.... Writing, however, is the bully in my playground... and on the day of my first final year exam he finally gave me a proper kicking.
>
> I am dyslexic. It's not how I identify myself normally—it doesn't feature heavily in my self concept and I certainly try not to use it for special treatment. Nevertheless, it unavoidably comes to the fore in anything academic. I'm not an academic but I am a good student, and my dyslexia is the reason for the distance between the two. I used to think that I got upset because I tried to write and couldn't but I've learned this year it is the other way round. Writing is my biggest weakness because I get upset about it—I worry, it knocks my confidence, and then I can't write.

Sophie's account is powerfully written and self-aware. Not only is it clearly meaningful to her and heartfelt in its honesty, it is also a clarion call to educational institutions to adopt alternative modes of study and assessment to ensure that students like Sophie are fully supported. Sophie is an interesting case because her challenge specifically lies in academic writing. Other forms (e-mails, memos, and texts) do not present an issue. She also notes that traditional examinations have their limitations as a means of testing someone's capability and knowledge but are a very good way of testing someone's exam technique. Sophie, being terrified in exam situations, fell foul of the system: "I didn't write for the first 35 minutes. Not a word. I panicked and couldn't find a sentence in the jumble of words and noise in my head." She had revised and prepared but had not practiced controlling her fear of exams, which led to a disappointing result. Stephen particularly resonates with Sophie's story with his own history of poor examination performances.

Sophie is not a lazy or incapable learner, and she makes it clear at what cost she gets tasks done. By paragraph 3 of page 1 of her story, she recounts she has spent four hours with pen in hand, listening to recordings of herself "blathering on about myself, to try and get some personality into it." The metaphorical kicking she alludes to stems from a mixture of panic and inability to control and release the information in her head. In her reflective analysis on the disaster that had been her examination performance she offers a dense and detailed narrative of how she picked herself up and what she learned would work best for her. Specifically, she realized how she needed to filter and retain information:

> Read about it, write bullet points, listen to a teacher, read some more, then I need to tell someone about it; in that order is best. There would not only be multiple sources of information but multiple types of input at varying levels of detail and information. This allows you to form a kind of detailed picture or idea—rather than the dreaded "words" of what you're trying to achieve or understand.

Sophie was studying business management, and it is interesting that she sees the multiple source approach as being without words, when words are so clearly present in discussion and listening, just not in a textual form. She also came to realize that dissertation writing taught her perseverance, while goal setting had shown her that realism and optimism went hand in hand.

> Realism, optimism, time management, problem management and technical writing skills; all improvements I have made this year which will doubtless help me in the workplace. I've even starting eating my crusts!

Sophie produced something in her essay that was a personal and insightful assessment of where her real challenges lay and how she would need to get to grips with them. She proved her ability to write in a different style and to tap into a metaphorical appraisal of her situation to produce a reflective essay that was both well informed and elegantly expressed. Writing the essay was not easy because she was "trying to avoid the bully," and reflecting on the year meant facing some sensitive areas of her life. However with determination she completed her dissertation successfully, which caused her no little satisfaction:

> The day I passed 10,000 words was the day I turned round and kicked the bully somewhere unpleasant. He ended up flipping burgers for a living, by the way,—and I'm headed for the fashion industry.

Sophie's essay is an illustration of the possibility of approaching a seemingly conventional essay with a little more leeway in terms of personal voice and style. She fulfilled all the obligations of the task in terms of a self-evaluation of her skills, strengths, attributes, year events, and future plans, but she did it metaphorically, having the courage to address parts of her way of learning that she did not want to go near. She did it honestly, with wit and style. Some teachers reading this story may respond that this is like creative writing, not an objective self-evaluation, and that it would not work with their students. This may be so, in which case it has perhaps been no more than pleasant reading that does not apply to practice. However, Alison did not ask Sophie to tell her story in this way; she simply gave her the space and the freedom to tell her story in the way she wanted to. Alison felt this elicited a far stronger impression of what Sophie was capable of than if she had recited her dexterity with Photoshop or Excel, or described what a great team player she was.

Reading essays like these demonstrate to us what Dewey (1933) calls "the other side of the stone," or hidden aspects of reflection, in terms of what our students are capable of and what else is going on in their heads besides what we are teaching them. Through the metaphors they use, they teach us to be alert to their passions and drivers. Some students much prefer a dry, businesslike, structured, and objective approach and, depending on who is going to see the final outcome, this may be much more appropriate for certain circumstances. For us, what is important is giving students the freedom to choose. Choice was very much the order of the day for students who contributed to the next example we look at.

Tell Us about It

Tell Us about It is an initiative that has been running at University of the Arts, London, for several years and is designed to invite high-achieving students from a range of backgrounds to provide a narrative in some form or another of their positive learning experiences while at the university. Its goal is to research the student experience in a way that would inform pedagogic and institutional strategies for supporting student progression, "to use their collective reflections of the learning experience as a lever for change within the organization" (Finnigan, 2009, p. 136). Students are asked to focus on the challenges they faced and describe how they overcame them, to identify what helped them learn, and to provide tips or strategies they could share for other students.

Students' responses identified familiar challenges—the tough transition from high school to college, homesickness, loneliness, responding to different ways of teaching and learning—but were expressed in very different ways. Many of the responses wrestled with changing identities. Rather than write a report summarizing these themes, Tell Us about It leader Terry Finnigan believed that the students' voice needed to be respected and that their work would be exhibited, rather than written about by academics. It was anticipated that students would most probably submit essays as the most traditional form of academic writing; however, the reality was significantly different. With many items now held in the Special Collections Archive at the London College of Communication, the variety of the Tell Us about It submissions can be clearly seen.

Exhibitions have subsequently been held to disseminate the way in which the student responses speak for themselves, including one curated by a student alumnus for a conference on culture and cultural capital. The pieces exhibited combine artistry and creativity with metaphors and symbols, including the familiar ones of journeys or roads traveled. The exhibitions include animated, narrated, and composed sound tracks for students' movies, compiled sketchbooks, invented allegorical board games, newly created websites, or designed artifacts. Some are noticeable for the different kind of media they have selected for their messages: inked baby wipes, embroidery or hand stitching of material samples. These often require a particular kind of visual literacy or map to be able to go beyond a surface appreciation of what is intended, which the provision of text makes less problematic. Is a thick, spiraling, coiled thread wound into a one-dimensional snail shell evocative of a black hole of melancholy, or does it convey the aesthetics of interconnected experiences? Some are less opaque, such as the "square pegs in round holes" fabric prints of a mature student returning to full-time education who used a familiar metaphor to signify the discomfort she experienced in returning to academe.

Some of the most interesting submissions to Tell Us about It are almost completely visual: a canvas wall-hanging combining text, graphic prints, photographs, stitch samples, or a Tube map. One tells the life story of a mature student in movie form, using the convention of a fairy story, but updated through a collage of old family footage, animation, and music. Delvina Mckinson created a mask to represent her two sides. For her "the sparkly sequined side of the mask represents the part of me that shines through well when I have confidence. The black painted side represents my reserved, quiet, shy and sometimes doubtful side."

Dale Allen's *Scratching below the Surface* is a wooden box painted white with a woven straw handle on top and oatmeal-colored ties to hold it all together. The box encloses interior layers, each of which adds to the depth of meaning of her piece. Once the lid of the box is removed, the first layer discovered is a printed story, hand bound as a paper book, which lays bare the significance of both box and title. In coming to study in the UK, Dale—a White South African—was experiencing what it meant to be categorized and confined by nationality.

The color of the box is surely no accident. According to Dale, during the Apartheid era, White South Africans described themselves as European. It was only on coming to Europe that Dale realized that she was "incontrovertibly *not* European. I am African." For her this meant that she did not long for a previous kind of ancestral culture, but rather that she is "the product of an amalgam of cultures."

> I relied on and drew from my cultural experience [South African]...at least I did until my course director strongly recommended a steering away from the African....I spiralled into a sense of confusion....It [my work] didn't belong to me and I didn't belong to it—as in the case of displacement, it felt as though my work and I were sitting in that area between space and place, where relationships between objects had not yet been formed.

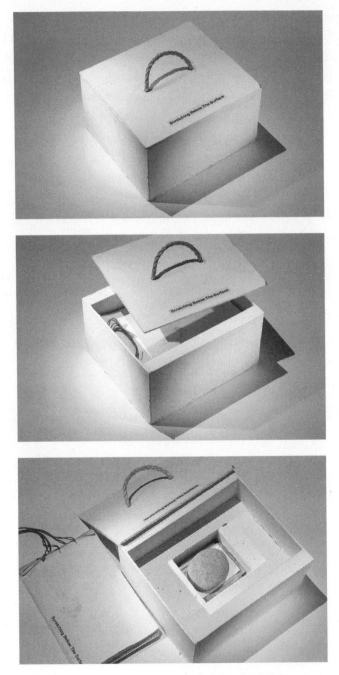

Figure 5.1   Three Views of Scratching below the Surface

Her reflections on this experience as embodied in the metaphor of the box, and the powerful, frustrated, thoughtful, and sometimes angry account contained within it, further note how she learned to play the game of keeping people (particularly a single tutor) happy by not exploring her African identity. Next in the interior layers is a stone, the significance of which is not made clear but can be imagined—perhaps a memento from home that has been included to symbolize her native land? Underneath the stone, wrapped in grease proof paper and nestling within a chunky square recess are waxy snippets of images perhaps indicative of her identity and practice as a fine artist. These also illustrate aspects of her story—abstract landscapes which are redolent of old historic photographs of wide prairie landscapes, brown legs, what appears to be wool, drawings, a white girl, and a quote by Okwui Enwezor, the Nigerian curator and theorist, on the marginalization or misrepresentation of contemporary African art.

Although the examples cited so far concentrate very much on the obstacles faced and impacts on learning, another submission focuses on guidance for new students. *U Is for University* is an A–Z

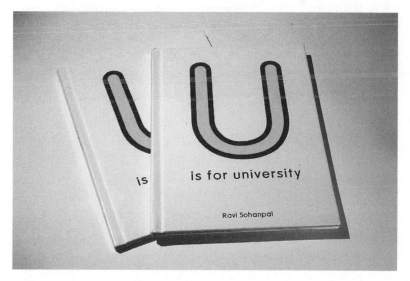

Figure 5.2   U Is for University

survival kit designed in the format of an early children's reader, with big words and simple short text in bold sans serif font and with artwork in keeping with the genre.

Diagrams as Story Triggers: The Change Curve

Visual aids can sometimes help to unleash a narrative flow, as when diagrammatic story triggers plot out a narrative trajectory or provide a skeleton or starting point for students to give a more imaginative chronology to their experiences. One example that bears many names is the *change curve*. Originally devised by Elisabeth Kübler-Ross (1997) as a five-stage grief cycle that would enable people to come to terms with the trauma of terminal illness, death, and bereavement, it has come to be used, with slight variations to its terminology, as a tool for understanding and facilitating change within individuals and organizations (see Figure 5.3). The terms used to describe the curve all effectively follow an upside-down bell shape or U-curve. Starting with shock at the top left-hand corner, the curve slides first into denial, then down into anger (and other negative emotions), bottoming out either with the ultimate low

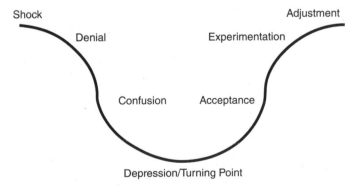

Figure 5.3   The Change Curve

Source: Adaptation of Kübler-Ross's Change Curve

point or depression, or, in more positive representations, with a turning point. The upward climb out of the bell on the right-hand side of the diagram follows the stages of experimentation and seeing new possibilities leading to acceptance of change and a new way of being.

The change curve is often used in therapeutic situations to help students navigate difficult personal circumstances. However, there are lower-risk situations that do not need the intervention of a trained clinician in which the change curve can guide student reflection. For example, there are close similarities to the stages typically identified in instances of transformative learning (Taylor and Cranton, 2012). Several students writing their reflective essays in Alison's final-year reflective module used the change curve to illustrate their academic experiences. For Alex, there was the initial shock in September of realizing the extent of the year's workload, especially after returning from a year's placement in Hong Kong. This was followed by a denial of what was required to get back into a work frame of mind and then confusion over framing a dissertation topic. The turning point in the curve was a tutorial in which a relaxed tutor enabled Alex to get past the paralyzing panic and into action. Acceptance took the form of framing a promising research proposal and adjustment.

Some students use the curve to plot the course of a specific essay, project, or dissertation, or to describe going through times of transition from one year to the next or preparing to leave the university. Retrospectively, it's also a means of looking back over experiences in a period of time to see whether, why, and how the change curve plays out, and to use it as the backbone for a reflective narrative. In addition, international students who have come to study abroad have found that using the change curve as a focus for exploring newness, change, and difference between their home and educational experiences and the host country, has been helpful in a number of ways.

This happened very usefully with a class of students from several Asian countries who were attending an evening seminar one bitterly cold November night in London. They had spent six weeks in the UK and had been rained on almost every day. Skies were leaden and the general greyness of everything seemed unremitting. The seminar was taking place right in the middle of what is known in the vernacular as "wobble week"—the point in the first term at university where students may start to doubt why they had come, miss home and friends, and when their reserves of energy, finance, and enthusiasm have started to run out. The class was politely attentive, but Alison feared it was also a little lost.

About halfway through the evening, however, the change curve appeared in one of Alison's slides. She had been using an array of exercises gathered together in the same slide show and had not intended to use the change curve in case students found it irrelevant that early on in their UK experience. As it had popped up on her screen she asked the group if they would be interested in knowing a bit more about it. As soon as she described the flow of the curve and what it might represent, there was a tangible shift in the atmosphere. The curve seemed to spark a response in all of them. They were looking at a simple visual that spoke to their own experience and were able and willing to voice where they found themselves on the curve and why. For most of them, they were somewhere in the shock, denial, and confusion areas, although this did not mean that these were entirely negative.

Seeing the stages mapped out on the curve, and being able to relate to them, was far more effective than having students respond to general questions about how they were finding things so far. The curve also provided students' tutors with useful feedback on their experiences to date, and helped both parties consider how they might approach the next phase of study. One very helpful by-product of the curve's use was to help students realize that they were not alone, and that it was not unusual to feel some or all of the things they did.

Timelines

The use of timelines has been popular in teaching history for several decades (Pryor, 2012). Here we describe it as a narrative tool to help students create the story of their own growth and development as learners. The exercise provides students with the opportunity to hover, helicopter-like, over a visual map of their experiences as they tease out certain recollections and important moments over a period of time. Although a timeline may appear chronological and linear in its final representation, its creation may come from a swirling whirlpool of memories and thoughtful extrapolations. It can be used to cover any duration, whether an entire life span, a year, semester, module, or week. It can even be used for a day, or at any time there is enough "life material" to allow the exercise to play out.

Students get a piece of paper, their mobile devices, laptops, or anything they can draw on and compose a single line, with specified starting and end points. They then mark out on the line key events. These may be of their choosing or guided by the teacher according to context. The goal, however, is for these events to be personally meaningful rather than routine or "official" milestones in that life experience. Line events sometimes cluster together; at other times they are spaced out far apart across the line.

The next step is for the student to map the dominant influences and people that surrounded these events. Looking at the resulting diagram, where as much detail has been plotted on as possible, the student then considers whether any patterns, themes, or trends emerge. For a costume student, this simple exercise helped her to realize that her decision to take a degree in her discipline area was not the random selection she had thought it to be, but resulted from a lifetime in performing arts. For a bystander, this may seem to be a conclusion that is so self-evident the student surely could have come to it without having to map it out; however, this exercise shows that it is sometimes the "obvious" that needs a little more eliciting than one would expect. As one student put it:

> I discovered something about myself whilst writing, something which I probably knew, but didn't give much credit to myself for it. I will take this knowledge with me, and with the risk of sounding ever so slightly corny, hope that it will make me a stronger person as I enter the world of work.

The purpose of a timeline is to help students to stand back and see cause and effect in operation. They come to see emerging patterns that perhaps they were less aware of, or to understand better why certain decisions were made or why situations played out the way they did. The benefits of using a timeline for creative reflection are multiple; it gives students a more interactive way of approaching their recollections, it helps them move away from a diary style regurgitation of experience, and it makes them be selective and questioning about the experiences they have had. Seeing where key events are positioned along the line offers a way of knowing when things may have come together in a very active, fruitful, or tumultuous period of life, and when there were gaps or quieter times. As a precursor to writing a longer reflection, it is also a useful means of gathering ideas and identifying the most important material that the writer wants to focus on, rather than getting mired down in too much superfluous detail.

Metaphor as Parable

As teachers we all have tricks up our sleeves to focus student minds on thorny or recurrent issues. Alison uses an activity she calls *Bad Math* to show students at the start of their final year that if you subtract weekends, holidays, part-time jobs, eating, sleeping, class time, and other distractions, they in fact only have ten days in which to write their dissertations. The calculation is entirely false, but it works well in galvanizing the group into starting to write their proposals!

Alex Irving, Media Production lecturer at Liverpool John Moores University in the UK, has resorted to similar creativity in order to press home to students the importance of punctuality and attendance. Like many of us, Alex believes that learning only really takes place when it has meaning for students. For her the most powerful way of communicating meaning is through metaphor. She adopts a playful but serious approach to attendance that has had far more impact than lecturing students on the foolishness and financial waste of not showing up for class.

Her ruse has been to "hi-jack" a colleague's session, under the pretense that the teacher has been delayed. Instead of just sitting and waiting for her colleague to arrive, Alex tells the students she wants to try some exercises with them to illustrate an earlier class on different thinking styles. They are all told to write their answers legibly for handing in; their papers will be marked and the answers confirmed at the end of the session.

She then asks the students questions requiring literal and lateral, knowledge-based and nonlinear thinking skills. To round the questions off, she includes a creative puzzle, such as joining the dots with only two straight lines without moving pen off paper, and then recounts a short story that needs two answers from the students as a result. These answers cover why they thought the events of the story had happened, and a sentence describing their personal responses to it. The story (fictional) that Alex tells is as follows:

> Apple has invented a new, cutting-edge digital gadget. Only fifty are being released onto the market in six-months time and then it will be a whole year before any more are made available. They will be sold from one shop to the first fifty people with the money on the

day and will cost £2000. An eighteen-year-old studying for A levels who is working in a bar decides she
wants one and puts in extra hours and works weekends
to save up. She goes without new clothes, days out,
and gets exhausted doing her bar job and college work,
until six months have passed until she has saved what
she needs. When the launch day comes she camps
outside the shop all night in the freezing cold and in
the morning she is one of the first in line. When the
shop opens she goes up to the counter, pays her money,
watches as her gadget is wrapped up, thanks the assis-
tant and walks out of the shop, leaving the item on the
counter. The End.

There is a pause while the students scratch their heads trying
to work out why someone would behave in that way and ask questions like "Did she just forget it?" They have been lured by the
previous questions into attempting to think laterally to find an
answer and are also distracted into thinking that the first question
(Why did this event happen?) is most important when it is really
the second one ('What's your personal response to it?') that is con-
sequential. They are unanimous in their contempt for the student,
who they condemn along the lines of "How could anyone in their
right mind do anything like that after all that hard work? She must
be a nutcase."

At this point Alex collects their papers and her colleague ar-
rives to take the session, following her "delay." A couple of hours
later Alex returns for the last fifteen minutes of the class, which
is still full, because everyone wants to know the answers to the
puzzles they had faced. Before revealing the metaphor of the final
question or story, Alex reads out excerpts from their answer papers,
many of which are very funny and a collective sense of ridicule is
shared by the class as they all laugh at their witty dismissal of such
a wasteful fool.

Once the laughter has subsided, Alex tells them that her story is a metaphor for something and invites them to guess what it might be about, only revealing after a few suggestions that it in fact relates to their own erratic attendance or, in some cases, extreme absenteeism. Waiting until the end of class to drop the bombshell is deliberate, because its effect is often powerful. As the students start to appreciate the parallels between the story and their own behavior, they are often stunned into silence. The realization sinks in that they have been "had," but in way that causes them to appreciate fully that what they had scorned with safe detachment as being someone else's idiocy was in fact a metaphor for their own desultory use of the assets, expertise, and teaching available to them that they were walking away from. If you had dreamed of going to university, planned and saved for it, made sacrifices and taken out loans, why would you not attend, or engage with the experience less than wholeheartedly? Not least when you knew that if you committed to learning with your tutors and working in the way they advised, the likelihood of you achieving your goal of a qualification was so much greater.

Purists may wish to debate whether Alex's story was in fact a metaphor, analogy, or parable, or to unpack the minutiae of the linguistic structures she was using. For us the exactitude of the terminology is not important; rather it is her belief that metaphor (for the sake of shorthand) seems to reach a more authentic part of our being and have a more palpable effect than a public nagging that may provoke a defensive mind-set or cause students to switch off until the worst was over.

Alison admired the creativity of this approach, which had been so much more effective in dealing with an age-old issue, than the tight-lipped, schoolmarm admonitions we may be tempted to convey to our lukewarm attenders. What she had done, quite legitimately in Alison's view, was to play with the students—just as a film does with the twist in the tale—and surprise them with a conclusion they had not seen coming.

Summary

In this chapter we have provided examples of narrative techniques through which students have been encouraged to choose their mode of self-expression. Effective leaders and good teachers both understand that people remember stories more than statistics, and that change agents marshal storytelling to move people to action. In the next chapter we stay with the project of effecting change, but look at ways this can be done more kinetically, through building Lego models and labyrinth walking.

6

Playing Seriously:
Legos and Labyrinths

Our focus turns now to kinesthetic forms of learning involving the body and the physical realm. We look at two techniques; using Legos to build metaphorical models, and living the physical experience of metaphors in the shape of labyrinth walking and its attendant activities. We begin by discussing our experiences using Lego building bricks as a creative tool to promote reflective thinking. Although Lego lends itself particularly effectively to metaphorical modeling (not least through its status as a globally known iconic toy and connection to childhood), the process can take place using any set of objects that are used to represent something other than their real nature. This will be apparent to anyone who has sat in a restaurant and used the salt and pepper cellars to describe a relationship, car maneuver, choice between two options, altercation, or offside rule in soccer. Buttons, sticks, candles, pots, peas, matches, or any other assortment of items that users find sufficiently rich to embody their ideas and convey their intentions work just as well. The point is that the user assigns specific meanings to the materials to illustrate some sort of process or relationship.

The Concept of Lego Serious Play

The name "LEGO" is an abbreviation of the two Danish words *leg godt*, meaning "play well," described by the company as its ideal. Play is considered to be not just about amusing oneself but about developing understanding and communication. Developed in 1996 by Kjeld Kirk Kristiensen, the owner of LEGO, and Bart Victor and Johan Roos, professors at the Swiss business School IMD, *Lego Serious Play* (hereafter referred to as LSP) was designed to generate more engagement, imagination, and playfulness in staff meetings. Since its inception it has been adopted by numerous high-profile organizations (Google, eBay, the International Red Cross, Roche, and NASA are some examples) as a business development process and an alternative to traditional planning meetings (see also Nolan, 2010).

An important distinction between traditional meetings and the Lego approach is that no business decisions are taken during the serious play. The operational side of matters is attended to outside the metaphorical modeling experience. In this way the creative engagement with the process—thinking outside the bricks, rather than the box, perhaps, or certainly through them— is not diluted or stunted by getting functional jobs done. In previous years the process was restricted to an official training course offered by LEGO in either Denmark or the US that involved annual accreditation fees. More recently LEGO has made the LSP techniques and sets of bricks available as open source materials for broader adoption. The intent is for the physical building process to unblock habitual thinking patterns that prevent solutions from emerging.

Serious play is not the building of literal models, but rather constructing metaphorical and symbolic creations that represent problems, solutions, realizations, and models of communication, among other things. Of equal importance to building, and almost impossible to extricate from the activity, is the ensuing discussion of how different models connect with each other, and how they can be adjusted. Nolan (2010) advises building models with fingers first, rather than designing in your head and then building with fingers. As the nerve endings situated in your fingers send messages to your brain, you are literally thinking through your fingers during the building process (Gauntlett, 2011).

There is a similarity here to creativity in music or art in which the physical enactment of the art (the feel of the brush on canvas or the fingers hitting the keyboard) is a crucial kinesthetic element of the craft. As a songwriter, Stephen finds songs are crafted as his fingers hit the guitar strings, the sounds of pickups and amps change, and his hands move around the fret board. He does not start with the song in mind—it emerges from the kinesthetic engagement with wood, wire, and electricity. We learn through our senses, and our thinking is formed through sensory engagement. When our senses are engaged differently, so our responses to the world change. In line with the learning-by-doing ethic in health care, engineering, sport, and creative arts, LSP posits that learning is deeper and more personal when we make something and that the mind learns best and retains more when people are actively engaged.

Lego Serious Play in Action

Let's turn to a concrete example of LSP in action for 130 international students on a diploma course designed to prepare them for progression to a UK degree program with a design, business, or media orientation. In this introductory course LSP was used to help these students make sense of the experience of studying abroad. It was part of an innovative program intended to engage students through drawing, visual research, and professional practice, and to introduce them to concepts of cultural and historical theory as well as more traditional academic components of study. The overwhelming majority of students did not speak English as a first language, and they came from a broad range of countries—China, Hong Kong, Singapore, Indonesia, Korea, Europe, as well as the US and Australia.

The context for the specific use of Lego building was a three-hour workshop run at the end of the year by Alison on personal and professional development, in which students reflected on how they had grown and changed during their study in the UK, and how their abilities, dispositions, and relationships had evolved. LSP was employed at a time of student transition when the participants were coming to the end of their preparatory studies and needing to consider options and next steps.

Students were split into groups of 10–12 and the workshops ran over a period of five weeks in a big studio in the East End of London. When students arrived in the studio, a large oval table was set up with an array of colored bags with drawstrings, full of an assortment of every kind of Lego brick—straight, bendy, animal, vegetable, and mineral. A gentle rumbling in the corner instantly drew students to a large white portable Pod structure, which would be the home of their video reflections at the end of the workshop. They were intrigued by the strangeness of it all, with one or two looking a little apprehensive. As the workshop leader, Alison was inevitably concerned with how using metaphor would work with different levels of English language capability, and how students might react to being thrust back to their childhood, at a big table in the company of semi-strangers with a bag of Lego facing them.

Metaphorical modeling demands attention, responsiveness, and management of the group interaction from facilitators who must know when to encourage, close down, ask for an extra metaphor or interpretation, question, increase, or slow down the momentum. An important task at the outset of the workshop was to emphasize that students would be doing a special kind of building—metaphorical—and that building and thinking were intertwined. As the facilitator Alison had to walk a fine line between offering a helpful structure within which to operate and being too prescriptive. Key to the workshop was stressing that students would be the architects and owners of their own meaning in relation to their bricks and their configurations.

Opening the Workshop

Alison began the building process by passing around little Lego owls, so that students could get a feel of the bricks and start thinking about what they were holding and what it might signify in their culture. Their varied homelands notwithstanding, associations with owls—wisdom, learning, study, death, seriousness—were quick to surface, often referring to literature and film (*Winnie the Pooh, Harry Potter*). Owls' particular physical attributes, like the ability to swivel their heads 270 degrees to literally have eyes in the back of their heads, also provided avenues for metaphors of students' experience regarding different ways of seeing the world.

Students then started an ice-breaking activity of constructing tall towers, conducted to make sure that everyone was able to fit bricks together and feel comfortable with the process. Inevitably, as towers grew they came crashing down for all kinds of structural reasons, and it was clear immediately that even a brief and supposedly trivial building activity was one that people invested in emotionally. The dismantling of models, whether accidental or intentional, could have a powerful effect on students' feelings, from disappointment and dismay to a sense of clearing away troublesome experiences or memories to make way for newer, more positive ones. Tower building was followed by building something with four legs and a face, after which everyone was told to pause to see how others were faring.

Inevitably groups varied in their confidence and alacrity in offering metaphors in English or from their own cultures. Some were excitable, and once started, could not stop, while others needed patience and a little cajoling. In one case a stimulus object, a chicken, circled the group three times with participants politely saying "pass" until seemingly out of nowhere a metaphor was suggested, and then the floodgates opened: "chicken and egg," "rule the roost," "ruffle my feathers" "a bird in the hand," and so forth. The chicken also spawned new associations, with its coxcomb representing a Mohican hairstyle, while apparently it also bore a close resemblance to someone's father. Students started to share metaphors from their own cultures, such as a Chinese metaphor for being happy ("a flower opened in his head"), or for the way people are protective toward their families: "Your arms are always in, not out." With confidence, the examples became more elaborate and imaginative, both with the use of recognizable objects and abstract symbols (one of which, reproduced as Figure 6.1, can only be described as a black splat).

The passing around of an elephant then engendered metaphors such as "the elephant in the room," "an elephant never forgets," to characteristics of elephants (afraid of mice, versatile with their trunks, gentle giant, big or little ears) or their putative qualities (grey—boring, invisible, neutral, or heavy, and possibly

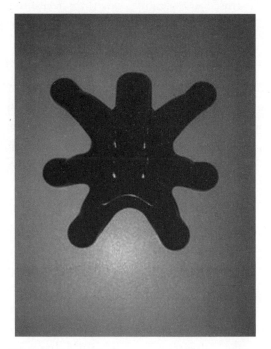

Figure 6.1 The "Black Splat"

blundering). The elephant could be taken to indicate an individual, culture, or system with which participants were working and the positives and negatives associated with that.

Beginning Metaphorical Meaning Making

Having established that participants were comfortable with using the bricks, were able to handle the concepts of metaphor and modeling, and were not struggling with their English, the focus turned to building a four-legged model. Students were instructed that it was now not just a basic model but that it represented a very good or very bad student. They were then asked to decide which kind of student their model represented and to explain this to the group. This threw students into the position of having to imbue meaning in a collection of bricks that they had assembled with less specific instructions.

Their stories varied from interpretations of cleverness that might be familiarly deduced (adding crowns, stars, and thrones to indicate success) to more abstract psychological justifications (explaining how unevenly proportioned bodies indicated a lack of development in certain areas of learning). Despite the instruction to create a good or bad student, many decided to offer a more complex evaluation of why their models was a blend of the two, which showed real engagement with the process of thinking metaphorically and imaginatively (see Figure 6.2). The purpose of this activity was not only to relax the group, but also to put them in the position of having to think on their feet and generate an interpretation solely from their imagination. This was a strategy designed to free up their thinking and embed the gently coalescing principles of metaphorical thinking into their builds.

At this point in the workshop students were advised that they had finished the preparatory skills phase and would be moving on to creating models of their own learning. As already indicated, workshops can be quite intense—getting to grips with the

Figure 6.2 Metaphorical Model with Coins and Skeletons

processes, thinking things through, responding to other people's models, and envisioning change—and participants and facilitators can get quite tired, however exciting the process might be. An important indicator of their level of engagement was that in many cases when they were offered a break halfway through the class, none of them chose to take it.

Creating Their Own Models

Alison then asked students to build their own Lego models as an opportunity to reflect on all aspects of their study in the UK. In particular they were invited to consider strengths and weaknesses in both their personal growth and the course itself, things they wanted to improve, and any kind of newness, growth, or change they felt they had experienced during this period. The

Figure 6.3   Lego Model of Student Journey

extra dimension of doing this with Legos was the ability to work
in three dimensions, layering, clustering, and connecting events,
thoughts, and people, in a way that had more richness than if
the reflection was articulated on a flat paper surface (see Figures 6.3 and 6.4). Alison was aware that exploring experiences
could bring all kinds of emotions to the surface and needed to
make sure that no participant felt threatened or uncomfortable
by reflecting in this way, not least because the unifying theme

Figure 6.4   Eye-Level View, Lego Model

in the activity was one of personal identity. Her mentor—Stuart Nolan—had advised her to avoid things getting too personal by keeping the discussions happening through the model; that is, by discussing the metaphors rather than getting literal about sensitive issues.

One way to generate deeper focus through LSP is to investigate parts of the model by metaphorically double-clicking on that aspect of the model. Double-clicking is the process of pausing to home in on specific details of the model, such as its size or color, the significance of its location, or its relationship to other parts of the build. This often involves comparing aspects of someone's model with another person's for similarities and differences. A fine balancing act was performed between allowing students to give generic interpretations so that they would not feel bullied into self-disclosure ("These are my skills and this is my goal") and gently encouraging them to give a little more personal detail. This act of moving students away from the generic to the specific is a recognizable dynamic in deepening reflection, no matter what the format. Once the models were built, students were invited to talk about their experiences through their models. Depending on the individual, this could be a quick, surface presentation, or a detailed self-evaluation. Questions from peers asking about what was embodied in specific parts of the model helped provide further elaboration, as did the double-clicking approach.

The follow-up activity to this build was to add in a detail about students' future aspirations. With one group, which had almost unanimously been quite generic in their interpretations and had not included any specific aspects of their learning development ("These sharks were my obstacles, but this is my bridge to my success"), this activity was tweaked to imagine a particular skill, character trait, change they would like to introduce, or next step they wished to take. This simple instruction engendered a move from generic statements as the group dived into deep, insightful comments about what they needed to do in different areas of their lives. One laid gold dust on a path to symbolize creating incentives to improve their time management; another (headless, as feeling a little lost) gained a head and a removable blindfold, for the times when they needed to see more clearly and shift their perceptions; a third built a "robot of control" to help with project management.

Many models included spatial metaphors representing the relationship between their home countries and the UK, while even more had issues of confidence and adjustment running through them. For some, the change was about integrating the two worlds—how they could bring their newfound knowledge back to their home countries, if that was where they were going. For one student the whole process had been about how change, and living abroad, had brought the paradox of missing the country you were not in, and yet feeling increasingly rootless while there. For another it was about reminding the group that distant goals were not necessarily practical but might be about life priorities—"to be wise and smart and grow as a human being."

Building Cohesion

Although the students were all on the same course, they were following specialist pathways and did not all know each other well before attending the workshop. A sign of the bonding power of the workshop was the way that through building they learned more about each other, in a short space of time, and at a level that "speed dating" at network events or normal group work does not allow. (See Figure 6.5.) They were guided to listen to each other's stories and models, rather than fiddling with and adjusting their own, when they got inspired to add more. The value of this was embodied in the final activity that involved creating a gift for someone else in the group—something that the giver felt was true about that person and that was missing from their model.

Figure 6.5   Building Shared Models for Collaborative Reflection

As a reflective act, this was more complex than just giving something nice or superficial. It required paying attention to the person's stories and being thoughtful and perceptive as to her needs, albeit in a playful situation. Part of the LSP protocol in gifting is to write the names of participants on paper and ask the group to select a name and keep it a secret (if they pick their own name they give it back and take another). Once the gifts have been built they are invited to describe their gift, say why they think it will suit the person, and only at the end say whom it is for. Gifts have included a holiday for the class perfectionist, an emergency kit for the student who was feeling a bit trapped and directionless, and a boat for the one who was torn between three research areas and did not know how to integrate them or navigate among the three.

One of the surprises of the LSP process has been the sheer pleasure that students get both from giving and receiving their gifts—not just in a trivial or jokey way, but at a deeper level. This was one of the many insights that came through the feedback that students offered at the end of the session. As mentioned earlier, during the workshop an inflatable Pod was waiting at the end of the studio for students to enter and record a video reflection on how they had experienced the workshop. Students had the option to talk freestyle or respond to one of several prompt questions stuck inside the Pod, and to go in solo or together. As guidance for this, Alison drew on Stephen's Critical Incident Questionnaire in a kind of CIQ-lite formulation, with the five main questions pinned up inside the Pod; these asked students what they had found involving, distancing, surprising, puzzling, and helpful about working with Legos and metaphorical modeling.

Students' Responses

From the mood of the workshops Alison was fairly confident that students would express enjoyment and interest, but she was not expecting the level of intensity expressed, nor some of the insights offered as to how metaphorical modeling had affected students' learning. Several noted that they had felt curious, awkward, or unsure when they had first entered the room and were not entirely clear on what they were letting themselves in for. But they repeatedly described themselves as "amazed," "fascinated," and "excited" by the experience. They had found more than just fun in the session. Recurrent thoughts included how "helpful" the process had been for interpreting self and others, for having visual ideas that symbolized the present and future, for understanding their learning more specifically, and for developing their self-perceptions and imaginations.

Learning about other people's perspectives on life, and the way colleagues offered each other views of how they were perceived, were both identified as insightful. A majority cited the gifting process as having made an impact on them in this regard, as well as the focus and the attention required when making a gift for someone else. Many expressed how the puzzlement they had experienced at the start of the session, when the prospect of an LSP workshop as part of university study did not make much sense, had been replaced with the realization that there was a deeper purpose behind the building processes. Many expressed surprise at how much you could say with just a few bricks.

The power of modeling to shift perceptions and introduce new ways of thinking was also a constant in their feedback. They saw this as a means of considering problems and identifying solutions, or of seeing different possibilities. A corollary of the session was the usefulness of the modeling approach for the development of their second language. Not only did students comment that they felt their English had improved just in the space of a few hours, but they also noted that they felt more courageous about speaking in front of people than they did when they were in traditional classroom situations, working in groups, or giving presentations with PowerPoints and handouts.

There were further unexpected benefits. Early in one session a student volunteered the detail that she had attention deficit disorder, with its characteristic fidgets, short concentration span, and ability to be distracted. One hour and forty minutes later, at the end of a shorter version of the workshop, the student had been entirely focused and participative, taking no breaks. When Alison mentioned how attentive she had been, the student replied, "It's because of what we were doing. When I can think with my fingers, I'm golden." She went on to say that any kind of traditional lecture with PowerPoints and handouts left her crawling up the walls, whereas anything that involved activity completely held her attention.

Overall, the success and effectiveness of the LSP approach was so significant that Alison trained as an accredited LSP facilitator and extended her use of the techniques with staff and students. This has been at all levels of provision and for multiple purposes—exploring good learning, building team identity, visualizing doctoral research, and strategizing.

Labyrinths for Creative Reflection

Labyrinths date from ancient times and are found all over the world. They take many forms: historic and contemporary, fixed and transportable, permanent or disposable (the latter made from chicken feed, mown out of grass, marked out with stones, or indicated with hay bales). The labyrinth at Chartres Cathedral dates from 1200 and has been a site for pilgrimage and repentance. Labyrinths in other locations have been used for local rites and rituals (including protection from poor fortunes or evil forces) as well as expressions of all kinds of faith. They are not the sole preserve of believers from all denominations, however, and have been used simply as tools for relaxation and meditation, or an agreeable experience, often in the fresh air. Whether you come to a labyrinth out of spiritual inquiry or secular curiosity, there is growing evidence to suggest that walking labyrinths in whatever way can contribute to stress reduction.

Labyrinths are sometimes confused with mazes, but whereas mazes have convoluted paths and high walls, and are often a puzzle to navigate, labyrinths have a single path, low or no walls, and are straightforward to walk. According to the Labyrinth Society website, mazes are associated with left-brain activities because of the need to decode them logically, while labyrinths are associated with the right brain, being creative, intuitive, and imaginative. To continue our theme of the metaphor, labyrinths are also seen as living metaphors for the journey of life, in whatever form that may take.

Despite having been in existence for more than 4,000 years, and despite that little is known about their uses in preliteracy periods, there has been a recent resurgence of interest in labyrinths as spiritual or contemplative spaces. One of the driving forces behind this reawakening has been Lauren Artress, a Canon of Grace Cathedral in San Francisco, and founder of Veriditas, a nonprofit organization dedicated to labyrinth work for personal healing and community growth. In the UK, the University of

Kent at Canterbury (see Figures 6.6 and 6.7) is thought to be the first university to adopt a labyrinth for learning and teaching, through the National Teaching Fellowship of Dr. Jan Sellers (Sellers, 2012, 2013). Jan wanted to introduce labyrinths to the university for three main purposes: as a means of providing much-needed quiet spaces for staff and students, as a technique for teaching and learning, and as an art installation. Wherever they are found, labyrinths are also considered to be a resource for spiritual development as well as personal reflection.

A labyrinth walk or workshop can contribute to learning modules, educational programs, and personal and professional development in a variety of ways that are adaptable for staff and students. Jan adopts a specific structure in her workshops that includes the following components: introduction to the labyrinth, its historical context, situating the labyrinth in the specific academic setting

Figure 6.6   A View of the University of Kent Labyrinth

Figure 6.7   Finger Labyrinth on Bench, University of Kent Labyrinth

in which participants are working, exploring agreed-upon themes, providing guidelines for walking the labyrinth, arranging complementary activities, and facilitating shared reflections and discussion. At the University of Kent, examples of cases when labyrinth walking has been used include the stimulation of creativity (creative writing; dance); professional reflection (BSc dental care; MA professional practice); exploring personal and professional values (educational development); and reflection on a life journey or on experience and aspirations (any discipline), art, applied theater, drama, symbology, and social anthropology.

Mathematics classes have also been held in the labyrinth because of the interesting calculations that underpin its construction. A law colleague of Jan's has held seminars and tutorials in the labyrinth, having found it a different experience to using a classroom, one that results in deeper, more thoughtful engagement.

Drama students have already used the labyrinth for performances, and in Summer 2012 the music department at the university delivered lunchtime recitals in the labyrinth for the first time. Bridging activities between school and university are also held for local students, using color, light, and music in the space as part of efforts to make the university seem familiar.

In the example of creative writing, the class combines walking the labyrinth with their writing activities, with mats available to be able to sit in the space and reflect after walking. Lecturer Sonia Overall has used both the indoor and outdoor labyrinths at Kent for creative writing seminars, encouraging the students to use the walk to focus on particular elements of their writing—for example, thinking about a theme, or working through a problem they have encountered—and then writing notes when they get to the center. She has also used the labyrinth to help students listen to their own work by reading workshop texts aloud as they walk. This helps them to think about pace, how long their sentences or lines of poetry are (they can visualize, and indeed "feel," how long it takes for them to deliver a piece of text), and so assists with discussions of economical writing, syntax and punctuation, enjambment in poetry, and so on.

In one creative writing module, students read an extract of Sebald's *Rings of Saturn* (1998), which uses labyrinth imagery. They then walked the outdoor labyrinth with Sonia so they could have a practical experience of how the space feels. The intent was to get them to consider the labyrinth as a metaphor for memory, and also to introduce Sebald's prose style—meaning at the center, approached in an apparently circuitous manner, with the walker/reader glimpsing it at various points before reaching it in the "middle" of the text. This might sound rather tenuous, but it was clearly a breakthrough for some of the students who had struggled with the text and found the physical aid of the labyrinth helpful. Standing above the labyrinth and looking down on the shape, with the "puzzle" of it solved, related directly to an image in the book—this was particularly useful.

In the US, Dr. Kay Sandor, professor of nursing at the University of Texas, uses labyrinths in a module on self-care (alongside journaling and meditation) to help with stress reduction. Situated on the island of Galveston, Professor Sandor has access to both a permanent brick labyrinth as well as a portable canvas one. However, because her teaching is entirely online, she also sends links to students so that they may use labyrinths closer to home. Alternatively, students can use finger labyrinths; this is often a better solution than making the time to physically walk the life-sized version. For Sandor, self-care in nursing is an essential aspect of self-protection, given that so many nurses leave the profession through burnout—a great loss to the workforce. White and Stafford (2008) claim that when they incorporated labyrinth walking into nursing training in Texas, it shifted students' reconceptualization of their practice from the reflective to the analytical and helped them manage stress. In medicine, as in law, labyrinths can be particularly useful for negotiating ethical issues. In dental care, students have found it beneficial for developing a professional voice and confidence in their professional practice.

Other examples include the American Psychology Association building in Washington, D.C., where a green roof and labyrinth were created in 2008 as a peaceful, reflective space for the community. At City University of New York School of Law, the Contemplative Urban Lawyering Program has incorporated the teaching of meditation and yoga to students to support the inner lives of students working hard to create outer change. Professor Victor Goode, long-established leader of the program, has overseen the shift from contemplative practices offered as extracurricular activity to their being incorporated as an accredited full-semester class entitled "Contemplative Practices for Social Justice Lawyers" that he teaches. Goode and his colleagues have a labyrinth in their "backyard," as he puts it, which they use for regeneration and "renewed intentionality"

(Anselmo, Bryant, and Goode, 2006, p. 62). The increased mindfulness that labyrinths encourage is also central to people being able to do their best work when interacting with people from diverse backgrounds.

In a further example from the UK and inspired by Jan Sellers, Professor Bernard Moss has considered labyrinths as learning tools rather than purely reflective spaces. For Bernard, it is important to think about the specific learning outcomes that result from using a labyrinth. In his work with professional development teams, a key question might be "As a result of using a labyrinth how will colleagues be able to reflect on the challenges of curriculum development and pinpoint next steps?" With this outcome in mind he uses a three-stage worksheet to accompany a labyrinth walk: the first stage outlines what labyrinths are about; the second is used after the walk has taken place and requires the participant to reflect on the issues and struggles that were taken with him on the walk, and the immediate thoughts and feelings that are surfacing. The third concerns actions to be taken as a result—"In a fortnight's time, where will you have gotten to with this (unblocking paths, removing obstacles, and so on)?" He uses a similar technique with social work students in a module on communication skills that also contains an element on dealing with stress. A two-level technique is used in which students walk the labyrinth and record on a worksheet the factors that are causing stress and the kinds of coping strategies that are emerging. A third situation in which he has found the labyrinth to be a powerful stimulus to clarity of thought and cogitation is during times of transition.

Moss notes that participants often record the extent to which the walk clears their minds and acts as a creative stimulus in a way that a stroll with the dog in the country does not. They believe that this is because the labyrinth offers a bounded space, in which other people are involved but not directly with you, and in which "silent shuffling" has an impact on your thinking and feeling processes. He notes the mysterious effect of a labyrinth walk—one that is not ascribed to magic but that eludes explanation.

Walking the labyrinth is for all faiths and none, is a voluntary activity, and harbors no secret religious intent that is being surreptitiously foisted upon walkers. Those who undertake a labyrinth walk bring to it whatever they wish to bring. Walking a labyrinth is a simple activity: it is a single path made up of one-directional circuits, you have only way to walk in and out. Diversely viewed as pathways to the "center of yourself" or as a pleasant environment in which to take time out, the walk may be regarded as having three phases: leaving your "baggage" at the entrance to the labyrinth, regrouping and recharging in the center, and returning to your present situation on the walk back out.

Although many people are happy to venture forth and walk a human-sized labyrinth, others prefer a gentler introduction to this form of contemplation. As an alternative to walking, finger labyrinths are equally soothing; the user can move her fingers through sand and along the grooves of a wooden board to trace the labyrinth shape, which also quiets the mind and can enable meditative thought. Drawing labyrinth shapes on paper using a set technique can have a similar effect and can perhaps seem less daunting than the physical involvement of walking an actual space.

Alex Irving: Challenges and Opportunities in Labyrinth Learning

Alex Irving, who created the parable shared in chapter 5, was introduced to labyrinths for contemplative purposes when she encountered one made in polished stone and laid out beside a beach at a creativity conference in Italy in 2008. The power of labyrinth walking crept up on her gradually, but also powerfully enough for her to feel it had transformed her life in terms of being able to think more fluidly, understand herself better, and find solutions to thorny problems.

Although she was keen to share her labyrinth experience with students in the hope that they too would find such benefits, she was mindful of potential pitfalls. The use of labyrinths is undertaken at different ends of the spectrum, from the trained facilitator such as Jan, who is involved with labyrinth organizations across the world, to enthusiasts such as Alex, who is well acquainted with the history and principles of labyrinth use but who prefers to work on instinct with the labyrinth and its users. Alex is wary of being intimidated, as she perceives it, by any notion of ritualistic or organized protocols that may accompany its use.

Alex and Alison both believe it is important to introduce students gradually to something like labyrinth walking and to work on a small scale with your champions and allies so that a creative innovation may "go viral" naturally. Alex had an interesting breakthrough using the labyrinth at a weekend event at the Museum of Liverpool (see Figure 6.8), with a wishing tree, craft table, and student volunteers, all of which demonstrated the success of the unforced introduction of novelty. She deliberately did not oversell

Figure 6.8   Candlelit Labyrinth at LightNight Liverpool, 2011
Source: Courtesy of OpenCulture. Photograph by Mark McNulty

the labyrinth to her students and just let them be aware that it was there, allowing them to build up curiosity and move toward exploring it in their own time. They began to ask more and more questions about it, and as the weekend progressed gradually went in and out of it many more times. As a result of this gentle induction, they are now keen to use it more, no doubt because they felt as though they had thought of it themselves, and now use of the labyrinth is spiraling.

For Alex, one of the reasons for persisting with labyrinths and other creative approaches in her teaching is that some of her students have very narrow views of what constitutes "proper" learning. This is in part because of the now-established view that the main driver for learning is assessment protocols and that our educational systems require teaching to the test. Students ask Alex "Why do we need to learn creative techniques when we can just come up with a few ideas and knock the job off our 'to do' lists?" They miss the point that they need to find novel ideas, not necessarily those that spring most immediately to mind, and that finding these—and generating the capacity to trigger them—will make a significant contribution to their employability. Alex and Alison share a commonly expressed fear that students are increasingly uncurious and lacking in imagination in their approach to their studies, even though they both know that making such sweeping generalizations does a disservice to many. Fostering creative reflection, innovatively, imaginatively, and playfully, is essential when the zeitgeist seems to favor auditing performance of previously determined learning outcomes, as opposed to generating creative and interactive ideas about learning.

Summary

In this chapter we have explored kinesthetic modeling techniques, building on the understanding of metaphor and its value in learning. Although our emphasis has been on the kinesthetic, either in the shape of building, or physically walking a space, other senses and learning modalities have of course come into play, not least the visual and discursive. A playful or nontraditional approach as epitomized in both Lego and labyrinth experiences as we have described them prepares the way for deeper and more engaging learning if the student is receptive to it.

We extend the discussion of learning spaces begun with our analysis of the educational dimensions of labyrinth walking in the next chapter. Here we will be meeting Pods, spliff bunkers, and *Quercus genius*, among other things—all experiments in varying classroom spaces to allow for deeper student reflection.

7

Playing with Space:
Pods and Patchwork

In this chapter we extend our consideration of spatial relationships to analyze the connection between interior and exterior
spaces; that is, the way that external spatial relationships encourage or inhibit internal reflection. In particular, we focus on the use
of video filmed in temporary inflatable spaces (Pods) to capture
on-the-spot reflections. We note the ways in which student insights and comments vary when talking to the camera as opposed
to writing text.

Learning Spaces

In her discussion of learning spaces, Savin-Baden (2008) aligns
different formulations of reflective space to different kinds of reflective thinking that she suggests are akin to Mezirow's (1991)
seven types of reflection. In keeping with Dewey's evocation of
reflection as troublesome, she posits reflective thinking as inter-
ruption, something that tends to "disturb our position, perspective
and views of the world" (p. 69). For Savin-Baden, reflective spaces
are preliminal or supraliminal; in other words, they either precede
or oversee moments of transition or change. In her view, changing
learning spaces can make us more aware of how we think about
experience and can lead to a transformational overhaul of personal
beliefs.

In recent years there has been renewed attention to the way that space and place on campus intersect with learning (Boddington and Boys, 2011; Boys, 2011; Chism and Bickford, 2003). Online education has forced a consideration of virtual space, and service learning has shown the importance of community spaces off-campus for various kinds of learning. The idea of the flipped classroom (Bergmann and Sams, 2012), in which students view prerecorded lectures at home, on the bus or subway, in a coffee shop, or wherever they find themselves, and face-to-face classroom time is used to discuss problems generated by that viewing, upsets traditional notions of learning space.

Gardens and natural spaces of all shapes and sizes are being nurtured to provide pleasant, restorative spaces and to make the best use of every available foot of institutional territory. We see this in the meadow labyrinth at the University of Kent, the green roof on the American Psychological Association building in Washington, D.C., and, on a much smaller scale, in the housing of beehives on top of the London College of Fashion in the heart of London's West End. Such steps are a small step toward redressing what Savin-Baden has termed the "marginalization of reflective spaces" in academe, not least for staff.

The link between learning and the design of institutional space has been recognized at the University of St. Thomas, Stephen's employer. In 1998 the university built a new school of education, for which faculty were invited to submit ideas regarding design. Overwhelmingly, faculty asked for classrooms not just with smart technology but with two specific design features: round tables that could be moved easily and comfortable chairs on wheels. Different departments teaching different levels of students all seemed to think that the depth of discussion would be enhanced by the possibility of breaking quickly into different seating formats for different kinds of small-group activities.

One unintended shift that occurred, however, was in the amount and degree of conversation occurring serendipitously between lecturers and professors across disciplinary boundaries. In the old school of education premises (a converted elementary school), all offices were on the same level and a corridor that was 15 to 20 feet wide ran the length of the building. Faculty mailboxes and the school's departmental office were both situated on this corridor, and as a result, this wide corridor was the route traversed several times a day by all members of the faculty. Consequently, faculty were continually bumping into colleagues from multiple departments, exchanging pleasantries, but also sometimes holding conversations of import.

It would not be unusual to walk the corridor and find clumps of colleagues holding unofficial meetings of cross-college committees, or dyads and triads troubleshooting how to deal with common problems, such as student nonattendance, student resistance to challenging learning, or balancing the demands of publishing and getting good teaching evaluations, both of which the university required to reward tenure. Stephen remembers several times walking past pairs or small groups of colleagues and overhearing them discussing situations they were struggling with. If these were ones that he had some experience dealing with, he would stop and contribute whatever ideas he could. Some of the best initiatives of his professional life—like the creation of schoolwide "Talking Teaching" groups (Brookfield, 1995)—were hatched in chance conversations in that corridor.

This kind of accidental talk has disappeared, however, in the decade or so since the new school of education was built. Faculty are now housed on different floors grouped according to department. Although there is a wide corridor entering the school, once you move into your office on your designated floor you typically see only colleagues from your department throughout the day. There are obviously still chance meetings and serendipitous conversations, but these are almost wholly within departmental groups. Hence, space is crucial not just for supporting student learning but also for teachers' professional growth and development.

Hello Cloud 9: The Reflective Pod

Our first example of the use of a dedicated space for reflection on learning is Cloud 9.

Cloud 9 was the name given by a student to the Reflective Pod, a puffy, white, inflatable beehive that stands more than six feet tall and that can be erected in five minutes in any location that offers an electrical outlet. Providing a temporary enclosure and coming in different sizes, the so-called Pod (see Figure 7.1) can offer a private space within social and learning environments where thoughts can be recorded. Its use as the space in which students could reflect "post-Lego" has already been alluded to in the

Figure 7.1   "Cloud 9": The Reflective Pod

previous chapter. Cloud 9 can house three people comfortably, more at a push, because its interior is shared with a waist-high pedestal on top of which sits a MacBook with Photo Booth software, ready for podcasting.

The Pod was first used at the 2007 annual show and critique of student work at the London College of Fashion. At the inaugural event students had an opportunity to step into the Pod at any time during the evening to record their thoughts on the experience of being critiqued. Any brave guest who also wanted to step inside the Pod and leave a reflective memento was also free to do so. There is no doubt that the novelty value of the Pod played a part in courting attention and attracting participation. The presence of a ceiling-high, gently whirring white inflatable in the exhibition space was never going to be overlooked. Even people who were not sure what is was for or whether they wanted to have anything to do with it could not help but wander over to investigate.

The Pod was, however, far more than shameless gimmickry. Two specific aspects of its use led to its adoption in many other situations since its introduction. First, the honesty with which students spoke was striking. There was something about being enclosed in a small, private, intimate space that seemed to provoke a much more open assessment of what students learned both from the critique itself and the way it was given. Second, Cloud 9 seemed to encourage students to articulate their reactions, concerns, and what they learned from these in a different way than they typically expressed themselves in written papers. These two factors spurred faculty on a new degree course to find ways of using the Pod to nurture, recognize, and value reflection in a form that was unique and personal to each student. Dr. Pod (Alison's alter ego) recorded a video guide to using the Pod that we have placed on our book website (http://www.engagingimagination.com).

Students took enthusiastically to using the Pod to make videos recording their reflections on learning that were gathered together in electronic portfolios or folders. Students could replay these videos as often as they wanted to review their personal and professional development over time. As well as helping them develop the content of their reflections, the videos showed a variety of ways to orchestrate reflection—sometimes as an off-the-cuff stream of consciousness, sometimes a presentation that was clearly prepared in advance and sequenced with visual prompts, and occasionally choreographed by a group with cards, movements, and turns to speak.

Students will say things in the Pod that they would not write on paper. The difference seems to be that the sense of enclosed privacy the Pod provides allows for both a freedom of speech and an immediacy of being able to say whatever comes into your head as soon as it occurs. Naturally there were vague, rambling, off-the-point, and un-illuminating contributions. Being extemporaneous is not the same as being profound. But there were also unexpected gems of self-realization and honest commentary that were a far cry from the unimaginative regurgitations of some obligatory reflective assignments.

Two important factors in the extended use of the Pod have been the judicious selection of time and place for its use, and a focus on how it should be used to audit different aspects of learning at different times. It is regularly inflated in Student Induction Week in lecture theaters to capture early expectations and impressions and in classroom studios at particular points of unit modules, with students concentrating on different learning outcomes or aspects of tasks and their own engagement with these. The first time it was used during Induction Week it was so enthusiastically received that course team celebrations in a local pub seemed called for at the end of the evening. During this time, the laptop on which the student videos had been stored was stolen from under their feet. Recovering from this blow, the team invited the students two nights later to repeat their Pod reflections, which they did. One young woman commented that she was sorry that the first video had been lost, because she had come so far in the four days since enrollment. For her, the experience of having started university was already something that was causing her to transform her self-conception and view of the world.

Sometimes students had free rein over what they wanted to talk about, while at others there would be specific questions for them to respond to. There was also the possibility that they could listen to the recordings of previous speakers to find out how those already documented experiences compared to the new ones being recorded. At key moments of the year, such as during the lead-up to producing final student projects, or prior to important deadlines, the Pod provided a welcome space to vent frustrations and voice panic over all aspects of the learning experience. This venting enabled speakers to clear their heads and identify a suitable course of action or recuperation.

As students gathered and built up their own visual repertoires of reflective files, faculty took the time to view the movies together and collate their feedback to students on their learning observations. Staff responses were always formative, often provided at midpoint of a course, and took the form of general conversations about group, as well as individual, progress. In response to staff feedback on their movies, students would then articulate their own responses, either in an additional movie or by mind mapping their progress at that point in the course. In this way a kind of asynchronous conversation around learning was established.

The Spliff Bunker

As any fan of punk rock knows, a variation of the Pod was used by punk band the Clash. When he entered the studio to record new material, Joe Strummer, the chief lyricist in the band, would form a *spliff bunker* somewhere on the studio floor. This was a collection of boxes, guitar and amplifier cases, equipment that was not being used at the session, coats, and anything else that could be used to create an enclosed space into which he could retreat.

The spliff bunker got its name from the fact that it was in here that Joe would roll his marijuana joints. Clearly, we are not advocating that teachers create classroom spaces for the pursuit of recreational drug use! What is interesting about the bunker, however, is how closely it parallels the form and function of the Pod.

First, the bunker was portable. You assembled it anew at each recording session from whatever materials were available. Its portability and accessibility were part of the reason why it was used and reused over the years that the Clash recorded. Second, it was a small, enclosed space, and something about the smallness and intimacy of the space seemed to get Strummer's creative juices flowing more freely. You could get maybe two or three people at most inside the bunker, just as you could get only that number inside the Pod. Third, and perhaps most important, the bunker, like the Pod, was private. There were you and the small amount of space around you, with the rest of the world effectively held at bay. Something about the privacy of these two spaces is important for producing honest statements.

One of the most difficult things to do in teaching is to keep the theater of the classroom—the performance anxiety surrounding trying to behave like the "good" (that is, smart and articulate) student—from stopping personal reflection. In a book Stephen coauthored on teaching through discussion (Brookfield and Preskill, 2005), he explored how, unless deliberate steps are taken to prevent this happening, students will assume that participating in discussion means speaking as often as possible. Equally, teachers will usually assume that silence is awkward, a sign that people are confused. The typical response is to fill the silence with speech (usually the teacher's voice) as quickly as possible. In the bunker and the Pod, however, there is no need to perform by speaking regularly. You click on "Record" when you have something to say to the camera, or you write down lyrics at the pace most comfortable for you. There is no pressure to act a certain way, so mental energy is not spent on performing the role of good student.

Other Forms of Reflective Pod Engagements

The Reflective Pod has been adopted in multiple programs for a variety of purposes. Although many Pod recordings focus on the specific and tangible—project management skills, relations with industry, responses to assessments, and so on—it is clear that the more students become confident using the medium, the more personal, intuitive, and self-revelatory their filmed episodes become. Students begin to talk about conflicts between their value systems and those of the wider field or profession, about their understanding of their personal identities, about how their identity is constructed and confirmed through their pursuit of sustainability agendas, engaging with research, linking to Amnesty International, advocating for corporate social responsibility, and so on.

The two examples following give very different illustrations of how speaking within the Pod elicits a different kind of reflection to that which is written. In the first, copied verbatim, the notion of authenticity is once again to the fore:

> Attending Reflective Discourse [a dedicated unit on reflection] and participating in the "POD" activity was one of the most insightful sessions. I realised I found it a lot easier to sit down and say what I thought into a camera than write it down on paper. I decided to keep a video diary and take a short clip a week to reflect on my feelings. I learnt that I keep a lot of my thoughts and feelings inside and don't share my emotions. Talking into a camera allowed me to say exactly what was on my mind. It was a true version of what I was thinking rather than a slightly fabricated written piece on my emotions. Looking through several clips was an easier way to establish my feelings and emotions through my attitude and facial expressions alone. I thought I'd be embarrassed to talk out loud to myself but actually found if I said what was on my mind I often relaxed and my mood calmed.

As this student continued, the idea of her video diaries was elaborated both into a metaphor of sanctuary but also tied in with her self-concept as head sibling (eldest of four) and responsible arbitrator of family interchanges. The Pod as a space where she could negotiate and express her feelings, or perhaps rehearse some of the things on her mind before acting, became invaluable.

The Pod was important to a second student for an entirely different reason. At an evening lecture on reflection for master's degree students studying a range of subjects from museum curating to media, the Pod had been inflated for trial reflections. At the front of the class was a deaf student with her signer, who had had the entire lecture mediated through British Sign Language. When the class was invited to enter the Pod, this student was one of the first to volunteer—delighted that she had been given a different way of expressing her views through signing to the camera as opposed to having to write something. For her, the video medium allowed her infinitely more freedom to express herself.

Although the Pod is mainly used for student reflections on learning, on progress through the curriculum, or on industry involvement, it has also been used for feedback on other aspects of the student experience, which is then harnessed to provide guidance for incoming first-years. A case in point has been the online Commonplace resource (http://commonplace.arts.ac.uk/) designed and created by students. Here students already in their junior or sophomore years tell new undergraduates all the things they wished they had known before coming to university. Siobhan Clay, Commonplace project leader, took the Pod to numerous university sites and found it a focal point for drawing in contributions from students:

> I've loved having use of it—thanks! The student response has been funny and mainly positive. I term it "the Venus fly trap"—they ask "what's this," peek inside

then they're "got"! As you know we use it to film students talking to camera about all aspects of going to
university. They are very comfortable to speak in there
and I think they do sometimes talk more honestly in
the Pod, it's a physical and psychological safe space to
speak. (Personal communication)

It has become clear in the years since its introduction that
there are obvious benefits as well as areas of sensitivity associated
with using the Pod. Students react in different ways to being able
to record themselves and their views; some are entirely comfortable, some are playful, and some use the Pod in ways the course
team had not expected. Student engagement has varied from an
individual, straightforward "to camera" recording, from pair or
group presentations, to song and dance videos, demonstrations of
texts or artifacts, and giving the Pod multiple nicknames. Students
appropriate the space and make it their own.

The Pod is not for everyone. Its unusual aspect can put some
people off rather than lure them in. Some struggle with the enclosed aspect of the Pod that is so unleashing for others, remark-
ing that it feels claustrophobic. Some hate the prospect of seeing
themselves talking to the camera, a discomfort that is not always
reduced by the capacity to transform their literal image into something abstract or kaleidoscopic. Sometimes there is a fear they will
be heard when speaking, or a concern over who might view their
podcasts. This is no different from the concern expressed by students as to "Who will read my journal?" and points to the con-
tradiction embedded in requiring reflective work to be submitted.
How can a piece of reflective writing be truly personal and honest
if students write for an audience other than themselves? Conversely, for some students it helps to have an audience, which is why
one wrote reflections in the form of letters to her tutor. She was
not expecting answers to these but found it a useful mechanism to
help her to write.

Postcards and Patchworks

The following two examples unite a number of multisensory, visual, and creative practices with the written word that are transportable and involve movement. The first is Shibboleth Shechter's use of postcards. As part of an introductory unit preparing students for the experience of higher education, Shibboleth asked her students to send her postcards of their own creation that included both image and text. The cards were meant to tell her about the connections students had noticed across different parts of the course and about the new knowledge or skills they were developing.

These postcards of learning were posted in a box specifically designed for this purpose, emphasizing the ritual and playful aspects of the task. Because the unit lasted ten weeks, and eighty students were enrolled in the course, by the unit's end Shibboleth had eight hundred 4-by-6-inch postcards. These varied enormously in message and decoration, but writing the cards had clearly helped students integrate and synthesize different elements of the course, such as connecting history and theory lectures to design practice. (See Figures 7.2 and 7.3 for examples.) The playful ritual of card

Figure 7.2   Reflective Postcard: Anna Samygina

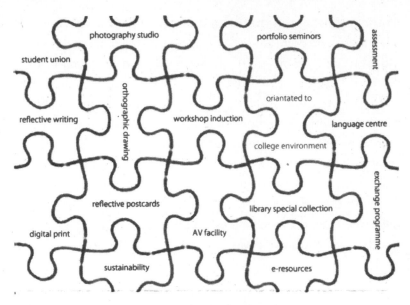

Figure 7.3   Reflective Postcard: Chiaki Matsumoto

writing was also a factor in making students sit up and pay atten-tion to what they were thinking and the act of physically posting the cards somehow made it more significant than simply keeping diaries that they took to class.

The use of patchwork as a physical and collaborative embodi-ment of students' personal and professional development is a second spatial variant on presenting students' reflections. The brainchild of Clare Lomas, lecturer in cultural and historical studies at the London College of Fashion, the patchwork activity brings reflection into the realms of the three-dimensional and invites students to think about questions of identity, learning, journey, and subject through decorating patchwork quilt squares with text and visuals.

Students are given an 8-inch square of fabric and asked to take it away for a week and personalize it any way that occurs so that it says something about who they are. They can cut it, draw on it, and dye it, or do anything else to it that occurs to them.

The following session they bring their squares to class and describe what they have done and what that means. Students then work in groups to join squares together in ways that work thematically or aesthetically.

This idea was adapted for a conference on motivating teaching and learning at the London College of Fashion, during which, and alongside other conference events, staff had the chance to create their own personalized patchwork square on the conference theme. As each square emerged from their handiwork, participants tied these together to form an instant collective and reflective artwork. (See Figures 7.4 and 7.5.) Created throughout the day, the patchwork was presented at the closing plenary as evidence of imaginative reflection in action. The resulting artifact can now travel to and from the different sites of the university, inviting responses and additional squares, to result in a joint reflection on learning.

Figure 7.4   The Motivating Teaching and Learning Quilt

Figure 7.5   The Motivating Teaching and Learning Quilt: Detail

Source: Courtesy of Sina Shamsavari

Quercus genius

The University of Kent's labyrinth, situated in green fields on a hill overlooking Canterbury, is not the campus's only example of innovative and creative use of the outdoors for learning and reflection. Tucked behind one of the teaching blocks in a small woodland is *Quercus genius*, or the outdoor seminar area, created by Dr. Ian Bride, lecturer in Biodiversity Management and the University's Conservation Society. (Figure 7.6 is a "before" picture of the woodland.) *Quercus genius* (the *g* is usually the italicized part of the name, with the first letter in lower case, in imitation of a scientific species name) came into being as a result of a survey of how people were occupying spaces on campus, which revealed a dearth of outdoor seating areas where students and staff could meet and relax. After one of the oak trees in a patch of historic woodland on campus fell down, Ian arranged for a local wood sculptor to work with students to fashion a teaching space whose boundaries are

Figure 7.6   *Quercus genius* "Before" Photo

Source: By kind permission of Ian Bride

now discreetly edged out by tree branches. (One of these branches had to be carried into place by two dozen students!) This space is now bookable for teaching or can offer a place for quiet reflection or socializing. (Figure 7.7 is the "after" photo.)

Figure 7.7   *Quercus genius* "After" Photo

Source: By kind permission of Ian Bride

The fallen tree was a fragment of an ancient bluebell wood in a natural dell whose timber has now been repurposed to offer rustic benches, a cluster of wooden mushrooms and carved artifacts, such as a stack of books on which up to twenty students can sit and study. (See Figures 7.8 and 7.9.) Tufts of grass and meadow flowers (and nettles, which have to be weeded) pad the woodland floor. It has been used for lessons within the field of biodiversity and has proved particularly popular with students who see it as their own social space. Lights have been erected for evening sessions, and those trees still growing around it constitute a natural canopy with their leaves in spring and summer. On the day that Alison visited, it was mottled with shadow, sunshine filtering through the new green of early summer growth, and was immensely peaceful and still. Even the occasional dog walker passing through on a path nearby did nothing to disturb the quiet and thoughtfulness. It is

Figure 7.8   *Quercus genius*, Spring 2012

Figure 7.9   *Quercus genius*: Book Detail

clearly a special space for reflection and learning that has an entirely different nature than traditional classrooms, even if, as Ian puts it, the spreading carpet of bluebells—and the interruptions from woodpeckers—can be a bit of a distraction in spring.

Spatial Design and Inner/Outer Space

Arts and design practitioners often say it is hard to separate reflection from creative work because it is so embedded in everything they do. This can be seen in a number of examples of learning in environments other than the classroom or studio. Dr. Nicky Ryan, of the London College of Communication, teaches a module on "Curating & Exhibition Design" that she conducts almost entirely outside the university. In a variety of museums her students look at objects in situ, using specific texts as the lenses through which to reflect on both the item and the space (that is, the museum) within which it sits. In this unit students visit a different museum every week and draw on a different text.

Using the British Museum in London as one venue, Nicky designed an activity in which students were asked to take "a ritual walk" as outlined in one of the course texts and to analyze the visual and spatial aspects of that experience—the layout of rooms, arrangement of displays, and so on. They were asked to consider how the museum's ensemble of art, architecture, and installation shaped the visitors' experience and to reflect on the way the values and beliefs inscribed in the "architectural script" of the British Museum concealed deeper ideologies. In Nicky's experience, this activity forces students to see with new eyes a place and an item they may already know well and to reconsider their responses and reactions. In another collaborative module on "Artefacts & Effects," students choose an archival item from a museum with which the college has a relationship and place it in the college gallery. They then create a response to it, whether in performance, sculptural, sound, or other format. At the heart of this response is the student's reconsideration and reappraisal of his or her relationship with that item and the framing of the message he or she wishes to communicate.

As a closing thought to these examples, Alison remembers seeing the same well-known art work in three very different settings—the home of the owner, a Victorian style house-cum-museum, and a modernist white cube gallery—in two very separate geographic regions. She was struck by the extent to which the change of context brought up very different thoughts and responses to the same work.

Inner Reflection on Outer Presentations

One of the job requirements in most professions is the need for its practitioners to make presentations to clients or colleagues. This is one reason student presentations are so ubiquitous in higher education. Presenting information and clarifying reasoning in a presentation is typically seen as part and parcel of the student experience. We ask students to present for any number of purposes: to demonstrate their grasp of ideas, pitch concepts, defend a thesis, get backing for a venture, compete for an award, impress a recruiting panel, or simply prove they have done their homework. Unpacking what goes through the head of the individual presenter is a useful means of enabling students to fully appreciate the extent to which they are operating on multiple levels simultaneously when apparently doing only one thing—making a presentation.

In our experience, students are unaware of the multiple processes they are managing simultaneously when giving presentations. For many of them, presenting to a group, large or small, is a stressful activity that plunders their reserves of nervous energy while challenging them to remember their content. They have to work at the intersection at which the pressure of displaying command of content meets the requirement to communicate clearly and engagingly. They need to get the content organized, use appropriately helpful examples, make sure important elements are highlighted, sequence explanations, and convey important shadings of difference and meaning. In terms of process, they have to make sure they are heard, that they direct eye contact around the audience, and that their voices are well modulated, all the while watching the reactions of audience members and wondering what their nonverbal gestures and body postures signify.

Clearly, then, a great deal of instantaneous decision making is going on as students make a presentation that is evidence of their engaging in embodied reflection or doing reflection-in-action (Schön, 1990). This helps students to realize that this is useful in enabling them to see how reflection is not simply a retrospective activity, but one that involves being in the present as much as looking back into the past. We both use student presentations not just to enliven classrooms and check students' understanding of content, but also to encourage them to take greater responsibility for their own learning. Part of this responsibility entails developing a mindful appreciation of the different variables they are juggling as they present and improving their capacity to make instantaneous decisions in the midst of presentations. Given the widespread use of student presentations across educational environments, we believe part of that exercise should involve helping students become more reflective about the process.

The following exercise works effectively as part of presentation skills training with individuals, small groups, or large cohorts of students and transfers easily across contexts.

- First of all, ask students why they think they have to present. (Answers should not just be to keep teachers happy, but to persuade, prove, clarify, win over, test out, inform, guide, and so on.)

- After their initial responses, ask them what is usually going on in their heads while they are presenting. The kinds of replies they offer will vary enormously, from comments about subject matter to thoughts and feelings about the process: Am I making myself clear? Does anyone care? I've just forgotten what I am going to say next. I have too many slides. She's smiling—at least someone agrees with me. The Web link's not working—What is plan B? None of these thoughts in and of themselves are particularly reflective, but the way in which the student responds to and acts on those thoughts—almost instantaneously and not always consciously—may well be. Input from teachers about any challenges they themselves have faced when speaking publicly are always well received, as are statistics, however inaccurate, about presenting being as stressful for humans as divorce, moving, or death.

- Having heard the various kinds of offerings from the floor, the next part of the exercise is for the students to think about how the examples they give of instantaneous decision making during presentations fall into various learning categories: learning how to manage practicalities, how to interact with the audience, how to convey content, how to manage their emotions, how to control nerves, and so on. These alone constitute five distinct learning tasks that operate concurrently and that require continual evaluation, analysis, judgment, and response from the presenter. If working with copresenters, managing a team relationship is a further category.

- As the learning categories and tasks are teased out, they are presented on newsprint or on the board so that students have a visualization of all the things they have to manage as they are presenting. Just knowing how much is going on internally as they try to present information engagingly and accurately, while at the same time presenting a confident and relaxed front, is helpful. The group can share their different strategies for negotiating the tensions they experience (imagine the audience naked, speak as if you're talking to just one person, take regular pauses to slow down, and so on).

The purpose of the exercise is twofold: first, to make students aware of the multiple conscious and unconscious functions they perform during the activity of presenting, and, second, to help them recognize the extent to which reflection in the moment is an intrinsic part of their actions. By unpacking experience in this way they recognize the inner world of thoughts, feelings, micro-decisions, and information processing that lies behind the outer world of public speaking. Realizing the complexity of what's happening to them, they often end up congratulating themselves for managing so many intricate processes under pressure. It can be a lighthearted means of tackling something that students often dread doing and enabling them to be reassured that they are not alone in feeling intimidated and confused. At the same time, those who thoroughly enjoy the performative nature of the event have a richer understanding of all that's involved.

An "al fresco" version of this activity can be seen at work in the attractively named "wild module," "Guiding and Interpretation," led by Ian Bride, who thought up *Quercus genius*. Here students across all subject disciplines can undertake to plan a guided walk outdoors, part of which they then conduct for their final assign-ment. Ian describes past offerings as including:

> a sculpture tour led by a deer-stalker-clad detective, a mobile lecture on understanding dogs, several nature trails, each with a focus on different flora or fauna (from trees to ants and birds to woodlice), a calamitous first-date picnic which requires several herbal remedies, and an introduction to ancient history involving a fully fledged Viking! (Personal communication)

The freedom of expression, interpretation, and creativity al-lowed by such a module has made it extremely popular and often oversubscribed. Not only do students have the chance to think up something inventive and entertaining, they need to engage with a number of logistical and philosophical aspects of their walk. They have to plan the walk itself, to determine how the audience might be cared for in an open environment, to structure and present the narrative of their walk, and to find their own voices in so do-ing. They also have to consider epistemological questions such as how they judge what they consider to be valid knowledge and how they believe such knowledge is legitimately acquired. Finally, they have to clarify the assumptions, beliefs, and messages that may permeate or underlie the tour. Ian says that although it is more demanding of his time than other modules, it is "an utter delight" to teach.

Summary

In this chapter matters of inner and outer space have spanned interior and exterior environments. We have looked at spaces that are portable, temporary, human-made, and natural, such as the Pod, spliff bunker, *Quercus genius*, and "wild" tours. These all involve students reflecting on how they learn to create and navigate different spaces in their lives. All the examples presented have invited students to collaborate with staff in determining how and why these spaces might be used. In our next chapter we leave the theme of space to consider one of the teaching processes that crosses many of the techniques we have considered in the book thus far: the use of questioning.

8

Asking Powerful Questions

At the heart of being imaginative is asking questions. Indeed, the practice of imagination rests on the question "What if?" Asking how we might do things differently, or what a situation looks like if we view it from a new perspective, opens us up to new possibilities and helps us approach old problems in an original way. In this chapter we want to look at the way that asking questions threads through so many activities that engage the imagination and to focus on two provocative bodies of work—personal construct psychology (PCP) and clean language—that both suggest creative questioning protocols.

Both of us value students asking good questions. A good question indicates an active and deep engagement with the material in which the student has identified potential blind spots, possible omissions, likely contradictions, and unresolved issues. So good questions used well are crucial for the extension of any kind of knowledge or exploration of ideas. Teachers yearn for good questions in students because they signify energy, enthusiasm, interest, and—above all—curiosity. To ask the question that may seem "from left field" or that we fear is stupid requires confidence, trust, comfort, and a little bravery from the asker.

For us a good question has multiple characteristics. First, it is one that neither the poser nor the responder has an immediate and clear answer for. Second, it's one that opens people up to new ways of thinking about a topic. Third, answering the question properly entails some act of learning to occur. We have to go and find something out, or change our ways of thinking about something, to give a reasonable answer. Fourth, a good question is one the hearer understands. She does not have to puzzle out what the questioner is really getting at, or what is really being asked. And, fifth, a good question is one that matters. It is not about inconsequential trivia or minutiae, but rather cuts to the heart of an enterprise. In this chapter we show how particular kinds of question can be powerful in eliciting understanding of how we, and others operate and how they encourage creative reflection in many contexts. We will also see the importance of responding in verbal, visual, metaphorical, or written form.

Students often view the raising of questions as a technical rather than creative task. In our experience they consistently underestimate the intellectual effort entailed in raising questions. Sometimes, as often happens with Alison, students ask teachers for a complete set of appropriate questions, rather than (to their minds) wasting the energy trying to come up with their own. Both of us have experienced making the mistake of asking groups what questions they have and then, when we're faced with an uncomfortably long silence, have proceeded to tell students what questions they *should* have asked. What makes things worse is when we then go on to answer the questions we've just raised.

Asking good questions requires time and introspection as much as it does familiarity with the material. Because they are so dependent on context we can never really know what questions will emerge until we start to explore new territory. We need only to look at how cultures frame questions differently to know that this is locally determined. However, general question templates can sometimes be helpful in starting students off on a reflective quest. For example, Stephen has published such templates in his work on critical thinking (Brookfield, 2011) and critical reflection (Brookfield, 1995). Reflections on learning often slip into habits and travel well-worn grooves—asking what went well, what went badly, what did you do before that you would change now, what new skills or knowledge did you learn, and so on. In this chapter we move away from such stalwarts of reflective questioning to examine decidedly different protocols and patterns in questions that can generate alternative ways of seeing situations, outcomes, or relationships.

We have already asked questions of practice and experience, implicitly and explicitly, in our previous chapters. Here we turn specifically to psychology and an aspect of clinical therapy to examine two further forms of questioning. These are found first in George Kelly's personal construct psychology (Kelly, 1991) elaborated in the 1950s. Although PCP is primarily used for clinical or therapeutic purposes, its use has been extended into diverse fields, including health care, education, business, and management. David Grove's framework of clean language (Sullivan and Rees, 2008) developed in the 1980s and 1990s through his work in psychotherapeutic counseling. Although different in origin and application, these two frameworks share some important common features. Both have been used successfully in a range of educational contexts, and both offer helpful additions to the repertoire of reflective practices staff and students employ together.

Personal Construct Psychology and Creative Reflection

Proponents of PCP use a range of techniques to help interviewer and interviewee understand how the interviewee is construing the world; that is, how his perceptions shape the way he processes, stores, and acts on information. Kelly's intent with PCP was to encourage people to have faith in their own constructions of experience. Yet the expert-dominated pedagogic approach, in which students assimilate whatever knowledge the teacher judges to be necessary, is still the preferred learning mode for many students. Even in higher education contexts, where one might expect a high degree of student self-direction, the need for teachers to define what counts as truth, and to certify whether or not students have understood it, is paramount.

Key aspects of PCP run parallel with work on reflective practice in that both stress students' development of their own metacognition. Using a PCP approach, an instructor, in either a pastoral, tutorial, or subject-related capacity, uses a range of questioning approaches and tactics to encourage students to elicit for themselves their own beliefs, and to determine what they want to change and what needs to be done to achieve this. As a reflective tool, PCP can be used in pair work, mentor–mentee and tutor–student relationships. Beverley Walker (1996) uses the metaphor of adventurers to describe people who use PCP processes to enter unfamiliar terrain and encounter unanticipated challenges in their quest for greater self-knowledge and authentic relationships with others.

Kelly's theory is organized around the idea that individuals create their own idiosyncratic realities based on their construal of previous experience. If this construal is invalidated by events, they have the choice (invariably made at a low level of awareness) to either change the way they construe experience, or simply to repeat the same construal and, inevitably, produce the same result. If this should sound like a banal statement of the obvious, let us emphasize that there are many other conditions and qualifications to the theory that expand it into a much more complex means of comprehending events.

Constructs are "the discriminations that we make between people, events or things in our lives" (Fransella, Bell, and Bannister, 2004, p. 18). They create mutually exclusive categories and binary opposites: effective and ineffective, student centered and teacher centered, correct and incorrect, and so on. The labels we give things, although these may not always describe adequately what we mean, represent the constructs we use. Sometimes categories and relationships are much more effectively construed in terms of images rather than words.

Our constructs are bipolar and dialectic (that is, each one has an opposite that it is defined in relation to) and do not roam freely in isolation. They are typically arranged in a hierarchy, with some being more concrete "subordinate" constructs and others being more abstract, value-laden "superordinate" constructs. Personal constructs operate through being connected to one another and are neither static nor finite. As situations around us change, we assume that many of our present interpretations of the world will be revised or replaced.

Just as students sometimes believe that there exists somewhere a comprehensive list of reflective questions that cover all situations, so others believe that their characters are fixed and their paths in life predestined, a matter of chance, fate, or victimization by the universe. In their eyes the power to change or choose is irrevocably constrained by external factors. By way of contrast, PCP stresses that how people respond in situations is governed not by the event itself, but by the interpretations they place upon it. This tenet is both crucial and revelatory to enabling students to identify options and explore other ways of seeing.

The major PCP technique used to explore a person's constructs is the repertory grid. Using these grids requires a degree of experience and skill, so for newcomers to the theory they may not be the best starting point. They are also difficult to use with large groups of students. Alison has found that merely raising awareness of some of the basic principles of PCP can in itself be of value in helping students expand their horizons by demonstrating that the things we take for granted about the world are not, in fact, set in stone. Through using PCP in this context, the aim is to help students:

- Recognize the power of their construing

- Become more aware of how their constructs shape their reflections on learning

- Understand how construing shapes responses to experience

- Highlight possibilities of control, choice, and change in how they respond to events

- Realize that the truth is not "out there" but is constructed

- Respect the perspectives and realities of others through credulous ("accepting at face value") listening

- Examine their, and others', assumptions, preconceptions, and value systems

- Learn what they can do for themselves safely using PCP adaptations without an expert supervisor

In the next section of the chapter we look at two techniques adapted from PCP that lend themselves to creative reflection in very different ways.

Self-Characterization

This is a powerful technique that steps away from the simple "Tell me about yourself" autobiographical narrative approach in which a student writes a personal profile in the first person "I." Kelly's instructions for writing a self-characterization were simple. If the student is named Harry Brown, he is told:

> Write a character sketch of Harry Brown just as if he were the principal character in a play. Write it as it might be written by a friend who knew him very *intimately* and *sympathetically*, perhaps better than anyone really could know him. Be sure to write it in the third person. For example, start out by saying, "Harry is…" (Kelly, 1955/1991, p. 323/242)

This technique can be used with students to help them clarify a sense of their personal identities. Alison has used it in writing workshops with journalists as a means of helping them focus on specific attributes, skills, and areas for personal and professional development. In that context students were told that they were to gather briefing notes on their fictional selves that contained the things that a documentary maker would need to know if they wanted to tell the inside stories of those persons. The principal task these students were engaged in was to create a broadcast production such as a film, editorial feature, or investigative story lending itself well to documentary.

Alison gives participants ten minutes to produce their self-characterizations. In disciplines in which writing is not at the heart of learning, this tight timescale might be problematic, so including time away from class to write has also been used effectively.

Once their self-characterizations are produced, students can either share them with someone or analyze them themselves, paying attention to content, context, and recurrent or dominant themes and motifs. This is not about carrying out a fake psychoanalysis, but noticing what a writer focuses on and what he or she avoids.

Even when students share their profiles with someone they know well, self-characterization can still provide powerful insights that throw into relief features of the writers that, even if articulated previously, have not been fully appreciated. Because of the revelatory nature of this kind of writing, safeguarding the individual is paramount, and students must consent to who has access to read it. Students can also have the option of writing a public and private self-characterization. One can be shared with peers and one can be for their own private reading, and students can then consider differences between the two.

Laddering

Another technique used in PCP is *laddering*, the attempt to discover the superordinate and subordinate constructs a person holds (Hinkle, 1965). This is done by asking questions as to why something is preferable, advantageous, or important to a person compared to something else. For example, if someone describes himself as hating confrontation, as opposed to liking a quiet life, this simple statement can be laddered through exploratory questions and probing phrases to elicit the values behind it.

Another approach is to explore the significant people in an individual's frame of reference, asking about their chief characteristics, and then probing what their opposites might be (for example, aggressive versus gentle). The individual is then asked which person she prefers to be. Whichever answer she chooses can be unpacked further to ask why she feels it's important to manifest those particular qualities. This can, in turn, reveal a deeper, more powerful meaning. Someone who hates confrontation may say she prefers to be like that because she gets uncomfortable in confrontational situations. The person who prefers to be aggressive may say it shows she or he is not a pushover. Someone who stresses hating confrontation may hate to cause pain to others because they have experienced pain themselves, while the person preferring not to be a pushover explains that this demonstrates power and control. Already, these simple examples show how moving from a superficial and slightly hackneyed description of actions and qualities can be deconstructed into much more fundamental constructs.

"Light Touch" Laddering

We have already noted that care should be taken with PCP techniques to avoid personal vulnerabilities that neither need airing in public, nor benefit from such exposure, being brought to the surface. Knowing when to halt in the laddering process is therefore an essential skill. Alison has successfully used a lighter touch laddering activity to elicit people's views about professional values. This is part of an exercise to move people away from providing trite throwaway comments about what they want to do for a living, toward helping them explore where they might flourish, or what it is about present circumstances that stops this happening.

This kind of laddering exchange is best conducted in a one-to-one setting in which the interlocutor can guide the respondent through a range of responses and flex these entirely to the respondent's needs. But laddering can also be adapted to student groups of any size, as participants work simultaneously with the lecturer to walk through the activity. Alison has conducted this exercise as part of a workshop on students' conceptions of professionalism and the multiple meanings that term holds for people. The obvious limitation to laddering with a group is that it is not possible for the lecturer to attend to every individual with questions or modifications or to engage in individual conversations to extend the reflective potential of the activity.

Here's how laddering with a group around professionalism proceeds:

- Students are asked to consider three aspects of a job they currently do. The example we use to illustrate this exercise involves a student working in fashion retail. The three areas of her work that she chooses are window dressing, customer service, and store room duties.

- Next, students are asked whether two of these three things had something in common that is not shared by the third. Our sample student—let's call her J—groups window dressing and customer service as a pair that had something in common not shared by store room duties.

- They are then asked which characteristic is shared by the two aspects. J groups the first two as *people oriented*, and when asked says that the opposite in meaning to *people orientated* was *process oriented*.

- Now students are asked which of these qualities they prefer and why; J replies that she prefers *people oriented* because it is about being *sociable and creative* (possibly two constructs) as opposed to *just dealing with things*.

- Students are then told to think about their preferred aspect and jot down why it is important to them. For J, being sociable and creative is a fundamental need, which gives her *energy and fulfillment* (also possibly two constructs).

- Finally, students are asked to consider what their lives would be like, or what they would feel like, without this preferred aspect in it. J replies she feels it would be flat and dull and she would feel "less like me."

In the case of J, we can see how laddering can move a person from considering external aspects of his or her work in superficial terms to exploring more deeply felt drives and needs. We have taken a single respondent as an illustration of how this process might work. However, J's responses that we've quoted were offered as part of a large (100-plus) lecture class, and, led by the teacher, the technique was used with multiple groups. When conducted in this way, groups can discuss what patterns emerge from their thinking, or whether they can see themselves moving from a superficial level of preference to understanding the deeper meanings of their likes or dislikes. A light touch laddering can help students articulate something that they feel instinctively but can't quite express.

Pyramiding

Laddering is often described as an exercise built around the eternal question "Why?" With *pyramiding* (Landfield, 1971), we are more concerned with questions around "What?" and "How?" These questions reveal more of the subordinate constructs of an individual, the concrete details and nuts and bolts of their experiences. (See Figure 8.1.) Pyramiding may be a useful technique that enables students to probe more deeply into the specifics of a situation, for example, finding out how they know when a person is exhibiting particular characteristics (easy going versus high

Figure 8.1   Construct Categorization Undertaken by Nick Reed, Sarah Holborow, and Charlotte Devereaux Walsh: Two Views

Source: Photographs by kind permission of Dr. Jean McKendree

maintenance), or how they decide on an object's features (fragile versus long lasting).

Nick Reed, director of the Centre for Personal Construct Psychology at the University of Hertfordshire, used pyramiding around the same theme of good student-versus-poor student that we explored in one of our metaphorical modeling activities with Lego earlier. He suggests that, unlike laddering, pyramiding has very little structure and there are few, if any, rules to guide the interviewer. The pyramiding process is principally guided by the purpose it is designed for. So if we want to find out what our students think of their peers, we could ask them to think of three students they know and then to identify a characteristic that two of them had in common that was not shared by the third. When we have done this, students often propose the construct: *good student versus—poor student.*

If we then want to know more about what students understand by the expression "good student," we can pyramid the *good* student pole (and possibly the *poor* student pole as well, if we thought it would be useful so to do), asking questions like:

> "How would you know that someone was a good student?"
>> "What would that person be doing in class?"
>> "What would he or she *not* be doing in class?"
>> "How would she behaving when she was not in class?"
>> "What would his written work or portfolio be like?"
>> "How would she prepare for examinations or assessment tasks?"

We could also go further and drill into aspects of student behavior and ask the question:

> "What is X (a student) doing or saying to make you think that she is not enjoying the course?"

This activity can be used to explore teamwork, group behaviors, or people's perceptions of learning situations. The subject under scrutiny continually shifts, but the same kinds of questions are asked, along with variations such as "How do you know when...?" or "How would you recognize...?" as follow-ups. (See Figure 8.1.)

Such questions may sound as if they are a little basic for a college- or university-level of inquiry. We have found that not to be the case. Not only do students get lazy in the way they express their conceptions of expertise, but we teachers do so as well. It is so easy to come out with "pat" or familiar answers that fit the ethos of the class, or embody the institutional mission statement, that the hard work of operationalizing what these abstract ideas actually look like is entirely avoided. Hazy generalities or the (risky) assumption that we both know what the other is talking about are often allowed to stand. Pyramiding puts the spotlight on the details of practice and action and pushes us to go further and articulate more clearly what is on our respective minds.

Clean Language

Although it is constituted very differently, *clean language* (CL) shares with PCP a respect for the individual, a desire to place power in the interviewee's hands, a wish to avoid imposing the interviewer's reading and value system on a situation, and the shaping of certain questions in a particular way. Clean language is also a means by which individuals can become aware of how their assumptions and intentions affect their engagement in all aspects of their lives, often through exploring the metaphors they use.

In both PCP and clean language the teacher or questioner or facilitator is asked to listen credulously; that is, to take things that are said at face value by suspending judgment and striving to understand the student's construing system from the inside. This is the same process described by Habermas (1987) as intersubjective understanding, and Mezirow (1991) as perspective taking. Clean language also uses a form of questioning that uses the speaker's words to frame new questions, an approach that has parallels with active listening. All these ingredients add up to a respectful and highly focused form of attention being paid to the speaker (client or student) in which understanding their construction of meaning is more important than overlaying them with the teacher's frames of understanding.

The originator of clean language—David Grove—noticed how therapists shifted their clients' terms of reference by rewording what they say. In their interpretation of his approach, Tomkins and Lawley (2000) describe how he came up with a limited number of simple questions as part of a technique to reduce assumptions to a minimum and allow for the clients' interpretation of events to stand firm. This process involved stripping questions of content and simply framing them around attributes, location, and sequence. Tomkins and Lawley further note that in tandem with the use of clean language, metaphors proliferated in the ways clients described their situations. As they put it:

> When Clean Language questions were then directed to the metaphors and symbols, unexpected information became available to the client, often with profound results. He found that the *less* he attempted to change the client's model of the world, the *more* they experienced their own core patterns, and organic, lasting changes naturally emerged from "the system." (Tomkins and Lawley, 1997, p. 1)

Clean language involves bringing as few of the facilitator's assumptions and interpretations into the dialogue as possible. In particular it means avoiding leading questions or suggesting what the speaker might mean. These are important elements shared with PCP and also with the approach to Lego Serious Play facilitation that we encountered earlier. The clean language approach encompasses twelve basic questions "covering space, event, category, attribution and intention" (Sullivan and Rees, 2008, p. 148). These are used in conjunction with listening attentively, avoiding advising or passing comments, and exploring people's metaphors and their responses. The full set of questions can be found in various publications (Tomkins and Lawley 2003; Sullivan and Rees, 2008), but the most commonly used questions are called *developing questions*. Examples of these might include:

"(And) what kind of X (is that X)?"
"(And) is there anything else about X?"
"(And) that X is like what?"

Adopting clean language's minimalist, reduced questioning style needs sympathetic handling, so that the inquirer does not come across as detached or awkward. We are, after all, talking about teachers here, and given that the situation is emphatically not a clinical one, we are deliberately avoiding terms such as *client* that would often be used with clean language in other settings. In common with Appreciative Inquiry, which we touch on at the end of this chapter, a clean language approach seeks out the positive aspects of experience as the focus for reflection or debate, such as "What do you want more of?," or "What you do well that you want to build on?"

Practicing Clean Language: Caitlin Walker

Caitlin Walker is notable for having brought the discipline of clean questions into a number of nontherapeutic, education, and business settings. She pays "exquisite attention" to individuals in groups and trains them to pay the same level of attention to each other. You could refer to her as a change agent, but she refers to herself as a "systemic modeler" who tries to foster growth and development in a variety of contexts. She tells her own story better than we can in her TEDX talk, broadcast in the UK in 2012, http://www.youtube.com/watch?v=aVvcU5gG4KU, in which she also explains her work with clean language.

Caitlin studied with David Grove and other clean language pioneers and set up the clean practice group as part of her work to reintegrate disturbed teenagers into mainstream education. She was determined to listen without judging, accept what she was told, and build questions around whatever these teenagers told her rather than tell them what to do. She was equally clear that she would not project a view to the group that she was okay but that they were not. As she told Alison,

> Violent kids outside the school system will have heard that they are not good enough. If I go in with an "'I'm OK you're not okay" message, I start from a position of contempt—starting from the system that exists already and not from a different place. I decided to try and do it a different way. Treat them as if they were not broken and they did not need me to fix them. (Personal communication)

Although she had been asked to do baseline math and reading assessments, and to produce action plans with the group, her instincts told her she needed to break the rules in terms of what was expected of her. She introduced herself as a "brain coach," telling them "My job is to help you find out how you do what you do, so you have more choice about it." She asked the group what they wished to change about their lives, and most of them responded that they wanted to stop losing their tempers. Her clean language dialogue proceeded this way:

> CAITLIN: "When you lose your temper, that's like what?"
> FIRST TEENAGER: "I go red."
> CAITLIN: "And when you go red, what kind of red?"
> FIRST TEENAGER: "Blood red."
> CAITLIN: "You go blood red. And who's not like that?"
> SECOND TEENAGER: "I'm not, I snap."
> CAITLIN: "What kind of snap?"

SECOND TEENAGER: "Real quick, one minute I'm walking down the road, the next someone's laid out on the ground."
CAITLIN: "And what happens just before you snap like that?"

Using just one or two questions with each individual Caitlin was able to help group members see how they are similar or different. By using clean language to explore the location and sequence of how these teenagers lost their tempers, they could build models of their experiences and then make changes and choices within items.

A segment of dialogue divorced from its video context and from any additional material on clean language may make this extract read strangely, and sound stranger. Hearing Caitlin's full version of this encounter in her TEDX talk referred to earlier gives an infinitely richer description of the process and the way each question and answer were developed from the preceding response; our snippet is included to illustrate the radical departure she embarked on. Although her approach was extraordinarily high risk, the students connected to it as a method that spoke to them. The way they explained what happened to them—what rage felt like and how it might be managed—was through metaphor.

Listening to Caitlin's "playback" of her conversations with the group shows how it is clearly the antithesis of a teacher–pupil exchange. At many points the volunteer participants ask her "Is that why I do X?," and she answers, "I don't know," which then prompts them to raise further questions. Caitlin assumed the keys to unlocking the meaning of these teenagers' experiences were firmly within the participants' grasp, but that the process of interpretation needed clear support. Their previous schooling had focused on math and English, which could be said to be a deviation from what they really wanted to learn, which was how to control the triggers that unleashed problematic behavior.

The snippet of dialogue presented here also illustrates the pared-down nature of clean questions, and the way that they throw into relief the loaded nature of our own "normal" questions. Clean practitioners all emphasize that less is more, and that one or two open questions are the most powerful tools teachers have. The less you clutter up a student's mind with the details of your question and position, the more space he has to work out what she thinks or wants to say.

With every member of the group, Caitlin used a set of clean questions to enable the students to "open up a space in their modeling mind and loosen all of their assumptions" (TED talk). Her concern was to enable students to represent their behaviors and feelings in their own words, and most definitely not according to the interpretations laid on them by external experts. Her reason for adopting this approach was quite clear: "Each of these kids belong to a social network of which I had no experience. If I decided they had to change I was not respecting the wisdom in their own systems. If I started without respect how could I expect them to develop it?" (TED talk).

Although it may have been logical to expect excluded students to be poorly behaved, dismissive, or truculent in the face of such an alternative approach, the opposite occurred. No one made fun of the process or each other, they all attended their sessions, and they paid real attention to the metaphors they were generating that described their own challenges and situations. They remembered these metaphors so well that one day, when they felt Caitlin was going too fast for one member of the group who needed slower input in order to be able to process the information, they declared: "Remember Miss, when Naomi is learning at her best she is like a millpond and she needs the millpond to settle—you're chucking rocks at her Miss." In a way that Caitlin herself can't entirely explain, the students found the process easy to adopt and became something akin to peer coaches to each other.

Not only did these students respond to the methodology, they also asked Caitlin how it might transfer into other disciplinary areas, such as mathematics. One boy found that numbers "spun" when he tried to add them and the group used the clean approach to find out how each of them made sense of numbers and to start generating new ways to do mental arithmetic more effectively. The outcome of the two-year project was that 60 percent of the students returned successfully to school and the venture won a European Community Safety Award.

The effectiveness of the clean language approach has been adapted to other initiatives such as Learning Conversations in Liverpool John Moores University. Under Caitlin's direction, educators there designed a workbook to help students make the most of their time in university. Among the materials developed were metaphor models for learning at one's best, ways to organize time, decision-making techniques, how to seek inspiration, and being self-motivated. Because Caitlin was adamant that modeling as a learning process would not be effective on students unless it was also used within their own staff teams, the activities were first carried out with team members. Then, in tutorial groups of ten, each staff member modeled his or her application of clean language approaches to help group members loosen their assumptions.

Clean language questioning was also integrated into staff lectures. For sports courses this could be asking questions about how learning takes place in elite athleticism, what learning at your best in peak performance looks like, how time is used in sport and business, sport and diversity, and so on. In a comparison of overall grades in the years since the program began, the percentage of students placed in the top two bands of academic performance increased from 49 percent to 75 percent. This reflected a tangible improvement in student performance and the staff behaviors supporting them.

As we have explained, clean language questions often focus on the metaphors people use to construe their experience. The two transcript excerpts following (both shared with us by Caitlin) show the richness of the analysis that flows from probing metaphors.

EXAMPLE 1: LEARNING LIKE A CHEETAH

Over three tutorials, one student noticed a pattern across his metaphors:

CAITLIN: When you're learning at your best, you're like what?

STUDENT: A cheetah.

CAITLIN: Is there anything else about you learning like a cheetah?

Student: I lie around for ages looking like I'm doing nothing, then something takes my attention and I'm super-quick, then go back to lying around again."

CAITLIN: Time is like what? Where's the past and the future?

STUDENT: Time doesn't really have a direction, it's like I'm in a big cloud of now and then suddenly something swings into view, gets all of my attention, I'm completely absorbed and then it's done and I'm back in my cloud again.

CAITLIN: And when you're making decisions, that's like what?

STUDENT: It's just like the last two—it's as though I don't really have the ability to set goals or make deliberate decisions. I'm either doing something that interests me or I'm doing nothing.

This student realized that operating this way was going to make the next three years, full of frequent external deadlines, a very difficult time. He then worked with his peers and his tutor to explore times when he had made smaller decisions such as saving money or training for sports events and used these experiences to help support him through assignments that didn't interest him.

EXAMPLE 2: COMPARING RESPONSES

Within a staff team at John Moores University, colleagues used clean language questions to explore their teaching styles and to develop a peer coaching practice:

CAITLIN: When you're teaching at your best, you're like what?

FIRST TEACHER: An actor whose lines and stage directions are clear—I've rehearsed them until I'm word-perfect and all my props are in place.

SECOND TEACHER: That is so not me—I'm like a child in a playground—the information is the equipment but I never know what order I'm doing things in and it all depends on how the students take to it—I love introducing them to it and watching them use it in a way it was never meant for.

After these comments the staff look at the benefits and costs of their teaching styles, both to themselves and to a diverse student body. The aim is not for them to change who they are, but rather to help them become aware of their unconscious mental models of practice. Being aware of these means they can share them with students who also know their own models and say, "This is the way I teach. Knowing this—and knowing your own learning style—what might you need to do to get the most out of my lectures?"

Some students may baulk initially at what seems like an unnatural way of talking to someone without the politeness that usually softens a line of inquiry. But our experience is that they end up noting how the pared-down nature of clean language questioning encourages them to think more clearly and specifically about something. They are not being led in any direction by these questions, in contrast to the way that "normal" questions often implicitly offer a range of possible responses.

Summary

As a bridge to the next chapter we say something about how the philosophy of Appreciative Inquiry (AI) relates to our theme of powerful questions and connects to the positive character of the clean language approach. David Cooperrider, the originator of the term (Cooperrider and Whitney, 1999), sees AI in part as an alternative to the deficit model typically used to determine directions and approaches for institutional change. In the context of our book we can replace what he refers to as "institutional change" with "individual development." Like clean language, AI asks us about what we do best, and how we can get more from this, through using the "unconditional positive question." This can be seen in the following sample of questions used in a corporate context: "When did you feel 'most alive, most engaged, or most successful'? Can you tell me the story? How did it unfold? What was it [organizationally] that made it stand out? What was it about you that made it a high point?" (Cooperrider and Whitney, 1999, p. 8).

While traditional approaches to change center on fixing problems, improving what isn't working, and redressing past injuries, AI focuses on envisioning a future that extends what we already do well. Although it is a change process that typically involves big numbers (thousands of interviews may be conducted as part of an AI program evaluation), it can also be used for individual conversations and small-scale reflections. If we transpose these questions into a format for student reflection, we can see how they become a positively framed analysis of personal experience. Rather than being a particular protocol, AI relates to a mind-set that emphasizes being open to thinking about what is going well. Just as with grounded theory, the analytical categories and data themes that emerge from an AI focus can offer unexpected insights and paths.

9

Building Reflective Communities:
Maps and Mazes

Many of the reflective exercises and approaches we have discussed so far involve solo reflection of one kind or another, although we do not suggest that they preclude being used by more than one person. In this chapter, however, we are interested specifically in social models of reflection—those in which students pay more explicit attention to reflecting on, and through, their interaction in real and virtual groups and communities. We both believe that identity is, in important ways, socially created in groups and communities of peers. Like Stuart Hall (1996), we believe the shaping of the self is not merely a "return to roots but a coming-to-terms with our 'routes'" (Hall, 1996, p. 4). In other words, who we are is in many ways a function of the communities to which we belong.

Wenger's Communities of Practice

Our thinking regarding the role of collaboration in reflection and the building of reflective communities is very much informed by the work of Etienne Wenger, in particular his key notion of *communities of practice*. The community-of-practice framework stems from Wenger's earlier work with Jean Lave on situated learning (Lave and Wenger, 1991), and examines the specific conditions under which people operate and learn together. His framework is complex and elaborate, so for brevity's sake we sketch out a few of its bare constituents, while urging anyone who wishes to delve into it more deeply to do so (Wenger, 1998; Wenger, McDermott, and Schneider, 2002; Wenger, White, and Smith, 2009).

A community of practice shares three main characteristics: mutual engagement, a joint enterprise, and a shared repertoire. Participating in communities "is a complex process that combines doing, talking, thinking, feeling and belonging. It involves our whole person, including our bodies, minds, emotions and social relations" (Wenger, 1998, pp. 55–56). Participation takes many forms, from being on the fringes of a community, for whatever reason, to being at its heart. Although community is an abstract entity, it is evoked in material objects that symbolize the identity, ethos, and values of the community that produced them.

Learning assessments in educational communities of practice often become externalized—what Wenger calls "reified"—as do many other items from the paraphernalia of learning. By this he means they exist outside of us, and separate from us, in the form of documents, videos, installations, and other artifacts. These reified assessments are experienced as artificial products created to fulfill an institutional requirement rather than authentic representations of who students really are. Here Wenger echoes Marx's notion of alienation in which the objects produced by workers come to take on lives of their own, existing over and above the individual worker (Fromm, 1961).

Reification often leads to deification and immunity from challenge, in which the object produced is considered to be so obviously desirable that it escapes any kind of critical inquiry. Reification also leads to ossification, or the transformation of something malleable into something rigid. This happens when an evaluative protocol produced in response to a particular learning environment becomes inappropriately generalized to a much broader range of situations. We might even argue that creativity, imagination, innovation, originality, and risk all become reified through our repeated requests for these to be present in student submissions.

People shape their identities within communities of practice, and Wenger examines how these shift as members move between different communities and change their purposes and activities. Sometimes the communities in which we participate are experienced as being at variance, one with the other, in terms of how we conceive our identities. As a result we withhold some facets of ourselves in certain environments that we feel able to give free rein to in others. Hence, in an academic community we may rarely curse. In the Twin Cities punk rock and rockabilly community of which Stephen is a member, cursing is often the chief mode of communication. Changing behavior to fit each context is not about dissembling, but about knowing when and what you can reveal of yourself.

Because of their purpose—working toward a shared goal—communities are also not static, and they may exist for different periods of time. Their membership changes as people move on, new members join, patterns of working change, and so forth. The same learner may take a very different role in different communities. For example, the student coordinator of a special interest group will take a central role in its coordination, while that same student on work placement, doing an internship, or going on an exchange will have shifted to "legitimate peripheral participation," or experiencing being gradually inducted into the community's workings.

For Wenger, we negotiate meaning primarily in our communities of practice. Doing this involves exercising imagination in a way that's considerably more complex than that of being able to conjure up images in our minds. He views imagination as the ability to see what might be rather than just what is, noting that people will imagine in different ways according to how their community frames their conceptions of who they are and what they are supposed to be doing. Playfulness is central to imagination, but so are intersubjective understanding and empathy, being able to walk in another's shoes and recognize patterns and connections across different experiences.

Maps, Membership, and Mazes

An experiment that Alison orchestrated around Wenger's key modes of belonging—engagement, imagination, and alignment—was Maps, Membership, and Mazes. This was the name of a project in a course with final-year students in business management. The project was designed to help students explore how they might usefully extend their ability to think more flexibly and creatively about their personal capabilities and support networks. *Maps* referred to the different kinds of communities they belonged to or moved between. *Memberships* referred to the ways they identify as members of particular communities that were sometimes overlapping, sometimes at variance. *Mazes* referred to the visual on the home page of Alison's online visual resource, Personal and Professional Development (PPD) Coach, http://www.arts.ac.uk/ppd) (see Figure 9.1), which helped students apply and make meaning of the reflective theories they were studying as part of their course work.

The goal of the *Maps, Memberships, and Mazes* combination was to help students understand better their performance

Figure 9.1   Screen Shot of PPD Coach

as learners and the conditions that enhanced or inhibited this. In particular it aimed to extend students' knowledge of how they operated with others to become more effective practitioners. The project was an attempt to "provide a context in which to determine what, among all the things that are potentially significant, actually becomes significant learning" (Wenger, 1998, p. 155). Identifying significance is at the heart both of creative reflection and of our use of the communities-of-practice framework with students.

Final-year students in any discipline are nearing the end of a sustained course of study, and it is entirely appropriate that one of the goals for that year would be to help them understand what communities of practice they have been members of during their studies. It is also important that they start to think about future community memberships that they may join when they enter the world of work. One way to get students to identify the many possible communities within their landscapes of practice is to have them plot out in diagrammatic or symbolic form their community memberships and the territories and overlapping terrains in which these are located. In drawing these maps, students are asked to indicate the ingenious ways in which they steer a course through the communities and terrains that overlap.

Overlaying the emerging visuals of diverse communities and students' routes through these are the boundary objects they use to facilitate their movements inside, outside, and between communities. Wenger (1998) defines the term *boundary objects* as "artefacts, documents, terms, concepts, and other forms of reification around which communities of practice can organize their interconnections" (p. 105). Such objects might be learning journals or portfolios that learners use to "take" their learning in a physical form and evidence from one community and present it to someone else (a tutor or a person in charge of an internship perhaps) in another one. In the UK, the concept already referred to as PPD—personal and professional development—can be seen as a boundary object that enables a person to move up the career ladder or into different roles or levels of study.

The point of this mapping exercise, beyond being an entertaining way to find out more about a group of students, is to establish whether applying the three basic tenets of communities of practice—engagement, imagination, and alignment—helps students understand better their own positions, movements, directions, needs, and interpersonal abilities. A secondary purpose of mapping is to find out how reflective thinking activities serve as useful boundary objects and brokering tools for students. For example, how can Lego modeling or clean language create useful entry points to a new situation? Investigating this entails helping students to make connections across their different communities and encouraging them to understand how they introduce elements of their practice from one community to another.

After introducing a skeleton understanding of the theory of communities of practice, Alison walked her final-year business management students through an activity in which students were asked initially to map out on paper the different communities and groups that they moved within. Although each student produced a very different map in terms of individual communities, there were also recurring themes such as work, home, and family, and, for international students, observations concerning differences in values, liberality, culture, food, and language among their cohabiting communities. Their instances of mutual engagement ranged from music making to revision groups, sporting teams, roles at work, and social hubs.

In narrating and plotting the existence of their different communities, students described behaviors that paralleled Wenger's outline of how claims processors negotiate meaning in their communities of practice: "They act as resources to each other, exchanging information, making sense of situations, sharing new tricks and new ideas, as well as keeping each other company and spicing up each other's working days" (Wenger, 1998, p. 47). Students were often surprised, however, to find that thinking about their social relations in terms of communities of practice brought to the surface tacit or unexpressed realizations about their personal and professional identities. As discussions of how membership played itself out unfolded, further aspects of the framework came into play; for example, students considering the different ways in which their participation evolved in different communities.

In studying their communities of practices, the student participants were, in the main, cheerful and curious, and prepared to envisage a different perspective on their social relations. This is not surprising. After all, it's helpful for them to see that some paths they take are ceasing to lead anywhere and will fall into disuse, while others are strengthening or being carved out from unexpected quarters. Mapping out movement across and between communities also illustrates the different trajectories involved in fashioning individual identity. Using Wenger's framework can help students understand the ways in which they operate within and across communities and their different modes of belonging. Investigating the environments and relationships of their communities of practice brought the intriguing complexity of life below the surface of their relationships sharply into focus.

The following vignettes give a flavor of the different communities and boundaries that some of the students were traversing and also show how discussing communities-of-practice principles highlights the impact of identity matters within our learning experiences.

Pia

Pia is a mixed-race South African ("My mum and dad are divorced, my dad's Indian and my mum's Portuguese, different cultures, he's Muslim and she's Christian") who drew multiple complex and interlinking communities. In hers were also the subdivisions of national identity that were manifested in her relations with three distinct groups of her countrymen: South Africans in South Africa, South Africans in London, and South Africans in fashion. She gave voice to the difficulties of multimembership alluded to earlier, noting that "even when I'm hanging out with these different groups I can't fully immerse myself in them because I have other aspects of me. Whereas they just seem to concentrate on that one aspect."

Her narration of her map was peppered with words evoking drive, ambition, and success, as well as joy at having become a high-achieving student in a UK university after an undistinguished earlier education at home. The complexities underlying how we choose or are constrained to choose to operate within certain communities of practice was illustrated when she chose to be identified as White in school because of the negative connotations surrounding being described as Black. Pia also kept her work and study worlds apart—aligning herself with hard-working students who were as motivated as she was in one context and with party animals in another. She noted too that UK students, although friendly, could not understand what she was going through as an international student, whereas her friends from outside the university and from other countries knew all too well.

Maria

Maria described herself as "Tex-Mex," a Mexican American whose different communities included Bible group, arts and crafts, and cultural groupings, with all of these sharing a common value of affirming family ties. She noted, however, a distinct separation between what she might share and reveal in one community and what she might keep within the confines of another—her Bible and arts groups being a case in point. She spoke of how "I feel kind of stuck sometimes in-between them and who I want to be. I feel a little bit more liberal." Her multiple communities and experiences of studying abroad had inevitably shaped her view of identity: "I used to feel very defined but I think the more I stay here the more cosmopolitan I feel." On the subject of alignment she observed that, "sometimes we fail to see how you are linked with the rest of the world, I think."

Li Hu

Li Hu was of Asian origin but had lived all her life in the UK, with a highly international friendship group whose communities were centered on faith, music, and dance. She defined herself as someone who was a "bridge" between multiple communities, most particularly between international and UK-based groups. Her life involved showing students how they could make connections across communities by introducing elements of practice from one community to another.

Samantha

Samantha's communities were geographically bounded, because most of her life experience had been either in her home town or at university in London, compared to other students who were more widely traveled. She noted the significance of impression management in her community participations, illustrated by her awareness of being a female in one male-dominated social group, of being a new member in another group, and of the need to adopt a "hard" personality in the workplace by definition of her professional role. As someone who was very shy and reserved, she found it hard to get to know people and operate in new situations without adopting a set of behaviors and a social "façade" to help her overcome a lack of confidence. Allied to her shyness was her attachment to friends from primary school who knew her "warts and all" and for whom, therefore, the façade was unnecessary.

Duncan

The links and dividers between Duncan's communities were oriented primarily around football and geographic location. He felt able to move in and out of any community of practice because of his interest in people and his ability to get along with anyone, irrespective of age, class, or other factors. He described his participation in communities in terms of vocal contributions, noting how he moves back and forward from the edges of activity according to the presence of dominant personalities. Having a relatively relaxed nature, Duncan did not feel the need to compete with flamboyant characters in a social situation and was happy to "move to the sidelines" and leave them center stage rather than compete. His community map was illustrative of Wenger's notion of brokering, or the ability of participants to move between communities without belonging as full members (Wenger, 1998, p. 105).

Lucas

Lucas described his various communities as characterized by the importance of image "because a lot of us are designers or models...." This had relevance in terms of being active on the clubbing circuit "as it's not just about the clubbing, it's about the way we look as a group." His reasons for membership of different communities of practice were highly strategic; in identity terms this manifested as a deliberate separation between what he described as his "fashion friends" and his "not so fashion friends." The former were strategically useful in achieving good grades and professional goals, the latter perhaps more comfortable to be with.

Additional communities he saw himself as a member of included the "newbies at work," in which he identified the colleagues he gravitated toward on the basis of their status as newcomers. While getting to grips with the responsibilities of their roles, they were able to share the psychological and emotional aspects of being new and inexperienced as well as the ways that they might question accepted practice or learn the rules of participation. Another community he defined was his "East London gay set," with an inner population of drag queens and performance artists. Lucas used different variations of his name as part of this separation across communities, with one for work and one for his home life. He was also frank about barriers to crossing boundaries across communities, not least because his shyness was often misinterpreted as snobbish aloofness.

Drawing a map of one's membership in different communities of practice is a "light touch" adaptation of Wenger's framework and has a specific, limited purpose. However, even with this lightest of touches, benefits were seen in a number of ways. Students welcomed using the concept of communities of practice and the way this fostered a new recognition of a different way of seeing and acting in the world. They made robust and creative links between their personal and professional development, their subject of study, their family lives, and the shape of their futures.

A condensed image that reflects four of the individual case studies described is provided in Figure 9.2.

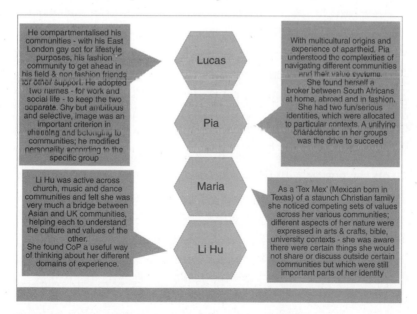

Figure 9.2   Communities-of-Practice Case Studies

Although the framework of communities of practice is complex, it can be used in a simple way to deepen reflective inquiry. In the examples we have given, the communities-of-practice tenets were applied in a short series of workshops or in stand-alone events. However, a much more detailed and systematic investigation of communities of practice as means of understanding identity, actions, aims, and relationships can also be undertaken. A different approach to reflection, which also took into consideration the life and functioning of a group, is explored next in the chapter.

The Picture Group

The Picture Group is an ongoing project originally launched as a means of overcoming gaps in cultural capital among *Widening Participation* (WP) students. In the UK, Widening Participation is a movement that seeks to ensure that no students who are academically able are excluded from higher education by dint of social or financial disadvantage. Efforts are therefore made to recruit students who may not have followed traditionally academic paths or whose families may not have a history of going to university. By creating a voluntary community of practice for such students to discuss the creative arts David Garner, course leader at the University of the Arts, London, hopes to prepare students to deal with the ambiguity they will inevitably encounter in their college studies.

The Picture Group project involves trips to galleries where students can engage with the works displayed, but also stand back and think about their own position and responses in relation to this engagement. Nichols and Garner (2009), writing on their experiences of instigating the Picture Group approach, note that it is rooted in the pedagogy of ambiguity "where embodied and tacitly held knowledge of practice-based subjects is seen as intrinsic to teaching in the arts. It can be difficult for students to recognize and access such as 'ambiguous knowledge', as it is more a way of being than a formula for success" (p. 101).

The Picture Group approach begins by using a mediating artifact like a painting, kinesthetic installation, or sculpture as a
prompt to encourage students to discuss a particular theme. For
example, instead of saying explicitly that "now we're going to talk
about your PPD," the Picture Group approach invites students
to say what they think about a particular artifact and then uses
these responses to lead into that discussion. An important aspect
of the Picture Group conversations is to create opportunities for
participation by all members. While the lead tutors prepare session
materials in advance, the discussion is not of the master-speaks-to-
apprentices type but is resolutely informal. A governing principle
is that it is student led, which obviously has implications for planning. For example, students engage in an initial activity or go to
an event or exhibition, and then have a say in determining where
they will be going next.

Relations between arts practitioners and educators involved in
the visits, and the student participants, are generally different from
sage–pupil relationships. The Picture Group visits an exhibition
and then has a conversation about the visit, with visiting practitioners bringing in their expertise only when relevant. Students'
responses drive the conversation and educators chip in to amplify
themes that emerge naturally. This approach seems to be a subtler
and less threatening way of operating for many students who feel
like impostors in higher education. If a student is already feeling
the lack of any kind of shared cultural capital, having this supposed inadequacy heightened by hearing an "expert" interpretation that differed from his own will stop him from developing his
own viewpoint.

This is why Marcuse (1978) believed that experiencing art
communally at a gallery, theater, poetry reading, or concert in
the company of expert educators who interpret the art for us and
point out subtleties we may have missed is inherently conser-
vative. Our responses to the artwork concerned are precondi-
tioned by the introductory comments from the experts, so we

think we are supposed to feel certain emotions as a sign that we have engaged correctly with the work concerned. But when a person experiences a deeply personal, completely private reaction to a work of art, she "steps out of the network of exchange relationships and exchange values, withdraws from the reality of bourgeois society, and enters another dimension of existence" (Marcuse, 1978, p. 4). This is the dimension of inwardness, of liberating subjectivity. Such subjectivity is liberating because we are moved by our own primal aesthetic and creative impulses, not the dictates of majority opinion or expert interpreters criteria of beauty.

Six Degrees of Separation

A very different model of collaborative working can be seen in this activity, which is used to introduce students to creative study skills, such as lateral thinking and making connections between seemingly separate parts of a subject. Used by creative director Rob Lakin, it takes its name from both John Guare's Pulitzer-prize-winning play (and later film) with that title, and also from the well-known game in which all filmic references can be linked within six steps to the American actor Kevin Bacon. As an algorithm of social networking theory, six degrees postulates that every person on Earth is connected to every other person by only six relationship links or steps.

The activity asks students to wrestle with plotting a path between two seemingly unrelated points, one banal, one "exotic." In its use in fashion courses, such "exotic" points are fashion designers, who need to be connected in some way to prosaic items—a power drill to Gianni Versace, Brussels sprouts to Vivienne Westwood, a shopping trolley to Stella McCartney. Students are introduced to the protocols of academic writing (attribution, organization of an essay, writing conventions, referencing of research sources in multiple forms, and so on) and then have five weeks in which to work in small groups to discover their six steps. Groups are given their two points of connection and tasked singly to go out and build a path between the two, making sure that they incorporate along the way at least one resource from music, film, book, report, image, and so on—covering as many research media as possible from a checklist. One of these has to be a physical place.

Having gathered as much data as possible, group members meet to share the many connections they have amassed and to choose from all the possibilities the single best step for each of the checklist categories specified as they build their route from A to B. They must strive to use the most inventive and least obvious connections and, as a group, to weigh up the various selections one against the other. There is an inevitable cross-fertilization of ideas as students learn how others have approached the challenge. The exercise prompts students to reexamine their perceptions of what constitutes legitimate research material and to broaden their channel of imagination to look in unexpected or very obvious places (whichever are less natural for them) for ideas. They realize that reflecting and researching are both iterative and multilinear processes and that creativity is often a matter of collecting existing insights, ideas, and information from disparate sources, pulling them together, and reworking them to make something new.

The *Six Steps* approach can be adapted to any topic, subject area, or discipline. Physics students could be told to trace the six steps between the Ashes cricket series between England and Australia and the Higgs Boson particle. Mathematics students could trace the steps between the four-color theorem and Rodney Dangerfield. Sociologists could explore how a Saguaro cactus connects to Georg Simmel's big lie theory, and so on. Six Steps is a creative exercise that gives students considerable freedom to conduct research in ways they see fit yet focuses on a predefined topic.

Wikis as Online Spaces for Shared Reflection

By the time this book is published, the use of wikis as collaborative reflective spaces may feel positively antediluvian, given the exponential growth in different kinds of innovative social media and apps. However, a brief mention of the use of wikis for creative reflection may be useful because they have been the forerunner of the social media we now use (and are still being used successfully in many contexts).

Wikis were revolutionary when they were first created, as spaces that were democratically owned and in which participants could, as we know, create and edit content together through shared access and permission to visit sites and materials. Politically, they have had an explosive effect through sites such as WikiLeaks, a conduit for the publication of classified information contributed to the site by anonymous sources. Wikipedia, their most famous exemplar, has seen its status shift from being a tool of academic ridicule and suspicion as a source of information, to one that is used carefully and critically as a learning tool in multiple disciplines. It has been invaluable as a means of getting students to distinguish between valid and reliable data and inaccurate gibberish, by learning to filter, verify, select, check, and triangulate.

Alison first presented the wiki as a more playful, friendly, and flexible means for students to carry out a year-long reflective activity. Her premise was that it would be a forum in which students could provide moral support for each other and share ideas and experiences. She believed it would also give students the freedom to express their views of the creative process and their experiences as learners in visual ways rather than just in an online diary or journal. Participants created their own pages and could see those of others, and students could read and comment on each other's entries. Students who wanted to write about private matters or raise them individually with their tutors did this through other means.

Initially the concept of the wiki as a friendly, communal space was not welcomed with open arms. Students were put off by the term *wiki*, which still sounded peculiar to their ears, and suspicious about the value of communal processes of reflection. Getting subscribed to the wiki offered unforeseen technical obstacles, and much cajoling and persistence was required to get students involved. This mostly consisted of maintaining a high level of teacher presence by Alison responding regularly to any postings or queries, either as herself, or as her alter ego Frank the Frog (see Figure 9.3), who kept his own reflective blog alongside the students' own pages.

Although it may seem unutterably childish for a garden ornament to feature as a reflective guide in a higher educational establishment, Frank the Frog proved unexpectedly popular and a useful means of bridging student distrust of the wiki's space. If nothing else, students may have thought that if their tutor was prepared to

Figure 9.3   Frank the Frog

abandon her dignity in this way, perhaps they could trust her when she said the space was for any number of creative forms of expression. Little by little, students started populating their pages, decorating them, and enthusiasm for the project grew. Postings increased, as did Frank's mailbox, and gradually students started commenting on each other's pages—usually following up an encouraging comment with an apology or disclaimer such as "Hope you don't mind me writing on your page?" By the end of the year students had come to understand the wiki as a place where you could share ideas without them getting stolen, and where thoughts or fears could be expressed with the knowledge that they would be commented on considerately. The wiki also provided an avenue for receiving useful feedback from their peers when students hit a creative wall or when they were stymied in making a difficult choice.

The Digital Transformations Research Project

David Gauntlett's *Digital Transformations* research project is a useful consideration of how social media could become as integral an element in learning to think reflectively and creatively as the traditional written paper. Gauntlett has proposed eight principles for building platforms that encourage their users to work creatively, all of which are highly relevant for reflective thinking and learning, whether formal or informal. His project's website (http://www.digitaltransformations.org.uk) contains rich examples of how these principles can be applied. Both of us regularly encounter questions regarding whether or not learning undertaken through the use of social media is sufficiently "valid" or rigorous. Questions of academic legitimacy are always going to be raised when there is an emphasis on displacing teacher authority in favor of democratic student engagement, particularly if learning is generated primarily from the student, with the tutor as facilitator.

Following are Gauntlett's eight principles for fostering creativity through digital platforms, followed by our comments:

1. Embrace digital media because we want to.

This is the now-obvious lesson learned from the wiki: that technology needs to be easy, instant, and intuitive. If students and staff take to it, engagement and creativity will follow.

2. Set no limits on participation.

A great example of creative reflection here, which was not billed as such, has been the *MyShakespeare* project, in which students have been commissioned alongside artists to "interpret, recode and remix" Shakespeare, with their work featured on the *MyShakespeare* digital platform (http://blogs.csm.arts.ac.uk/snapshot/2012/05/21/csm-students-recode-shakespeare-for-a-global-audience/). The project has had a global reach, allowing people who had never encountered Shakespeare before to respond to texts and artifacts alongside diehard enthusiasts.

3. Celebrate participants, not the platform.

A great example of this is Process Arts (http://process.arts.ac.uk), an experimental space online set up by Chris Follows where anyone who wants to contribute material and thoughts on creative arts practice can do so. Students across all years can comment on, and share, work alongside creative practitioners, and alumni can upload videos from their creative workplaces.

4. Support storytelling.

We discussed this extensively in chapter 5.

5. Some gifts, some theatre, some recognition.

For Gauntlett, gifts may be an actual artifact or text, but may just as easily be the creative intent that has gone into the creation of said object. Theater is about how we manage and promote the impressions of ourselves that we share—our "bios" on Twitter, Facebook photographs, LinkedIn profiles, our blog aesthetics, and so on. It is also about interaction with an audience of some kind; in this sense Frank the Frog and Dr. Pod are both mildly theatrical examples of how this interaction might be mediated. Recognition comprises the ways people respond to our posts by following, by replying, by citing, or any other ways in which others show they have heard us.

Lego and the Reflective Pod are two examples of this gifting principle at work as students save their photos of models and their reflective "Pod"-casts and reuse them in blogs, diaries, online pages, and so on. The theatricality (however subtle, it does not have to be overblown) of some kinds of creative reflection processes is an important element of the experience. We see recognition as important in the form of feedback and commentary (as in Frank the Frog's mailbox) or the spikes and tides of followers on Twitter feeds that give students the feeling that their voices are being heard and valued.

Our sense of how we are recognized has changed inordinately through the advent of digital media. We see playfulness at work in the countless videos on YouTube that have appropriated and repurposed well-known characters or film footage. One of our favorites is using the *Pirates of the Caribbean* films as a means of illustrating Bloom's taxonomy of learning (we make no claims as to the copyright status of these creations).

6. Offline to online is a continuum.

All our reflective activities demonstrate this blurring of distinctions.

7. Reinvent learning.

This area is too vast for our specific focus; however, its relevance is clear for creative and reflective thinking. The advent of mobile devices gives different opportunities to connect and learn from unexpected, as well as traditional, sources. Although the reflective journal has not been made redundant, digital tools allow for a one-stop capturing of experience either through writing or visually. Apps allow us to sit with a student, draw something, discuss it, photograph it, upload it, share it, adjust it in the light of commentary, and so on.

A prime dynamic in the reinvention of learning is in the mixing up of expert and amateur, and the increase in collaborative, constructionist practices. A good example of this is Paul Lowe's NAM project on Process Arts, exploring the theme of "Conflict and Media" (http://process.arts.ac.uk/content/conflict-and-media-nam-project-development). In this project students use the Stanley Kubrick and other photographic archives to re-mash and reframe materials to tell stories of the Vietnam War. New films are created through commenting, blogging, tagging, and posting, during which a great deal of peer learning and re-flection occurs. Students in the Conflict and Media project have collaborated with staff in building an open source website, the "front end" of which is the public face, and the "back" end" the space where students share and collaborate on work, provide feedback to each other, and reflect on the meanings of the arti-facts they are producing.

8. Foster genuine communities.

Our consideration of Wenger's social learning theory in this chapter looks at how students appraise their movements between and across different communities.

Summary

Creative and reflective thinking rarely happens entirely alone. We need peers to bounce ideas off, to ask us productively troubling questions, to introduce us to new possibilities, and to alert us to omissions in our thinking. Our experience is that when these things happen in face-to-face and online communities learning is galvanized. Of course, communities also contain tensions and contradictions, and we have seen classroom cohort communities split into deeply divided camps. How we might manage the ups and downs of group learning and steer students through the various peaks and troughs of learning to exercise imagination is the content of our next chapter.

Part 3

Negotiating the Emotional Realities of Engaging Imagination

10

Keeping Energy and Morale High

Creative and reflective thinking, although they can be wonderfully energizing, can also be extremely tiring. In this chapter we look at how energy can be maintained for this kind of learning, and also at ways that students can manage the troughs they experience—the times when the demands on them, and the difficulties they face, become overwhelming. The link between energy and productivity is well known in the study of elite athleticism, team dynamics, and collective leadership. For students, however, the elements of self-awareness that are most absent from their repertoire are those having to do with biofeedback, with being able to manage their energy levels for maximum learning effect.

Despite the upsurge in flexible, distance, and online learning, the majority of courses in higher education still follow the established pattern of daily study between 9 and 5. Institutional habit is so strong that despite research into the importance of somatic aspects of learning, and evidence connecting biorhythms to attention span, motivation, and readiness to learn, little has changed in terms of most colleges' and universities' day-to-day routines. Yet, as the following extract from one of Alison's students shows, what works best for individual learners often has nothing to do with institutional rhythm.

> I worked so much more this year that I have discovered lots of little facets which help me. I work best from 10 am–6 pm, at 6pm I hit a wall; I work best for an hour

and a half at a time, then need something with chocolate in; I need small incentives (milestones) to pass; I compartmentalize the dyslexic and the non-dyslexic in me; going to the gym really helps—the physical exercise counteracts the hours of sitting in front of a screen. There are more, but the point is the more you work the better you understand how you work, though inevitably there'll be a few "misses" along the way.—*Extract from a student's reflective essay*

Frogs and Bats

One of Alison's favorite exercises to warm students up to learning, taken from Hilary Wilson's *Little Black Book of Career Success* (2007), involves asking students whether they are a frog or a bat. The surprise on students' faces when confronted with the question alone makes it worth asking! However, its real importance is as an opener to a consideration of individual work patterns and energy levels. As a whole lecture activity it is a quick, effective, and often entertaining, way of galvanizing a group into thinking quickly about how they operate.

For Wilson, the key differences between the frog and the bat lie in their modus operandi, specific talents, and makeup. These can be elaborated into discussions of the frog as the "'strong, silent type" sitting on the lily pad, ostensibly doing nothing but acutely aware of what is going on in its environment. (See Figure 10.1.) The frog expends energy economically and is astute—if a fly goes by too close, their tongue can shoot out, and it is all over for the insect. But immediately afterwards, you would not know that the frog had moved. Frogs are amphibian and can therefore operate in different environments and have remarkably sharp vision. If you approach one sitting at a poolside they leap into the water at the slightest indication of movement from you. As Alison can testify,

Figure 10.1   The Frog

Source: By kind permission of Hilary Wilson

having found frogs in her bath, shoe, and laundry (live and indignant presents from her cats), they are also remarkably agile and hard to catch.

Bats, however, seem to have a problem, in that they are almost blind. But this handicap converts into one of their greatest gifts—astonishingly sharp hearing and the ability to fly on sonar through the night. They sleep upside down and are highly driven, fast in flight, and great at hunting. (See Figure 10.2.)

The naturalists and biologists among you can no doubt take issue with the accuracy of any of the details presented. However,

Figure 10.2   The Bat

Source: By kind permission of Hilary Wilson

the point of taking such liberties with nature is for students to find a playful analogy that describes their own pace and style of operating. The "frogs" may be the quiet ones in lectures, not looking as though they are engaging but absorbing everything and picking their moment to get involved. They may not say much, but when they do it is worth hearing. The "bats," however, are great energizers and may be enthusiastic "doers"—eager to get started and be active, without needing preliminary thought or planning. They may be quite strategic and good at plotting a path or instinctively responding to opportunity.

Once students have had a chance to decide which they are and why, they often want to know which is the right answer, or whether they have picked the "right animal" or the "right characteristics" of learning. Alison usually points out that it really does not matter which they are as each has some kind of "truth" or relevance for them. They may also be "frats" or "bogs," mixing features from both, or sometimes they will be one and then the other, according to context. Alison also often starts the exercise by asking the question and then asking students (1) why they think she has asked them such a thing, and (2) which creature they might pick and why, even in the absence of knowing the reason for the question. If nothing else, this always grabs their attention.

The animal analogy is an old one that crops up in lots of different places—from the archetypes of the owl student who livens up as the day goes on and can "pull an all-nighter" to get an essay in, or the lark student, affiliate of the dawn, who springs out of bed at the earliest hour, alert and ready for action, but who probably runs out of steam as the afternoon progresses. Stephen used to be an owl, then a lark. Now he is an owk or lowl. Alison has never, ever, been an owl. Isaiah Berlin (1993) famously compared the fox and the hedgehog; the fox has lots of different perspectives and can never boil things down to a single idea, while the hedgehog views the world through one defining idea and has a clear understanding of how to negotiate dilemmas on the basis of that model.

Michalko (2006, 2011) compares kittens and baby monkeys in terms of stress and reaction to change—the kitten, who mews and waits to be bailed out of a situation, and the monkey, who jumps on its mother's back and hitches a ride to safety. Using animals to focus attention on patterns of behavior is not just for individuals either; the same question can be asked of teams in regard to how they manage individual energies, and the activities that most contribute to building team momentum.

In addition to animal analogies (and students often come up with their own preferred creature as alternatives to the ones offered) the owl-versus-lark metaphor can be further applied to get a more precise picture of when someone is at the top of his or her energy levels. This includes knowing the best time for them to tackle more demanding tasks and knowing when their reserves of focus and application are dwindling and they should switch to less strenuous activities. Students can adapt a variety of creative approaches using visuals, charts, graphs, or lines to map out their energy patterns. This might involve using colors and markings to block out when you sleep, and when energy and productivity are high or low. A version of this can be found on Alison's PPD Coach website (http://arts.ac.uk/ppd) under the Learning section, with "how-to" guidance and student examples.

Plates, Timelines, and the Reflectionaire

A different approach to developing students' self-awareness of their biorhythms is Pat Francis's (2009) exercise with paper plates. Francis suggests taking plates and dividing them into the hours of the day, with different segments marking how you spend your time. She also offers a very simple exercise of taking a line, just like the one you might find on a heart monitor, and using it to represent activity through time. We saw a more elaborate version of this with the Timeline exercise in chapter 5, but what is important with Pat's line is the depiction of time as movement and intensity

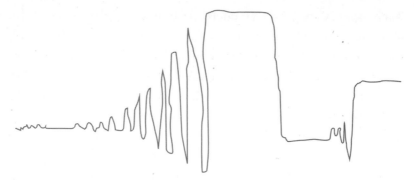

Figure 10.3   Alison's Input Line on the First Manuscript Draft, October 2011–12

of activity rather than as details of specific events. Adapting this approach, Alison's line depicting the act of writing the initial draft of this book might look like the one in Figure 10.3.

If this was a heart-monitor reading, you might be a little concerned at the wonky lines, although thankfully there are no prolonged periods of flatlining (however it felt mentally). As with other visual depictions, the importance of this exercise lies not in its final outcome, although this will mean something to the individual, but in the act of producing it. It is quick and easy to do anywhere, and if you are dissatisfied with its appearance you can start over again immediately. When Alison looks at her line, it reminds her instantly of early stages of planning and discussion, of competing teaching commitments in the early parts of 2012, and then a burst of activity sustained until Stephen's second trip to the UK. After this, progress plummeted almost to a standstill for a month (a family wedding is hidden in this bit) before picking up again to achieve an August deadline. It also evokes for her in each section the emotions and states of mind that may not be visible to the outsider, although they can probably make an educated guess.

Another flexible tool created by Francis (2009) is the Reflectionnaire, a self-created, self-administered reflective questionnaire, which lends itself to as many uses as you can think of. A

Reflectionnaire on time (Francis, 2009, p. 86) includes questions about when the student finds it easiest and hardest to work, his relationship with time, whether he is a linear or a simultaneous worker, and so on. Her Reflectionnaire on writing (2009, p. 83) drills deeper into such preferences, to think about favorite implements and surfaces for writing, speed and style of writing, shape of handwriting, feelings about writing, and so on.

Appreciative Inquiry and Strengths-Based Learning

We have already introduced our thoughts on *Appreciative Inquiry* (AI) in chapter 8, and we return to Cooperrider and Whitney (1999) for a definition of AI:

> In its broadest focus, it involves systematic discovery of what gives "life" to a living system when it is most alive, most effective, and most constructively capable in economic, ecological, and human terms. AI involves, in a central way, the art and practice of asking questions that strengthen a system's capacity to apprehend, anticipate, and heighten positive potential. (p. 3)

We see strong points of commonality between AI, clean language, personal construct psychology (PCP), Lego Serious Play, and what is called a *strengths-based approach*. In particular, AI ties in with the *strengths* position, elaborated by Buckingham and Clifton (2005), that our greatest area of strength is likely to yield the most fruitful area for growth and success. In their 2001 Gallup study of "the best of the best," Buckingham and Clifton (2005) noted that such individuals spend most of their time working in their areas of strength. In these areas they overcome obstacles, find partners to work with to compensate for their weaknesses, and invent ways of capitalizing on their strengths in new situations. In this last feature we find evidence of the creative, innovative, intuitive, imaginative flexibility that marks out some high achievers. We consider this group in a more detail shortly, but first of all clarify what a strengths approach entails.

A strengths approach overturns the deficit model of education by saying that we should focus on our talents and the things we do best to achieve really significant goals. This is opposed to our "traditional" Western model that concentrates on closing the gaps between our present weaknesses in performance and some designated level of future capability. This is often seen in advice to students "not to worry" about X or Y subject because they are doing fine in it, but they should really pull their socks up in A and B because those are the ones they struggle with. In their reflective pieces students typically spend far more time agonizing over their areas of deficit than documenting their successes. The moments of real success are celebrated, but rarely to the same extent that moments of setback or disappointment are articulated.

When helping students become more aware of their biorhythms, an approach that focuses first on what students do best, and when they do that best work, is likely to have more immediate impact (and to be more pleasurable) than one framed in the deficit model. To identify their strengths students can use an online questionnaire or similar kind of tool, or simply consider these four questions:

1. What have you learned most easily?
2. What do your friends most admire in you?
3. What do your tutors compliment you on?
4. What fascinates or excites you?

Having considered their responses, students can then describe times when they have done something really successfully, of which they are proud. Strengths-based learning practitioners also ask the question that we have seen posed through clean language: "What does it feel like when you are at your best?"

The questions and guidance described are both available on-line in Alison's reflective resource PPD Coach (http://www.arts. ac.uk/ppd, under Learning) and have been drawn from the work of Dr. Gary Pritchard, vice principal of the Condé Nast College of Fashion & Design in London. These materials are all intended to identify and develop individuals' strengths and talents that can then be channeled into learning, intellectual growth, and the pursuit of excellence. This happens through the development of self-awareness, self-efficacy, and self-confidence, the three touchstones for successful deep learning.

A STRENGTHS-BASED CASE STUDY

Dr. Gary Pritchard on "Why All Students Are Talented"

In his research for his PhD, Pritchard (2011) noted that although the United States has generated much data on strengths, there is scant emphasis on qualitative studies highlighting students' voices. His own strengths-based study investigated the specific personal impact of a strengths-based educational intervention on students. In a series of workshops and activities conducted over a four-month period, using, among other things, the Clifton Strengthsfinder tool, Pritchard found that, in general, data on the impact of the strengths approach are missing rich descriptions of personal experience. Such descriptions are precisely those that we argue can be generated through the kinds of multisensory and multimedia activities described under our umbrella of creative reflection here.

In his study Pritchard's participants noted the occurrence of learning epiphanies, during which they experienced a significant personal moment of revelation or an intense intuitive leap of understanding. For one student this took the form of a reconception of behaviors that had hitherto seemed to be problematic but that could be reframed as having positive potential through the lens of strengths. In one example a student who experienced personal and academic traumas underwent a shift in perception of herself that she

(continued)

deemed life changing, from being someone prone to self-sabotage to someone who could see and value her own potential. Pritchard observed that one of the most powerful outcomes of the study for students was the impact of the intervention on their self-reflection around questions of identity and self. One student described "not feeling crazy any more" because they understood why they were the way they were, and another viewed the strengths approach as being given keys to internal superpowers.

Pritchard also noted how easy it was for students to map their strengths onto their everyday lives and how this was manifested in an upsurge of self-efficacy and, concomitantly, confidence as a result of identifying where their strengths were at work in all aspects of their lives. This in turn generated appreciation for the skills and attributes of others, which sometimes translated into greater tolerance of difference. This has the motivating effect of being able to relate something quickly and meaningfully to one's own experience.

Strengths and Flow

The mapping of energy and mood levels has been famously analyzed through the work of Mihaly Csikszentmihalyi in his book *Finding Flow: The Psychology of Engagement with Everyday Life* (1998). In the 1970s, at the University of Chicago, Csikszentmihalyi devised the Experience Sampling Method (ESM) to investigate the flow of energy in everyday life. *Flow* is defined as the state of utter absorption, timelessness, and engagement on a deeply fulfilling level that is achieved when we have the skills to address complex tasks and challenges successfully. For Csikszentmihalyi, increasing the number of flow moments in human lives is the key to a more enriching existence. This is why Stephen plays in the 99ers (Figure 10.4), while Alison gardens and rides horses (Figure 10.5).

The ESM method has been used with thousands of participants in studies across Europe and the US, in which they were equipped with booklets and beepers emitting random signals. When the

Figure 10.4   Stephen and the 99ers

Figure 10.5   Alison and Harvey

bleeper went off, the participant had to write down a range of observations as to where they were, whom they were with, and what they were thinking about, and then rate their state of consciousness on a variety of numerical scales. Some of these states included their level of happiness, their intensity of concentration, state of motivation, self-esteem, and so on.

Flow intersects with people's strengths and talents because when we build on strengths or deploy our talents we are likely to be working with levels of skills and challenge that are higher than the ordinary—doing something that we really love. We experience a sense of being pleasurably driven that we have seen described in the approaches of high-achieving students. It is similar to Marghanita Laski's (1980) notion of everyday ecstasy, small daily acts of participating in a creatively uplifting experience.

Flow is characterized by complete involvement in the task or experience, in knowing exactly what needs to be done, and in a feeling of serenity and timelessness—the feeling that everything else you are aware of has fallen away. One of Csikszentmihalyi's goals is to elaborate the ways that each person can experience more flow in their everyday lives, and we suggest that some of the creative reflection approaches we explore in this book may enable this, even in a small way. Although Julian Burton did not use the term *flow* in his discussion of visual dialogue in chapter 4, his question "When you are at your best how can you stay there?" relates closely to a desire to remain in a state of flow for as long as possible.

What flow looks like, and how it's experienced, is highly individualistic, so there is no prescriptive list encapsulating particular behaviors or characteristics of flow. The change curve regularly illustrates the dips and peaks that can occur in an individual's confidence levels, whether in the space of a day or over a longer period of time. The fundamental quality of flow, however, seems to rest in the notion that if you are doing something you are passionate about, you are likely to be in flow at some point in that experience. For Csikszentmihalyi and Laski, this equates to a state of ecstasy, something that Gauntlett (2011) refers to in slightly more reserved terms as joy. Cooperrider and Whitney (1999) also question why joy is not included as a desired outcome of change, given the centrality of positive emotions to organizational, as well as individual, well-being.

When the Going Gets Tough: Techniques for Building Confidence

In the 1985 adventure film *Jewel of the Nile* starring Michael Douglas and Kathleen Turner, the soundtrack trumpeted the rallying cry "When the going gets tough, the tough get going!" This bouncy exhortation is probably something that we would all like to think we enact. However, we all have times when we think we lack the resources, energy, and confidence to face another challenge, or we find we're juggling too many priorities already. Perhaps we simply feel lost and do not know how to begin. A lack of confidence is not just confined to students who are struggling; many of the high-achieving students interviewed in Alison's study expressed worries over confidence, often linked to a fear of failure or losing control. Stephen has written and spoken frequently of his own sense of impostorship that he is not a "proper" academic despite having won academic honors, been awarded honorary doctorates, and being named an endowed chair.

Handling the tough times is not just about having sufficient skills or information to deal with a particular situation, but rather with feeling the calm, confident self-belief necessary to focus on tackling an issue. Developing students' confidence after they have suffered setbacks is not something that subject disciplines tend to include as part of the curriculum. They tend to rely instead on support services to provide this kind of input to students in the form of workshops, advice, counseling, and so on. The closest academic teachers usually get to helping students with confidence issues is through their pastoral care role, usually exercised in individual advisement conversations.

Several years ago Alison remembers seeing a tea towel imprinted with Henry Ford's famous slogan "Whether you think you can, or think you can't, you're right." It is a truism now to state that one's frame of mind is a deciding factor in the success of one's endeavors, which is why useful clichés such as "Mind over matter" are so widely accepted. Benedicta Kilburn, counselor at the University of the Arts, London, and co-deliverer with Alison of a confidence course for undergraduates, suggests that students ask themselves the following questions to help them become more aware of how their mental state frames what they see as possible in their work:

- What is confidence? Who has it? Who hasn't? Look around you. How convinced are you by the presence and depictions in everyday life and the media of confident people? How much is a façade?

- Rate yourself on a scale of 1 to 10, with 1 being the least confident and 10 the most. Where are you now and where would you like to be?

- Where have you come from? Our childhood experiences and how we are treated, conditioned, or brought up to see the world will affect our confidence levels later in life.

- We situate ourselves and repeat patterns in our relationships even if we are not aware we are doing it. What role do you adopt with parents, particular friends, siblings? Advisor, clown, defender, martyr, victim, aggressor, placator, or mediator might be just a few.

- Notice your body. The way we breathe and hold ourselves has been much written about. There is the stooped, protective, "disappearing" stance of the person who does not want to be noticed or picked, compared to the straight, relaxed posture of someone who is prepared to take up space without being invasive. Analyze a video of yourself to see how you respond to stimuli around you.

- Listen to your voice. What are its sounds and variations—tone, volume, pitch, speed, and silences? Do you speak in a monotone or are there multiple inflections? Do your words tumble out rapidly and erratically, or are they expressed clearly and slowly?

- Spot what causes your dips in confidence and how you react. How effective are the responses you adopt? This may include behaviors and feelings associated with low confidence—anxiety, use of alcohol, self-consciousness, physical reactions under stress, and so on. (Lego modeling and conversations with clean language can help here.)

- Ask yourself how you can minimize unhelpful ways of thinking such as the perfectionism often described by high achievers. Watch out for all-or-nothing thinking, overgeneralizing, comparing yourself to others, procrastinating, labeling, overpersonalizing, imagining catastrophic consequences, discounting the positives, jumping to conclusions, and negative self-talk.

- Ask yourself how you will change unhelpful ways of interacting, such as not saying what you want to say, not expressing your desires, putting yourself down, not standing up for yourself, giving up, not looking after yourself properly, making bad choices, not being able to say no, not being able to accept praise and compliments, and not praising and rewarding yourself. How can you incorporate assertive language that

is clear and concise, which means using lots of "I"
language, for example, "I think, I feel, I would like, I
choose…" Unassertive language is less direct and more
oblique, for example, "People think, one feels…"

Techniques for Troubleshooting: The Life Wheel and Covey's Circles of Concern

A different way of looking at where our energies are being expend-
ed and how to channel them to our greatest comfort is seen in
Lynne Dorling's interpretation of the *Life Wheel* discussed in the
Life Coach section of PPD Coach. This exercise can be found in
a great many forms and as many visual representations. Just as Pat
Francis divided a paper plate into segments to show the different
elements of someone's commitments and activities, so our version
of the Life Wheel (Figure 10.6) allows you to represent and evaluate how satisfied you are with where you are spending the most
time and energy.

Even more famous, perhaps, than the Life Wheel, is Stephen
Covey's *Circles of Concern and Influence*, discussed in his book *The
Seven Habits of Highly Effective People* (1994, pp. 81–85). These
circles appear in habit 1, "Be proactive," and offer a simple and
evocative means of getting to grips with a situation, task, or commitment. A Google search reveals that a plethora of versions of
these circles exist in addition to Covey's, and Alison has produced
her own on PPD Coach, in the "Identity" section. Alison has often
used them with final-year students getting ready to embark on their
dissertations, or with students commencing any projects.

The activity starts with students creating a circle in which they
put all the tasks facing them. This is their circle of concern. They
then create a second circle and think about how many of the things
in their first circle can be moved over into this by their being able
to take some control over them. This is their circle of influence.
The overall aim is to be able to identify as many issues as possible

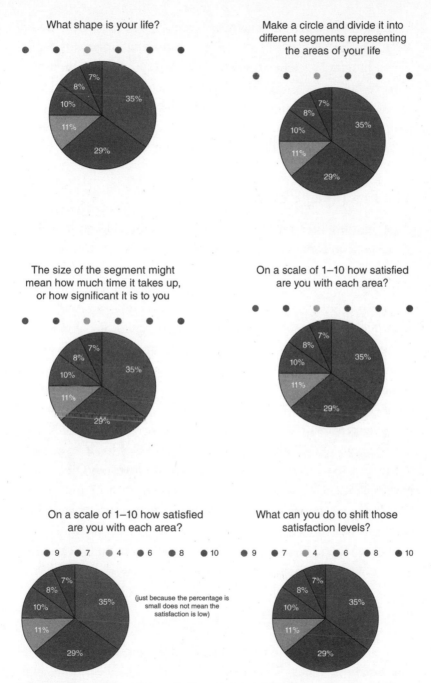

Figure 10.6   What Shape Is Your Life? A Version of the Life Wheel

that fall within a person's sphere of control, and to recognize those about which they can do nothing. In a lecture situation with more than a hundred students, this exercise can be a useful demonstration of who has included similar tasks (time management, generating income, conserving energy), and hear some of the more esoteric issues that are occupying people's minds (for example, having enough bookshelves in their new apartment).

The Emotional Pathfinder

Emotions have been present in surface or subliminal forms in all our discussions, and an exercise in which the emotions are identified and reflected on using a systematic protocol rooted in theory can be seen at work in the *Emotional Pathfinder*. This is deeply connected to theories and psychology of the emotions and based on Noam Austerlitz's work in studying the emotional power relations playing out in architectural design tutorials and studio practice in Israel. The elements that he identified in more than three hundred interviews were formulated into a six-aspect technique that was then applied to a similar number of students' reflective accounts of their personal and professional development during their undergraduate study in the UK.

The Emotional Pathfinder is now used as a tool to alert students to the ways in which their emotions may affect learning, even when not appearing to be directly emanating from the subject under scrutiny. It can be applied to verbal and written accounts of events and is set out below, in three stages; the first stage sets out the framework, the second maps it onto a student reflection, and the third is a piece of text to which you can apply the framework yourself.

The Emotional Pathfinder Framework

Students are first of all asked to define the emotions they feel, a task almost as tricky, if not more so, as defining reflection. Using their suggestions, the teacher maps these around a structure for explaining emotions—defined by Austerlitz as an operational mode that humans experience that involves their whole being. We all use emotions to weigh up information we are receiving through all our senses, and to process these—sometimes instantaneously—as we decide how to act on, or voluntarily respond to, thoughts, people, and events.

Students are then asked to think of times when they had been emotion-free. Although we describe ourselves as emotionless or numb at times, the extent to which this is true can be questioned. After all, shock or indifference is an emotional state. The point of this question about being emotion-free is to establish, if there were any doubt, that humans are affective beings and that our emotions are an inextricable part of our processing of experience. This is not to suggest that they are infallible radar as to the "truth" of an event; rather, students are asked to think about the role of emotions in propelling the trajectory of actions and events. Sometimes particular emotions are the straws that break the camel's back and lead to significant change. At other times they are small setbacks that cause huge distress.

Students can use the Emotional Pathfinder to review past accounts of experience or to interrogate those they are currently undergoing. In either situation it is a means of studying what might have been going on under the surface of their actions and responses. The pathfinder comprises six aspects labeled A–F and are set out in the Table 10.1.

There might be a temptation to look at this framework and observe that the comments are simply common sense, and the questions are ones that would naturally occur in the mind of the person reflecting. Although this may be true in some cases, feedback from Alison's students suggests that exploring the links between events and emotions in a structured way is helpful to prepare students for the emotional ebbs and flows that they will experience in future workplaces. Furthermore, students typically feel unable or not permitted to make room for the emotions in relation to their learning activities, and this is one means of allowing recognition of the

Table 10.1   The Stages of the Emotional Pathfinder

A. The dominant emotion	Where in your story can you locate the main emotions that color this recollection? What are they?
B. The cause of the emotion	Was this affected by your hopes or expectations of the event? The ways other people behaved? Things to do with how you feel about yourself?
C. The object or focus of concern of the emotion	How did this emotion find expression? For example, if someone was rude to you, were you upset because it was a friend whom you thought would never talk to you that way? The actions of the friend would be your focus of concern, rather than just the rudeness.
D. The emotional intensity	How strong were these emotions?
E. The way the emotional response evolved	If you failed an assignment, for example, how did you react—shock and numbness, followed by tears or anger, then frustration at having to do the work again, ending up with determination?
F. The effect on aspects of the student's learning	Sometimes we do not realize that the effects of our emotional sense making of experience have far-reaching effects on how we learn, what we decide to do, our confidence and appraisal of our capabilities.

affective domain at work. This kind of technique for burrowing deeper into the hidden layers of experience and causality is akin to detective work and is a simple means of bringing to the surface elements that may have been sensed but not confirmed in a reading of events.

Reflection as Speculation: Modeling Cause and Effect

Teachers exercise imagination and creativity like magpies, continually looking out for and raiding resources that they modify and adapt to their own ends. We admitted to doing as much ourselves at the outset of this book, which is why it contains such an eclectic range of materials, activities, and readings. So, in this chapter we draw on the National Endowment for Science, Technology and the Arts (Nesta) Creative Enterprise Toolkit, (http://www.nesta. org.uk/areas_of_work/creative_economy/creative_enterprise_ toolkit_startups) as another source of activities.

This toolkit is an online resource to teach students enterprise and entrepreneurial skills in order to set up their own business. Nesta is a UK charity with a mission to bring great ideas to fruition, and their Creative Enterprise Toolkit is one approach to making this happen. Within it is an Evidence Modeling sheet, which offers a simple four-word approach to interrogating a business proposal, project idea, or academic proposition. Alison has modified her use of it from its original focus of looking at "your business idea" to something broader; that is, to help students explore possibilities for research proposals, dissertation topics, subjects for major negotiated projects, or consultancy work with companies. It is a simple means of getting students to interrogate the subjects they have chosen, the solutions they are outlining, or the ideas they might have had, to make sure they are exploiting the full scope and potential they may hold. For the less fortunate, it may be a means of revealing dead ends or limitations to ideas that are quickly exhausted or are likely to be less fruitful avenues of enquiry.

This activity can work as a one-to-one tutorial, or as a group activity, with the amount and nature of discussion time dependent on which mode is used. Students begin by taking a piece of paper and housing their general ideas or starting points in a circle in the middle of the sheet. They then send out four equidistant lines from the idea to the corners of the page. At the end of each line, one of four words is marked in capitals: ENHANCE, REPLACE, REVIVE, and BACKLASH (see Figure 10.7).

This tool has been adapted for use with second-year students embarking on business consultancy with a company that might benefit from their services. They research the organization, identify

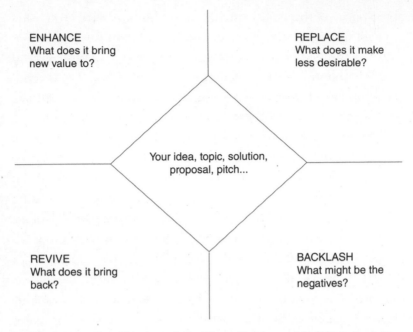

Figure 10.7   Our Version of the Nesta Evidence Modeling Activity

Source: Adapted originally from Marshall McLuhan's Tetrad model by Nesta, for inclusion in their Creative Enterprise Toolkit, available at http:// www.nesta.org .uk/enterprise-toolkit

a need or change, pitch it to the relevant team, and undertake a consultancy exercise to show how this idea might work in practice. This approach has been an extremely successful means of building student–enterprise relationships and benefiting both parties in different ways. The stories of their endeavors are fascinating, but, alas, not the subject of this chapter, so they must be told elsewhere. For us, the important thing is how this technique can benefit student inventiveness at the early stages of their thinking through what they might be able to offer external organizations.

Starting with the proposition, and discussing the four words in turn, students often find that their point of departure is somewhat woolly or too broad, and that it needs significant refining and re-framing. Students can start in any corner; however, we tend to start with ENHANCE, because this is likely to be the first thing that students have thought of—that something might be better than it is at present, or to make something else better. Having thought through, and generated as many possibilities for improvements that have been questioned or commented on in peer discussion, we then move on to thinking about what their proposal might RE-PLACE. In business terms, this might be a product, strategy, form of marketing and communications, or services arrangement. With dissertation students, it might be about reframing ways of thinking about a subject as much as physical change.

The third word, REVIVE, in fashion terms might be a self-evident one of revisiting past trends or styles, while in organizations it might be about values or foci that have received less attention or fallen by the wayside. BACKLASH is defined in the original text as "What could be the negative effect when pushed to extremes?" This is a little hard to interpret and so has been reformulated as something simpler: "What could the negatives be?" This last activity encourages students to speculate and second-guess, reflecting into the future to work out both imaginatively and methodically what the downside of their proposed interventions might be.

The beauty of this simple exercise is the minimal amount of language used but the maximum amount of debate and collaboration generated that surround the consideration of each word in relation to any idea. It is also often a bonding experience for students who realize they are not alone in trying to find a suitably appropriate business proposition and that their peers are also struggling to market their own ideas persuasively enough for a company to allow them to test out their skills.

Summary

In this chapter's somewhat eclectic selection of thoughts and approaches, we have selected techniques to focus on how we can recognize our natural or preferred patterns of behavior and use that recognition to understand how these patterns assist our learning us or hold us back. We want to end by emphasizing, however, that there are no value judgments about right or wrong ways of "functioning." There is a wide range of difference that is just that—difference. Although some patterns might fit the rhythms of organizational or community life better than others, this says more about organizations and communities than it does about individual characteristics. In some respects, this chapter has really been about how mood and vitality can permeate any of the activities explored throughout our book, and the ways that the peaks and troughs of personal confidence have a significant effect on performance, self-evaluation, and learning.

11

Engaging Our Own Imaginations as Authors

The two of us have deliberately written ourselves into this text, so it seems fitting that we end it with some personal commentary on how our own imaginations have been engaged as we co-authored the book. We do not know each other well, and our face-to-face time together comprises three meetings and occasional Skype sessions. Working with an ocean and a time difference of six to seven hours between us has meant that our writings—and their multiple redrafts—have been the chief way we have communicated. Two processes have been central to this: intersubjective understanding and imaginative extension.

Intersubjective understanding is a term popularized by Jürgen Habermas (1984) to describe the way one person strives to get inside another's meaning, to understand the arguments and experiences of another person as closely as possible to the original way these arguments were constructed, and these experiences interpreted, by that person. In transformative learning theory, this is sometimes referred to as *perspective taking* (Mezirow, 2012). One important way our imaginations were engaged, therefore, was through our attempt to place ourselves inside each other's heads and to look out on each other's world through this different set of eyes. Our worlds are very different. Alison works at a UK college of fashion, Stephen at a US Catholic university. Alison teaches reflective practice and personal and professional development, research methods, cultural and historical studies, and presentation skills. Stephen teaches critical theory, leadership, and organizational development. Alison works primarily within a humanistic philosophical framework, Stephen primarily within a radical one. We both, however, draw on the pragmatist tradition in believing we need continually to rethink and experiment with how we organize and practice our teaching, and how we support our students' learning. Alison is comfortable with kinesthetic and experiential modes of learning; Stephen privileges primarily cognitive ways of learning.

What connects us is our shared interest in the way people learn and the myriad ways that learning can be supported. As we strove to understand each other's worlds, a process of imaginative extension came into play. The more we learned about each other's practices and assumptions, the more we were able to suggest to each other a different perspective, a new take, an unexpected resolution to a problem. As each of us received feedback from the other that challenged our usual ways of thinking about, and doing, our teaching, our imaginative capacities were engaged and extended in multiple ways. We were forced to look at our usual words sideways or upside down, to ask ourselves "What would it mean if we thought differently about this practice?," and to follow each other's analyses through to conclusions that often took us by surprise.

In the next section of the chapter, Alison begins by outlining the ways her imagination was engaged during the writing of this book. She then talks of her deepened understanding of creativity, reflection, and imagination. Prime themes for her are the use of visual images and metaphors to engage students, and the need to attend to unexpected and serendipitous events in learning. Honoring these events means building on them as opportunities for learning rather than trying to erase them from a predesignated plot line. She talks of the need to learn to live with failure and the ever-present nature of potential student resistance that arises whenever innovative visual, kinesthetic, and imaginative approaches are first introduced in a classroom.

Alison

I think the prime realization for me in writing this book has been that engaging the imaginative capacities of students by using techniques of creative reflection (many yet to be discovered) is at the core of who I am as an educational practitioner. This does not necessarily make it easy to nail my teaching as representing any one philosophical approach. But I think that engaging imagination happens when we do three things:

1. We use creative, often nonlinguistic, means (artistic, 3D, performative, visual, or dialogic) to help us understand the assumptions we hold about what constitutes "proper" learning or good practice.
2. We deliberately seek out learning and teaching approaches from domains, contexts, and disciplines that are very different from our own and consider what elements of them might be applied to help our students extend or deepen their knowledge of a topic or their development of a skill.
3. We take a range of different thinking techniques, models, and stimuli and apply them with the purpose of (1) generating alternative ways of seeing familiar situations and practices, and (2) creating new opportunities for self-expression.

By scrutinizing my own engagement with imagination—and the creative reflection it has entailed—I realize this has enabled my own development as a teacher. In particular, I have been encouraged to

1. Engage students using playful and unusual activities
2. Seek ways to expand my—and their—imagination and creativity
3. Learn from the unexpected, sometimes in unexpected places
4. Respect, and act on, serendipity
5. Appreciate the diverse realities of others

6. Take nothing for granted
7. Try to connect disparate lessons and experiences
8. Think different things through using different media
9. Remain open to new possibilities
10. Wonder at a richly complex world

I won't unpack each one of these singly, nor in order, as some of the comments I make apply to several of these simultaneously. Many of these insights, themes, and feelings are woven through our discussions and demonstrations in previous chapters. While I am experienced and comfortable with more formal structures and styles of learning, those that I find most enriching, enjoyable, and productive with students are those that are playful, unusual, some-times unconventional, curious, and unsettling that challenge our perceptions of how things are. Opening up imagination is redolent of the philosophy of constructive alternativism expressed through Kelly's personal construct psychology discussed in chapter 8. Its reminder that there is always another way to construe experience does not make relativists of us all, but it does remind us of our own unconscious subjectivity.

Harnessing imagination and creativity has shown me how we can make the most of unintended learning outcomes, those that originate in unexpected places. To illustrate this I wrote the fol-lowing story and include it here because the point it makes has relevance for this book:

> As a mature adult (and I am using both of these terms loosely) I learned to ride a horse, which taught me many unexpected things. Most of the surprises came from the animal, however others involved thoughts about how I was learning to do it and had unforeseen resonance for my own teaching. Over and above how to stay put on horseback, insights related to managing confidence when several feet off the ground, self-consciousness

(in a lesson full of fearless eight-year-olds who thought falling off was a hoot), the prospect of my own mortality and/or ineptitude and the impact of negative feedback ("You're really not getting this are you?"). And persistence—I got there in the end. What I also got was a vivid reminder of how it felt to be out of that clichéd comfort zone, to learn with a different set of resources and develop different capabilities to the ones you have relied on in the past. As someone most comfortable with reading and writing I quickly realized that kinesthetic approaches and good old learning-by-doing would be obvious keys to my success; what I did not anticipate was the extent to which a technique like visualization could be crucial to being able to fully imagine what I was trying to do in order to be able to pull it off.

It was important for me to capture exactly what it had felt like to be that learner, in that situation, and to draw more insight from the memory than the localized mastery of a skill. Visualization appears in many forms and techniques, and for myriad purposes, as we saw in chapter 4. At that particular time it was, for me, about fully conjuring the experience of being on horseback and mentally evoking particular movements in order to reach a goal that had been imagined using all my senses. However, my familiar and preferred ways of learning had not indicated to me that this approach would be useful.

Imagery and metaphor have become central to my use of techniques and my conception of professional activities as well as to my broader writing and thinking processes. They have run through many of the techniques that we have included in previous chapters and have also infiltrated my own approaches, ranging across visual, verbal, three-dimensional and written practices. I have drawn pictures, made Pod movies, built Lego models, and kept a journal, including one dedicated to the production of this book, ironically entitled DOMO, or Diary Of My Opus. DOMO was the place where I spilled out the euphoria and horrors of the writing process, challenging content, philosophy, and certitudes at every turn. Its sheer length revealed that I write volumes when worried, and next to nothing (other than "to-do" lists) when I feel in control. In naming it, during a period of writer's block, I had tried to find the words that would spell the acronym DOOM but only managed Diary Of Opus My—due, no doubt, to my "condition." In hindsight and with more chutzpah I could have called it Diary Of Our Masterpiece, but I couldn't muster the nerve.

A substantial challenge I reflected on a great deal is one that many colleagues also contend with, which is how and when to write, if you don't have the luxury of dedicated time. My own writing became a patchwork of snatched hours, mostly carved out of early risings, when I boiled the kettle, shifted the cat(s) from the laptop, and buried my head in the silence until Leviathan (aka the family) awoke. Summer leave gave me space to write and the welcome reminder of how different our thinking processes are when unencumbered by competing intrusions. My moments of truth were not necessarily greater then, but my sense of clarity and understanding the journey, as well as the whole, were infinitely sharper.

Things were different from September, as I confided to DOMO:

> Back in the maelstrom of the Autumn term and my feelings about how I am engaging with our project take the form of ghost ships floating on a long black lake. I can see the pale silhouettes and I know vaguely what they are but I can't quite reach them and they seem ephemeral. These are the times when I feel challenged by my inability to ditch things and just get on with it. Periodically tiny orange lanterns can be perceived on the smooth surface—these are my bursts of writing; the

darkness of the water is the times when the files are unopened and the chapters hang in suspended animation, waiting for my next burst of freedom to take things further.

Respect for serendipity and the unexpected has been engendered in a number of ways. One involves how we came to write this text. I introduced myself to Stephen in 2011 via e-mail to let him know that I had included a version of his Critical Incident Questionnaire in my website PPD Coach and to make sure he was happy with this. He replied positively; we arranged to meet on his next trip to London and from that point our collaboration began. But what if I hadn't e-mailed? What if he had not been disposed to sharing? What if he hadn't come to London, had time for coffee, found enough of interest in our conversation to suggest that there might be sufficient material for a book? The episode, having as it did productive and agreeable outcomes, made me ask myself how many other things I have not done in life, because I feared that the approach might rejected or the endeavor (whatever it was) might potentially be unsuccessful.

This happy and unexpected outcome was accompanied by an even greater realization for me as to the nature of my teaching interests. I have tended to view myself in career terms as more an opportunistic traveler than a strategic planner. This has brought me a whole range of experiences and encounters that have been fascinating in their own way; however, at times I have criticized myself for having lots of items in my pedagogic basket but no single overriding specialism. It took my conversation with Stephen in a London coffee bar to understand that perhaps all the approaches, methods, perspectives, and philosophies that had most inspired me in the past two decades (and some career experimentation in the one preceding them) were united by some common imaginative strands. I have a focus on identity and self-construction, an interest in whole-person learning, a desire to use techniques with therapeutic origins in nontherapeutic contexts, and a continual faith in the power of creative, interactive, and playful approaches to learning and teaching. Writing this book helped me see how these converged. It was as if all the dots had finally joined up.

Writing long distance with Stephen has been a pleasure and a mystery, conducted through e-mail, online file sharing, Lego movies, and infrequent meetings. As strangers with different academic trajectories, initial questions milled in my head as to how we would write as "we" that were naturally resolved as our chapters took shape. As he mentioned earlier, we approached our subject from complementary traditions and different positions. His evaluation and synthesis of ideas resulted in a range of new insights, including his suggestion of my affiliation with American pragmatists. This had not occurred to me previously but made sense. In collaboration you learn from the modus operandi of another. I learned from him about the effect of quiet thoughtfulness in feedback and the ability to listen and pick out what matters without superfluous words; valuable counterpoints to my own style that can be voluble and Tiggerish, in the manner of the *Winnie the Pooh* character. Communicating through Lego models was an unplanned but helpful way of sharing visually with him some of the thoughts in my head while also demonstrating a technique at work.

The sense of mystery alluded to was born from nothing more dramatic than the inevitable gaps and pauses between meetings and communications and the possibility that when two people are working cooperatively and respectfully they might never fully reveal to the other what they actually think of their ideas and material. As George Bernard Shaw observed, "The single biggest problem with communication is the illusion that it has taken place." His early admission of the authorial skeptic in our joint voice—our suspicion of the uncritical celebration of everything labeled reflective—was a position I could identify with, and was also unnerved by. Whenever we put forward our ideas or practices there is always the fear that these may not be well received. This is an inevitable consequence of "sticking your head above the parapet," whether through publication, presentation, or in taking a lead on a daily task. As someone who manages to deconstruct even the most positive experiences if left alone long enough, writing and sharing inevitably involves me questioning assumptions and approaches that I hold dear. This is a scary undertaking because it means drilling into the philosophical backbone of my own educational practice. The painfulness of this process was rendered worthwhile, however, by the sense afterward of having been forced to "cleanse" my thinking and purge it of any inauthentic or fuzzy pronouncements.

The need to question and to write truthfully involved interrogating my own relationship with some of the theoretical positions and approaches we have discussed. Sometimes I experienced a competing tension between wanting to write about something that fascinated me and the legitimacy of my opinions when I was feeling more novice than master. Sometimes a period of self-questioning was a natural ally to my writing process. Similarly I found myself moving back forth, down and across the change curve in a myriad different situations. Some techniques I took to like the proverbial duck to water, others I struggled with, though not in such a way that I lost sight of the potential of the approach.

As Dewey warns us, drilling into our assumptions as to "how life is" is not a comfortable exercise. Writing this book, I often found myself critiquing imaginative approaches both in how they related to my own way of operating and in terms of their efficacy for others. This engendered a strange sense that somehow I was solely responsible for ensuring that people liked the techniques and found them of benefit, despite the logical impossibility of this. In the course of workshops on one or any of our themes, I would invariably be asked "Do they work for physicists/welders/lawyers?," to which I could only respond that I believed it depended on the physicist/welder/lawyer.

We have been frank in accepting that, according to the individual, engaging imaginative techniques may produce anything from enthusiasm to ambivalence to resistance. Although I have announced that I welcome the unusual, this is not, strictly speaking, true. A colleague once described going on a team-building event when she and several others were asked to work in a group to contort their bodies into the shapes of different pieces of office equipment. This would fill me with dread. Ambivalence in its strongest form is what has come to be known as having "the Marmite effect," a reference to the salty food spread that people either really love or really hate.

Imaginative approaches tend to create complex, and often contradictory, responses. One of the few teachers to object strongly to using Lego was a fine art practitioner who spelled out firmly for me the extent to which it was uncreative, fixed, linear, and limited in its plastic form, notwithstanding the curves, colors, and flexibility of its latest product range. These limitations were expressed in the context of an activity in which we had used the metaphorical modeling approach to explore what doctoral students wanted their research to look and be like. The complainant had been highly dissatisfied with his build and slammed the technique as unappealing and ineffective.

I pointed out another student's creation that was highly abstract and roughly resembled a wavy wand. This particular student had used Lego to embody the multidirectional, spontaneous, and subtle ways she was hoping her research would evolve and have impact. These complex impacts were illustrated by the student waving her creation in the air as she narrated her thoughts on what her model was intended to represent. "What did you think of that?," I asked the fine artist. "Amazing. It's so creative," she replied, indicating that she had not reconciled her dislike of the methodology with her admiration for the ability of someone else to adopt it imaginatively.

My own explorations of techniques that I admired in the hands of experts and longed to use effectively were not always a roaring success either. One attempt to conduct a "clean" conversation to use as an exemplar in our chapter on questioning had an unpropitious start. Although I had used clean language in lecture situations quite helpfully, a one-to-one interview on employability resulted in no richer insights than if I had just asked the respondent to make a list of her skills and qualities. Having seen clean language experts at work, I knew that the fault would lie in my inexperience, and I asked Caitlin Walker to talk me through where I was going wrong. She agreed. Our only chance to swiftly dissect my experience was to meet at a major London railway station in its outdoor café concourse— Caitlin between trains to the other end of the country and me between meetings.

She instantly pinpointed what was wrong. I had already fixed in my mind what I wanted to achieve, rather than starting where my respondent was and allowing her to reach the outcome that she wanted. I had sensed my interviewee was subtly resistant to the process and wondered whether it was because I was recording our conversation. Caitlin disagreed, noting that this was much more likely to be because I had an intended outcome that the respondent felt she was not meeting and that at some deeper level she believed her answers were not good enough for me. I had to take the conversation at her pace and only use the right kind of "clean" questions when she was ready—what Caitlin called "meeting someone at their attention." I was rushing into "clean" questions before my respondent was comfortable.

Caitlin then talked me through the kinds of questioning approaches we could use, and we modelled some "clean' conversations as people ate swift lunches in the chill air. This one exercise made me question other situations in which I had perhaps hurried students along to a predestined conclusion rather than allowing them a freer choice of conversational destination. Although I knew it is never possible to stay completely unbiased, my meeting with Caitlin was a useful reminder to break open and explore the reasons why we do things the way we do.

There was an endnote to this conversation that tied it to our thoughts about flow and spaces for reflection explored in earlier chapters. My absorption in my conversation with Caitlin seemed to relate closely to the flow experiences alluded to in chapter 10. In my curiosity and focus on finding out more, I had blotted out, excluded, almost everything around me. I was so focused on the relief of having my problem solved and soaking up every suggestion as to how I could avoid trouble in future, I had paid no attention as to where we were sitting. I would have walked away still oblivious had it not been for two girls who asked shyly if we could move our feet so they could check the wording carved under our stone bench. I had failed to notice the engravings telling us that the stone from which our bench had been made came from Everwaterslate in Cumbria and that it was potentially 450 million years old.

This intrigued me, and I wanted to know more. Once home I learned from a Google search that we had not just been sitting on any old municipal seat, but one of four benches constituting a public artwork by Paul de Monchaux. Made from different kinds of stone, each one is labeled by type and age, one of them Jurassic and apparently displaying many fossils. Not only this, but I learned that the station itself—Euston—is a site of great interest to amateur geologists both for these benches and the stone used elsewhere in its construction.

Finding out that I had been sitting on something with such creative and ancient origins produced two competing emotions: delight at an unexpected revelation, and mortification at my lack of observation. These both served to reinforce the lesson that Caitlin had been teaching me over lunch—that creative reflection is also about observing and picking up clues from people's behaviors and stances as well as their words. As teachers we need to "parse" someone's body language, as much as we carefully ponder their words, when we seek to understand that person's arguments and experience. I had written off my environment as an inconvenience rather than a source of enlightenment, and in my zealous pursuit of an answer had almost missed something quite enriching—the questions and wonder that arise from an unexpected presence or treasure in the midst of our routine activities. Csikszentmihalyi (1998) stresses the importance of the quality of our attention in flow moments, noting that those who have made important discoveries have often done so through paying attention to something that is different from the familiar or expected. This too reinforced for me the importance of creative reflection as a means of unlocking such flow opportunities in lives and learning.

Stephen

My reflections are the last thing written for this book and they come at the end of a two-year authorial journey. I suggested a co-authorship with Alison because I wanted to push myself to be more open to playful and creative ways of engaging students. This is because I know that I teach very much informed by who I am. As a person I am organized, focused, good at planning and executing on time, and a lover of words. These are great strengths in some venues and have served me well as an academic writer. But they have their dark side too. I'm sure that part of my suffering from depression is linked to the need always to control what happens in life. I think too that my style suits people who share these learning preferences but that it doesn't work well with visually inclined or kinetic learners. I rarely present information in a visual style, my PowerPoints are typically lists of words, and anything requiring body movement is way out of my comfort zone.

These traits also mean that I typically teach in an organized and sequenced fashion. Over the years I've gotten better at being open to unexpected events in class, and also to broadening my teaching repertoire. Now I have a live Twitter feed set up in class and I check this every few minutes to respond to questions that students post. I'm also finding it easier (though not yet easy) to use visuals. I love drawing and collaging discussion, and the Chalk Talk exercise—in which we hold a discussion solely on a blackboard or whiteboard with no speech allowed—is one of my top five favorite teaching techniques.

I have to say, though, that I was completely unprepared for most of what Alison threw at me! Inflatable Pods? Building models out of Legos? Paper tearing, plait making, and labyrinth walking? What on earth do those things have to do with teaching engineering, physics, theology or, for that matter, critical theory and leadership? I dealt with that question by using one of my favorite authorial devices; to imagine there are readers over my shoulder (Graves and Hodge, 1979). In other words, as I think and type I have several people figuratively peering over my shoulder to see what I'm writing. One who is a constant is George Orwell. Whenever I start to get wordy, to throw around Latin terms, or introduce unnecessary jargon I hear George saying "Come off it, Brookfield, who are you trying to impress?"

As I worked on *Engaging Imagination* George was certainly present. But others just as important were there. I imagined that some of the most cognitively inclined, focused people I've worked with were standing behind me. I thought continually about the reactions my words would generate from colleagues in some of the venues I've visited—the Butte School of Mines, the Marine Corps, the Milwaukee School of Engineering, ARCO (the oil corporation), the General Army Staff Command College, the Chartered Accountants Annual Conference, Computer Associates (a global software company) all spring to mind—and how I would seek to convince them that these approaches were worth considering. Interestingly, by the way, some of the most creatively reflective training approaches I've ever seen have been in these same venues.

It was, perhaps, a much more personal event that convinced me of the value of these approaches to helping people reflect on the meaning of their experiences. Just over midway through the book I was diagnosed with prostate cancer. The tests and eventual surgery this necessitated meant canceling a crucial trip to meet with Alison in London to work on the evolving manuscript, and also set the schedule for completion of the book back by at least six months. Those who have cancer know there's at least a whole book to be written about that experience, and I don't intend to try an unsatisfactory précis of what that book might be as I conclude *Engaging Imagination*. But what I will say is that while I was using the language of medicine and treatment (Gleason index scores, PSA scores, radical prostatectomy) to describe what was happening to me, I found myself thinking far more in visual and emotional terms.

As an example, every time I met with a new specialist and the cancer became more of a reality, I drew on drama to ask for a "script" that was as realistically optimistic as possible so that, like a method actor, I could learn, internalize, and *believe*. Probably the best thing that happened in my appointments was any time I was given that script. So a device drawn from drama—repeating the script—was extraordinarily helpful in keeping me from plunging back into the debilitating depression that is something else I deal with (Brookfield, 2012). I also found that I was focusing on images of what a life living successfully with cancer looked like. The diagnosis also meant canceling a long anticipated trip to Grenada in Spain to visit Moorish temples, so to offset this I saw myself in my mind's eye in shorts and sandals wandering through mosques and gazing at Moorish tile work in dappled sunlight. When I was unable to eat much other than a liquid diet I saw, and imagined in an olfactory way, the taste and smell of my favorite unhealthy foods—fish and chips, pecan caramel rolls, Krispy Kreme doughnuts, all accompanied by a mug of builders tea, preferably Taylor's Yorkshire Gold.

Perhaps most strikingly in contrast to my usual mode of going online, reviewing sources, buying books, and conducting an extensive, self-directed search for all relevant information, I did the exact opposite. Not once did I type "prostate cancer" into Google or even do more than a cursory reading of the literature I was provided with. Something told me that the best thing I could do for myself was to visualize a healthful future full of pleasing images and to repeat a script like an actor learning my lines. I also realized that humor had to be found. There were black moments (such as the days I was erroneously diagnosed with lung cancer) when humor and visualization failed completely. But most of the time I had fun joking with friends and family about the penis pump I was required to use (no more details—look it up for yourself!), and the Kegel exercises I did in the middle of teaching or meetings while supposedly explaining or discussing some intellectually heavy content.

I also knew that my band, the 99ers, was going to be even more important than ever. I've always known that expressing myself musically tapped into a part of me that had nothing to do with reason and totally to do with pleasure. But music also makes me feel powerful—empowered—in a manner very different from what happens when people tell me how my work has helped them in some way. Crashing a power chord, feeling the band kick in as we tear into a raucous chorus—these are things that make me feel as though something that matters is happening. To have that as a regular experience—even if it only happened on my own when recording a demo in my basement, or at practice when the only others present were Erik and Chris (my bandmates)—was crucial in making me feel there were aspects of my life where I was in control and not governed by the dictates of my body or the health system.

I think it's no accident that the drama, visualization, and music that helped me negotiate cancer were all used and valued as this book was being written. These things were not accompaniments to my usual preference for cognitive analysis; they *replaced* it! I'm actually astonished to read back over that last sentence. My six decades on the Earth had trained me successfully to be a highly effective piece of cognitive machinery, very good at using words to build arguments, explain ideas, and convey meaning. Yet here I was turning my back on all those things and instead using exclusively the sorts of approaches we talk about in this book.

All those experiences bled into my teaching. I found myself for the first time writing to students in syllabi and in assignment instructions that I welcomed visual and auditory assignments. For example, instead of asking students to write about their understanding of hegemony and provide written examples, I told them to stream a video, write a poem, submit a piece of music, or create a sculpture, collage, or drawing. My anal side did not disappear totally; I sensed that if on future accreditation visits someone asked to see examples of my student assessments, I needed to have these creations accompanied by some written interpretation and explication. But that political judgment was now balanced by a desire to open things up to the whole range of creative expressions.

In class and in keynote speeches and workshops I used narrative and story even more intentionally. I also decided to be the dissertation chair of the first ever Scholarly Personal Narrative (SPN) dissertation at my university, a project detailing Sandra Unger's developing understanding of the nature of reciprocal relationships as she moved her ministry from the White suburbs to a predominantly African American inner-city neighborhood. An SPN dissertation privileges personal narrative and views it as an intellectually rigorous medium of communication and one that holds the promise of affecting practice in meaningful ways. I don't think I would have been ready to put my personal reputation on the line had it not been for the narrative models provided to me by Tom Fish, my teaching colleague in Minnesota, and Alison's well-argued rationale for story and metaphor in chapter 5.

Let me end with one final thought. We cannot hope to create an engaged classroom involving multiple modalities of teaching, learning, and assessment unless we as teachers are ready to move out of our own comfort zones. If I had the unilateral power to man-date professional development for teachers, I would buy out at least one course a year and ask teachers to spend the time this granted learning a skill far outside their intellectual comfort zone, and to do that in a way that departed from their preferred ways of learn-ing. I would then ask them to meet with a few colleagues across the disciplines who were also having this experience to talk about its meaning for their teaching. How did it feel to be a fish out of water, feeling like a novice impostor? What was it that teachers did to help you negotiate those feelings? And how could you incorporate some of those same actions and activities into our own teaching? Conversely, what did teachers do that was confusing, that raised anxiety, or that created resistance? Do you do those same things in your classrooms? And, if so, how could we reframe and reorganize our own practice to make sure we keep those things to a minimum?

So, although it undercuts much of my own work to say it, I am convinced that reflecting on what unexpected learning feels like would do far more to create imaginative classrooms than attending workshops on engaging students taught by people like me, or by reading books like this one. But, on the assumption that you wish to follow up something you have read in the preceding chapters, we both urge you to visit the website we created to accompany this book—http://www.engagingimagination.com—where you will find videos, testimonies, demonstrations of activities, and interviews with some of the educators we have profiled.

References

Alexander, B. *The New Digital Storytelling: Creating Narratives with New Media.* New York: Praeger, 2011.

Allen, K., Scheve, J, and Nieter, V. *Understanding Learning Styles: Making a Difference for Diverse Learners.* Huntington Beach, CA: Shell Education, 2010.

Anselmo, J., Bryant, S. J., and Goode, V. M. "Connection to Purpose, Law in the Service of Human Needs: Social Justice and Contemplative Practice," 2006. http://www.aals.org/am2006/program/balance/anselmobryantgoode.pdf.

Argyris, M., and Schön, D. *Theory in Practice. Increasing Professional Effectiveness.* San Francisco: Jossey-Bass, 1974.

Arnheim, R. *Visual Thinking.* Berkeley and Los Angeles: University of California Press, 2004.

Atherton, J. "The Limits of Reflection." Video presentation made for the Education Development Unit, 2012. http://vimeo.com/39123277.

Austerlitz, N., and James, A. "Reflections on Emotional Journeys: A New Perspective for Reading Fashion Students' PPD Statements." In N. Austerliz (ed.), *Unspoken Interactions.* London: Center for Learning and Teaching in Art and Design, University of the Arts, 2008, 245–57.

Ayers, W., Kumashiro, K., Meiners, E., Quinn, T., and Stovall, D. *Teaching toward Democracy: Educators as Agents of Change.* St. Paul, MN: Paradigm, 2010.

Bamford, A. *The Visual Literacy White Paper.* Commissioned by Adobe Systems Pty, Australia and published by Adobe Systems Incorporated, 2003. http://www.adobe.com/uk/solutions/white-papers/education-k12.html.

Barkley, E. F. *Student Engagement Techniques: A Handbook for College Faculty.* San Francisco: Jossey-Bass, 2009.

Bean, J. C. *Engaging Ideas: The Professor's Guide to Integrating Writing, Critical Thinking, and Active Learning in the Classroom*. San Francisco: Jossey Bass, 2011 (2nd ed.).

Bell, L. *Storytelling for Social Justice: Connecting Narrative and the Arts in Antiracist Teaching*. New York: Routledge, 2010.

Bergmann, J., and Sams, A. *Flip Your Classroom: Reach Every Student in Every Class Every Day*. Washington, DC: International Society for Technology in Education/Association for Supervision and Curriculum Development, 2012.

Berlin, I. *The Hedgehog and the Fox: An Essay on Tolstoy's View of History*. Chicago: Ivan R. Dee Publishing, 1993.

Besheti, J., and Large, A. (Eds.). *The Information Behavior of a New Generation: Children and Teens in the 21st Century*. Lanham, MD: Scarecrow, 2013.

Bessette, H. "Revisualising Pedagogy: How Drawings Document Complex Educational Phenomena and Promote Change." Workshop delivered at Pedagogical Research: Enhancing Student Success, First PRHE Conference, May 2–3, 2006, at Liverpool Hope University, UK.

Boddington, A., and Boys, J. (Eds). *Re-shaping Learning: A Critical Reader—The Future of Learning Spaces in Post-Compulsory Education*. Rotterdam, The Netherlands: Sense Publishers, 2011.

Bohannon, J. "Dance versus PowerPoint: A Modest Proposal." TED talk, November 2011. http://www.ted.com/talks/john_bohannon_dance_vs_powerpoint_a_modest_proposal.html.

Bonner, F. A., Marbley, A. F., and Howard-Hamilton, M. F. (Eds.). *Diverse Millennial Students in College: Implications for Faculty and Student Affairs*. Sterling, VA: Stylus, 2011.

Boys, J. *Towards Creative Learning Spaces: Rethinking the Architecture of Post-Compulsory Education*. New York: Routledge, 2011.

Bradbury, H., Frost, N., Kilminster, S., and Zukas, M. (Eds.). *Beyond Reflective Practice: New Approaches to Professional Lifelong Learning*. New York: Routledge, 2010.

Brockbank, A., McGill, I., and Beech, N. (Eds.). *Reflective Learning in Practice*. Aldershot, UK: Gower, 2002.

Brookfield, S. D. *Becoming a Critically Reflective Teacher*. San Francisco: Jossey-Bass, 1995.

Brookfield, S. D. *The Skillful Teacher: On Technique, Trust and Responsiveness in the Classroom*. San Francisco: Jossey-Bass, 2006 (2nd ed.).

Brookfield, S. D. *Teaching for Critical Thinking: Tools and Techniques to Help Students Question Their Assumptions*. San Francisco: Jossey-Bass, 2011.

Brookfield, S. D. "When the Black Dog Barks: Adult Learning in and on Clinical Depression." In T. Rocco (ed.), *Challenging Ableism, Understanding Disability: Including Adults with Disabilities in Workplaces and Learning Spaces*. San Francisco: Jossey-Bass, 2012.

Brookfield, S. D., and Holst, J. D. *Radicalizing Learning: Adult Education for a Just World*. San Francisco: Jossey-Bass, 2010.

Brookfield, S. D., and Preskill, S. J. *Discussion as a Way of Teaching: Tools and Techniques for Democratic Classrooms*. San Francisco: Jossey-Bass, 2005 (2nd ed.).

Buckingham, M., and Clifton, D. *Now Discover Your Strengths: How to Develop Your Talents and Those of the People You Manage*. New York: Simon & Schuster, 2005.

Chism, N.V.N., and Bickford, D. J. (Eds.). *The Importance of Physical Space in Creating Supportive Learning Environments*. New Directions for Teaching and Learning, no. 92. San Francisco: Jossey-Bass, 2003.

Claxton, G. *Wise-Up: The Challenge of Lifelong Learning*. New York and London: Bloomsbury, 1999.

Claxton, G. "Creativity: A Guide for the Advanced Learner and Teacher," 2003. http://www.guyclaxton.com.

Claxton, G., Chambers, M., Powell, G., and Lucas, B. *The Learning Powered School: Pioneering 21st Century Education*. Bristol, UK: TLO, 2011.

Cockell, J., McArthur-Blair, J., and Schiller, M. *Appreciative Inquiry in Higher Education: A Transformative Force*. San Francisco: Jossey-Bass, 2012.

Conrad, R., and Donaldson, J. A. *Engaging the Online Learner: Activities and Resources for Creative Instruction*. San Francisco: Jossey-Bass, 2011.

Conrad, R., and Donaldson, J. A. *Continuing to Engage the Online Learner: More Activities and Resources for Creative Instruction*. San Francisco: Jossey-Bass, 2012.

Cooperrider, D., and Whitney, D. "A Positive Revolution in Change: Appreciative Inquiry." Appreciative Inquiry Commons, 1999. http://www.appreciativeinquiry.case.edu/practice/toolsPackDetail.cfm?coid=2159.

Covey, S. *The Seven Habits of Highly Effective People*. London and Sydney: Simon & Schuster, 1994.

Csikszentmihalyi, M. *Finding Flow: The Psychology of Engagement with Everyday Life*. New York: Harper Collins, 1998.

Csikszentmihalyi, M. *Flow: The Secret to Happiness*. TED talk, 2008. http://www
.ted.com/talks/mihaly_csikszentmihalyi_on_flow.htm.

Csikszentmihalyi, M. *Flow: The Psychology of Optimal Experience*. New York:
Harper Perennial Modern Classics, 2008.

Debes, John L. "The Loom of Visual Literacy." *Audiovisual Instruction*, 1969, 14,
no. 8, 25–27.

Dewey, J. *How We Think*. New York: Dover, 1933.

Digital Transformations. http://www.digitaltransformations.org.uk/.

Dilthey, W. *Descriptive Psychology and Historical Understanding*. Trans. from
the German by R. M. Zaner, K. L. Heides, and with introduction by
R. A. Makreel. The Hague. Martinus Nijhoff, 1977.

Dray, W. H. "On the Nature and Role of Narrative in History." In G. Roberts
(ed.), *The History and Narrative Reader*. London: Routledge, 2001.

Dungy, G. J. "A National Perspective: Testing Assumptions about Generational
Cohorts." In F. A. Bonner, A. F. Marbley, and M. F. Howard-Hamilton
(eds.), *Diverse Millennial Students in College: Implications for Faculty and
Student Affairs*. Sterling, VA: Stylus, 2011, 5–24.

Eide, B. L., and Eide, F. F. *The Dyslexic Advantage: Unlocking the Hidden Potential
of the Dyslexic Brain*. New York: Plume, 2012.

Elkins, J. (Ed.). *Visual Literacy*. New York: Routledge, 2007.

Erben, M. (Ed.). *Biography and Education: A Reader*. London: Falmer, 1998.

Finnigan, T. "Tell Us about It': Diverse Student Voices in Creative Practice."
Art, Design and Communication in Higher Education, 2009, 8, no. 2, 135–50.

Forster, E. M. *Aspects of the Novel*. Harmondsworth, UK: Penguin, London, 1927.

Foucault, M. *Discipline and Punish: The Birth of the Prison*. New York: Vintage
Books, 1977.

Foucault, M. *Power/Knowledge: Selected Interviews and Other Writings, 1972–
1977*. New York: Pantheon, 1980.

Foucault, M. "The Subject and Power." In H. L. Dreyfus and P. Rabinow (eds.),
Michel Foucault: Beyond Structuralism and Hermeneutic. Chicago: University
of Chicago Press, 1982.

Francis, P. *Inspiring Writing in Art and Design: Taking a Line for a Write*. Chicago:
Intellect Books, 2009.

Fransella, F., Bell, R., and Bannister, D. *A Manual for Repertory Grid Technique*.
Chichester, UK: Wiley, 2004.

Frazel, M. *Digital Storytelling Guide for Educators*. Washington, DC: International Society for Technology in Education, 2010.

Fromm, E. *Marx's Concept of Man*. New York: Frederick Ungar, 1961.

Gardner, H. *Frames of Mind: The Theory of Multiple Intelligences*. New York: Basic Books, 2011.

Gauntlett, D. *Making Is Connecting: The Social Meaning of Creativity, from DIY and Knitting to YouTube and Web 2.0*. Cambridge, UK: Polity, 2011.

Goleman, D. *Leadership: The Power of Emotional Intelligence*. Florence, MA: More Than Sound, 2011.

Graves, R., and Hodge, A. *The Reader over Your Shoulder: A Handbook for Writers of English Prose*. New York: Random House, 1979 (2nd ed.).

Habermas, J. *The Theory of Communicative Action, Vol. I: Reason and the Rationalization of Society*. Boston: Beacon Press, 1984.

Habermas, J. *The Theory of Communicative Action: Vol. II: Lifeworld and System—A Critique of Functionalist Reason*. Boston: Beacon Press, 1987.

Hall, S. "Who Needs Identity?" In S. Hall and P. Du Gay (eds.), *Questions of Cultural Identity*. London: Sage, 1996.

Hinkle, D. "The Change of Constructs from the Viewpoint of a Theory of Construct Implications," 1965. http://www.pcp-net.org/journal/pctp10/hinkle1965.html.

hooks, b. *Teaching to Transgress: Education as the Practice of Freedom*. New York: Routledge, 1994.

Jacobs, M. *Key Figures in Counseling and Psychotherapy: D. W. Winnicott*. Thousand Oaks, CA: Sage, 1995.

James, A. "Reflection Revisited: Perceptions of Reflective Practice in Fashion Learning and Teaching." *Art, Design & Communication in Higher Education*, 2007, 5, no. 3, 179–196.

Jensen, E. P. *Brain-Based Learning: The New Paradigm of Teaching*. Thousand Oaks, CA: Corwin, 2008 (2nd ed.).

JISC TechDis Staff Pack. *Checking the Accessibility of Your E-resources*, 2005. http://staffpacks.jisctechdis.ac.uk/Staff%20Packs/Checking%20Accessibility/Icebker%20Accessibility.xml.

Kane, P. *The Play Ethic: A Manifesto for a Different Way of Living*. New York: Macmillan, 2004.

Kelly, G. *A Theory of Personality: The Psychology of Personal Constructs*. New York: Norton, 1955.

Kelly, G. A. *The Psychology of Personal Constructs*, Vols. 1 and 2. New York: Norton, 1991.

King, S. *11/22/63: A Novel*. New York: Scribner, 2011.

Kolb, D. *Experiential Learning: Experience as the Source of Learning and Development*. Englewood Cliffs, NJ: Prentice Hall, 1984.

Kübler-Ross, E. *On Death and Dying*. New York: Scribner, 1997.

Landfield, A. W. *Personal Construct Systems in Psychotherapy*. Lincoln: University of Nebraska Press, 1971.

Lakoff, G., and Johnson, M. *Metaphors We Live By*. Chicago: University of Chicago Press, 2003 (2nd ed.).

Laski, M. *Everyday Ecstasy: Some Observations on the Possible Social Effects of Major and Minor Ecstatic Experiences in Our Daily Secular Lives*. London: Thames & Hudson, 1980.

Lave, J., and Wenger, E. *Situated Learning: Legitimate Peripheral Participation*. New York: Cambridge University Press, 1991.

Lodge, D. *Thinks: A Novel*. New York: Penguin, 2001.

Long, I. *Blob Life*. Raleigh, NC: Lulu.com, 2012.

Love, C. T. "Dialing into a Circle of Trust: A 'Medium' Tech Experiment and Poetic Evaluation." In M. Golden (ed.), *Teaching and Learning from the Inside Out: Revitalizing Ourselves and Our Institutions*. New Directions for Teaching and Learning, no. 130. San Francisco: Jossey-Bass, 2012, 37–52.

Mandler, J. M. *Scripts, Stories and Scenes: Aspects of Schema Theory*. Hillsdale, NJ: Erlbaum, 1984.

Marcuse, H. *The Aesthetic Dimension: Toward a Critique of Marxist Aesthetics* Boston: Beacon Press, 1978.

Mergen, B. *Play and Playthings: A Reference Guide*. Westport, CT: Greenwood, 1982.

Mezirow, J. *Transformative Dimensions of Adult Learning*. San Francisco: Jossey-Bass, 1991.

Mezirow, J. "Learning to Think Like an Adult: Core Concepts of Transformation Theory." In E. W. Taylor, P. Cranton, and Associates, *The Handbook of Transformative Learning: Theory, Research, and Practice*. San Francisco: Jossey-Bass, 2012, 73–95.

Michalko, M. *Thinkertoys: A Handbook of Creative Thinking Techniques*. Berkeley, CA: Ten Speed Press, 2006 (2nd ed.).

Michalko, M. *Creative Thinkering: Putting Your Imagination to Work*. Novato, CA: New World Library, 2011.

Miles, M. *Herbert Marcuse: An Aesthetics of Liberation*. London: Pluto Press, 2012.

Moon, J. "We Seek It Here: A New Perspective on the Elusive Activity of Critical Thinking—A Theoretical and Practical Approach." Paper on the Escalate Subject Centre website, 2005. http://escalate.ac.uk/2041.

Moon, J. *Learning Journals: A Handbook for Reflective Practice and Professional Development*. New York: Routledge, 2006 (2nd ed.)

Mortiboys, A. *Teaching with Emotional Intelligence*. New York: Taylor & Francis, 2007.

Nash, R. J. *Liberating Scholarly Writing: The Power of Personal Narrative*. New York: Teachers College Press, 2004.

Nash, R. J., and Bradley, D. L. *Me-Search and Re-Search: A Guide for Writing Scholarly Personal Narrative Manuscripts*. Charlotte, NC: Information Age, 2011.

Nash, R., and Viray, S. *Our Stories Matter: Liberating the Voices of Marginalized Students through Scholarly Personal Narrative Writing*. New York: Peter Lang, 2013.

Nichols, C., and Garner, D. "Encouraging Reflexive Practice: Alternative Ways of Embedding PPD within the University." *International Journal of the Arts in Society*, 2009, 4, no. 4, 99–107.

Nolan, S. "Physical Metaphorical Modelling with LEGO as a Technology for Collaborative Personalised Learning." In J. O' Donoghue (ed.), *Technology-Supported Environments for Personalized Learning: Methods and Case Studies*. Hershey, PA: IGI Global Publishing, 2010.

Noonan, S. *Leadership through Story: Diverse Voices in Dialogue*. Lanham, MD: Rowman & Littlefield, 2007.

Ohlson, S. *Deep Learning: How the Mind Overrides Experience*. New York: Cambridge University Press, 2011.

Palmer, P. J. *The Courage to Teach: Exploring the Inner Landscape of a Teacher's Life*. San Francisco: Jossey-Bass, 2007 (10th anniv. ed.).

Personal and Professional Development (PPD) Coach. http://www.arts.ac.uk/ppd.

Pink, D. H. *A Whole New Mind: Why Right Brainers Will Rule the Future*. New York: Penguin, 2008.

Pink, D. H. *Drive: The Surprising Truth about What Motivates Us*. New York: Riverhead, 2011.

Preskill, S. J., and Brookfield, S. D. *Learning as a Way of Leading: Lessons from the Struggle for Social Justice*. San Francisco: Jossey-Bass, 2008.

Preskill, S. J., and Smith-Jacobvitz, R. *Stories of Teaching: A Foundation for Educational Renewal*. New York: Prentice Hall, 2000.

Pritchard, G. M. *A Grounded Theory of the Factors That Mediate the Effect of a Strengths-Based Educational Intervention over a Four-Month Period*. Ann Arbor, MI: ProQuest UMI Dissertation Publishing, 2011.

Pryor, R. M. *Teaching for Recall and Analysis: Advanced Floor Timelines for U.S. History*. Chicago: Pryolino Press, 2012.

Reitz, A. *Art, Alienation and the Humanities: A Critical Engagement with Herbert Marcuse*. Albany: State University of New York Press, 2000.

Robinson, K. "All Our Futures: Creativity, Culture & Education." 1999. Report. http://www.sirkenrobinson.co/pdf.allourfutures.pdf.

Robinson, K. *The Arts in Schools: Principles, Practice and Provision*. Lisbon, Portugal: Calouste Gulbenkian Foundation, 1982.

Robinson, K. *The Unlocking Creativity Initiative*, 2000. http://www.dcalni.gov.uk/index/arts_and_creativity/unlocking_creativity_initiative.htm.

Robinson, K. *Changing Education Paradigms*. RSA Animate on YouTube, 2010. http://www.youtube.com/watch?v=zDZFcDGpL4U.

Robinson, K. *Out of Our Minds: Learning to Be Creative*. Chichester, UK: Capstone, 2011.

Savin-Baden, M. *Learning Spaces: Creating Opportunities for Knowledge Creation in Academic Life*. Maidenhead, UK: Open University Press, 2008

Schön, D. *The Reflective Practitioner: How Professionals Think in Action*. New York: Basic Books, 1987.

Schön, D. *Educating the Reflective Practitioner: Toward a New Design for Teaching and Learning in the Professions*. San Francisco: Jossey-Bass, 1990.

Sebald, W. G. *The Rings of Saturn*. London: Harvill Press, 1998.

Sellers, J. "The Labyrinth: A Journey of Discovery." In P. McIntosh and W. Digby (eds.) *Creativity in the Classroom: Case Studies in Using the Arts in Teaching and Learning in Higher Education*. Bristol, UK: Intellect Press, 2012.

Sellers, J. "Quiet Time, Quiet Space: A Labyrinth for Your University or College." In R. Sewell, J. Sellers, and D. Williams (eds.), *Working with Labyrinths: Paths for Exploration*. Iona, UK: Wild Goose Publications, 2013.

Silver, H. F., Strong, R. W., and Perini, M. J. *So Each May Learn: Integrating Learning Styles and Multiple Intelligences*. Alexandria, VA: Association for Supervision and Curriculum Development, 2000.

Smith, H. I. *Borrowed Narratives: Using Biographical and Historical Grief Narratives with the Bereaved*. New York: Routledge, 2012.

SooHoo, S. *Talking Leaves: Narratives of Otherness*. New York: Hampton, 2006.

Sullivan, W., and Rees, J. *Clean Language: Revealing Metaphors and Opening Minds*. Bethel, CT: Crown House Publishing, 2008.

Taylor, E., and Cranton, P. (Eds). *The Handbook of Transformative Learning Theory*. San Francisco: Jossey-Bass, 2012.

Tomkins, P., and Lawley, J. "Less Is More: The Art of Clean Language." First published in *Rapport, Journal of the Association for NLP* (UK), issue 35, February 1997. http://www.cleanlanguage.co.uk/articles/articles/109/1/Less-Is-More-The-Art-of-Clean-Language/Page1.html.

Tomkins, P., and Lawley, J. *Metaphors in Mind: Transformation through Systemic Modeling*. Highgate, UK: Developing Company Press, 2000.

Vickers, A., and Bavister, S. *Essential Neuro Linguistic Programming: A Teach Yourself Guide*. New York: McGraw Hill, 2010 (3rd ed.).

Walker, B. M. "A Psychology for Adventurers: An Introduction to Personal Construct Psychology from a Social Perspective." In D. Kalekin-Fishman and B. M. Walker (eds.), *The Construction of Group Realities*. Malabar, FL: Krieger, 1996, 7–26.

Ward, V., and Hough, A. "London 2012: Helen Glover Only Began Rowing Four Years Ago." *Daily Telegraph*, August 1, 2012. http://www.telegraph.co.uk/sport/olympics/news/9444529/london-2012-Olympics-Helen-Glover-only-began-rowing-four-years-ago.html.

Wenger, E. *Communities of Practice: Learning, Meaning, and Identity*. New York: Cambridge University Press, 1998.

Wenger, E., McDermott, R., and Schneider, W. M. *Cultivating Communities of Practice: A Guide to Managing Knowledge*. Cambridge, MA: Harvard Business School Press, 2002.

Wenger, E., White, N., and Smith, J. D. *Digital Habitats: Stewarding Technology for Communities*. Portland, OR: CP Square, 2009.

West, T. G. *In the Mind's Eye: Creative Visual Thinkers, Gifted Dyslexics and the Rise of Visual Technologies*. Amherst, NY: Prometheus, 2009.

White, M. J., and Stafford, L. "Promoting Reflection through the Labyrinth Walk." *Nurse Educator*, 2008, 33, no. 3, 99–100.

Wilson, H. *The Little Black Book of Career Success*. Radcliffe, UK: Cheeky Monkey Publishing, 2007.

Winnicott, D. W. *Playing and Reality*. New York: Routledge, 2005 (2nd ed.).

Woods, M. *Personal Best: How to Achieve Your Full Potential*. Chichester, UK: Capstone, 2006.

Index